Pioneer Performances

Pioneer Performances
Staging the Frontier

Matthew Rebhorn

OXFORD
UNIVERSITY PRESS

OXFORD
UNIVERSITY PRESS

Oxford University Press, Inc., publishes works that further Oxford University's
objective of excellence in research, scholarship, and education.

Oxford New York
Auckland   Cape Town   Dar es Salaam   Hong Kong   Karachi
Kuala Lumpur   Madrid   Melbourne   Mexico City   Nairobi
New Delhi   Shanghai   Taipei   Toronto

With offices in
Argentina   Austria   Brazil   Chile   Czech Republic   France   Greece
Guatemala   Hungary   Italy   Japan   Poland   Portugal   Singapore
South Korea   Switzerland   Thailand   Turkey   Ukraine   Vietnam

Copyright © 2012 by Oxford University Press, Inc.

Published by Oxford University Press, Inc.
198 Madison Avenue, New York, New York 10016
www.oup.com

Oxford is a registered trademark of Oxford University Press

Library of Congress Cataloging-in-Publication Data

Rebhorn, Matthew.
Pioneer performances : staging the frontier / Matthew Rebhorn.
p. cm.
Includes bibliographical references and index.
ISBN 978-0-19-975130-3 (cloth : alk. paper) 1. Theater—United
States—History—19th century. 2. American drama—19th century—History
and criticism. 3. Frontier and pioneer life in literature. 4. West
(U.S.)—In literature. I. Title.
PN2245.R49 2011
792.0973'09034--dc23
2011017717

1 3 5 7 9 8 6 4 2

Printed in the United States of America
on acid-free paper

To Mom and Dad,
and
Alexandra,
for extending my frontiers

CONTENTS

ACKNOWLEDGMENTS

While this book bears only my name, many people contributed to this project and to my development as a scholar. Let me briefly thank, first and foremost, Andrew Delbanco, for his intellectual guidance, his generous support, and his productive skepticism. To Jonathan Arac, I owe special thanks for making me accountable, sometimes reluctantly, for each word I used. Rachel Adams, Katey Castellano, Amanda Claybaugh, Laura Lewis, Eric Lott, Martin Meisel, Heather Nathans, John Ott, Julie Stone Peters, Martin Puchner, David Savran, and Ezra Tawil also helped focus and sharpen my argument, and I am indebted to them for their contributions.

Productive discussions of my work at the American Dissertation Seminar and Theater Seminar at Columbia University, and at the American Studies Brown Bag Series at James Madison University, also helped illuminate the issues and contexts of my work. I would like to thank the members of those seminars for their contributions, especially Lisa Hollibaugh, Matt Laufer, Jen White, and Laura Henigman for their critical insights and their warm friendship. At the Huntington Library, I would like to thank Peter J. Blodgett for giving me an interpretive road map, and Jen Huntley-Smith, Joshua Piker, and David Wrobel for giving me the historian's perspective. At the Harvard Theatre Collection, I'd like to thank Betty Falsey, Rachel Howarth, and Denison Beach for their tireless assistance in helping me track down primary material. To the knowledge and help of the reference librarians in the Boston Public Library, New York Historical Society, Columbia University Rare Book Room, and the New York Public Library's Billy Rose Theatre Collection, I am also deeply indebted.

I also thank the Jacob Javits Fellowship and the Andrew W. Mellon Foundation for their generosity in giving me the time to develop this project, and I am likewise grateful for the support of the Stanley J. Kahrl Fellowship in Theatre History from Harvard University and the Edna T. Shaeffer Humanist Award and Faculty Leave Award from James Madison University for providing me timely support in bringing this project to a close.

Material from Chapter 1 and Chapter 4 appeared in the journals *Comparative Drama* and *The Journal of American Drama and Theatre,* respectively. I appreciate the editors at both journals giving me permission to reprint portions of articles in this book. I'd also like to thank my editor at Oxford University Press, Brendan O'Neill, and the anonymous readers for instructive and illuminating feedback. I'd like to thank my copyeditor, as well as Molly Morrison, and the entire production staff at Oxford University Press, for their help in turning this manuscript into a book.

My biggest debt of gratitude, however, goes to my family, whose unswerving support and ceaseless love have kept my journey into the frontier from being lonely. To my parents, Wayne and Marlette Rebhorn, I owe an enormous debt, which I can only begin to repay by thanking them here. They have both guided my development as a scholar and as a person, and I would certainly not be who I am today without their support. To my wife, Alexandra, I owe everything, plus a little more. Critic and confidant, sparring partner and kindred spirit, she helped me work through the ideas and my presentation of them from the project's inception to its conclusion. Without her confidence and commitment, this project could never have been completed. To my children, Phoebe Violet and Erik Benjamin, I also owe my love for understanding when daddy had to work rather than play.

These people offered me insight and aid; like many authors before me, I consider the mistakes wholly my own.

Pioneer Performances

INTRODUCTION

⌒

Manifest Destinies

Buffalo Bill, Gowongo Mohawk,

and the Genealogy

of American Frontier Performance

One of the most provocative moments in the story of the American frontier and in the history of American performance never actually occurred, though it easily might have. Frederick Jackson Turner, the historian most closely identified with the frontier throughout the twentieth century,[1] and William F. "Buffalo Bill" Cody, the sensational performer who essentially invented the western as a performative genre, were both in Chicago in 1893 for the World's Columbian Exposition.[2] It was at this same cultural event that Turner delivered his famous lecture on the closing of the American frontier—the essay that would help crystallize what has become known as the Turner Thesis—while not half a mile from the midway, Buffalo Bill was performing in his celebrated show, Wild West.

Turner's ideas about the frontier were shared, of course, by a number of other nineteenth-century historians. Francis Parkman, for instance, had penned an eight-volume history of his own encounters and observations on the Oregon Trail, starting before the Civil War and with the last volume published just a year before Turner's address. "Like George Bancroft before him," Joy S. Kasson relates, "Parkman worked within a framework that celebrated the triumph of Anglo-Saxon conquest and saw English, and later American, domination of North America as a story of the progress of civilization over savagery and the extension of freedom over the continent."[3] Even amateur historians, like Theodore Roosevelt, had expounded on the frontier's symbolic values in his four-volume *The Winning of the West*

(1889–1896), and yet it was Turner's definition of what the frontier meant to Americans at the meeting of the American Historical Association at the 1893 exposition that has captured the minds of critics.[4] So initially successful was the thesis among historians, as Rosemarie K. Bank relates, that, by the 1930s, "the American Historical Association was branded one great Turner-verian."[5] Perhaps one of the reasons that Turner's definition of the frontier has been so highly popular is its simplicity. "The frontier is the outer edge of the wave" of American advancement across the continent, Turner wrote, "the meeting point between savagery and civilization."[6] For Turner, the frontier is a world of easily discernible binaries, a line clearly separating who "we" are from who "they" are, who is civilized from who is savage, not a "middle ground," as Richard White has suggested, or a "contact zone," as Mary Louise Pratt has argued.[7]

Moreover, for Turner, the clarity of this line helps us see more distinctly the genesis of the American character, for it is the "line of the most rapid and effective Americanization" (3–4). In the "crucible of the frontier," he argues, immigrants and other "foreigners" are forged into Americans, that is, "a mixed race, English in neither nationality nor characteristics" (23). Turner also then obliges us by outlining exactly what those new frontier characteristics of Americans are:

> The result is that to the frontier the American intellect owes its striking characteristics. That coarseness and strength combined with acuteness and inquisitiveness; that practical, inventive turn of mind, quick to find expedients; that masterful grasp of material things, lacking in the artistic but powerful to effect great ends; that restless, nervous energy; that dominant individualism, working for good and for evil, and withal that buoyancy and exuberance which comes with freedom—these are traits of the frontier, or traits called out elsewhere because of the existence of the frontier. Since the days when the fleet of Columbus sailed into the waters of the New World, America has been another name for opportunity, and the people of the United States have taken their tone from the incessant expansion which has not only been open but has even been forced upon them. (37)

Hearing these American traits—coarseness, strength, practicality, energy, individualism—expounded on in Chicago in 1893 audience members at Turner's lecture were encouraged to merge their ideas of what constituted an American with what defined the frontier. How they defined the frontier became synonymous with how they identified and defined themselves. As Turner put it: "This perennial rebirth, this fluidity of American life, this expansion westward with its new opportunities, its continuous touch with the simplicity of primitive society, furnish the forces dominating American character" (2–3).

The audience members would have also heard Turner's tacit invitation to further conquest and domination even as the frontier, in his words, was coming to a close. If the effectiveness of the Turner Thesis is at least partially due to its simplicity, then his paean to conquest comes as a natural outgrowth of the American frontier's drive toward "incessant expansion." "Movement has been its dominant fact," he concludes about the American nation, and so it is natural and expected that its citizens will continue to push that line of civilization beyond the continent, that "the American energy will continually demand a wider field for its exercise" (37). The Turner Thesis thus became just another name for Manifest Destiny and went hand in hand with the U.S. government's seizure, just five years later, of Cuba, Puerto Rico, Guam, Wake Island, and Manila, as well as the suppression of a colonial uprising in the Philippines that would last from 1899 well into 1902. The Turner Thesis would become most pointedly enacted in 1903 when Turner's fellow author, Theodore Roosevelt, then president of the United States, assisted Panamanian separatists to dissolve their bonds with the Colombian government in exchange for American rights to extraterritoriality over the Canal Zone.[8] The American people—at least as represented by Roosevelt's political maneuverings—had, indeed, demanded and seized a "wider field" for the implementation of their frontier ideology.

While fervently opposed to the kind of academic elitism of Turner, Cody and his Wild West nevertheless proved a perfect ideological mate for Turner in 1893. For the thirty years from 1883 to 1916, Buffalo Bill's Wild West was one of the nation's largest, most popular, and most successful performative ventures (Slotkin 66–67), and part of its popularity no doubt sprang from the way, as Paul Reddin notes, it "provided a simplified, patriotic, and believable national epic that blended history and mythology and legitimized the view of Manifest Destiny that sanctioned the use of force."[9] If we turn to some of the material Cody used to promote his show, we see a striking parallel with the same ideas that Turner was proposing just a few hundred yards away in Chicago in 1893. From the program for the show, for example, we can read the following:

> [While it is] a trite saying that "the pen is mightier than the sword," it is equally true that the bullet is the pioneer of civilization, for it had gone hand in hand with the axe that cleared the forest, and with the family Bible and school book. Deadly as has been its mission in one sense, it has been merciful in another; for without the rifle ball we of America would not be to-day in possession of a free and united country, and mighty in our strength. (qtd. in Slotkin 77)

While Kasson argues that Cody and Turner disagreed about the idea of the frontier as a "process" and that Turner insisted on a much more fluid notion of the frontier and the way it necessarily changed the settler (119), it seems clear that while the nature of that process was not identical, that like Turner, Buffalo Bill's Wild West positioned Cody as the embodiment of the frontiersman who had "passed through every stage of frontier life," as Turner argued the true pioneer did. "The notion," argues Warren, "that the frontier developed in 'stages' was never more explicit than in the show's first indoor performance, in 1886," where the frontier as process was evidenced by the show's billing as "A History of American Civilization" (51). Like Turner, therefore, Cody also suggests that the frontier is not a place so much as a process in which "civilization" meets "savagery" and conquers it. Also like Turner, Buffalo Bill gestures to the ways in which the frontier is responsible for Americanizing the nation, for if there were no frontier, Cody's logic insists, then there would not be a "free and united country." Turner and Cody part company, however, in Cody's making explicit and spectacular what Turner keeps implicit: the use of violence in the "civilizing" endeavor.[10] As Cody demonstrated every time he performed his acts of marksmanship and every time he staged the violent rebuffing of the raid on the Deadwood Stagecoach by Native Americans, violence is crucial to the frontier: As he succinctly puts it, the "bullet is the pioneer of civilization."

If Turner lectured about Manifest Destiny, drawing simple connections between the American character and his understanding of the frontier, Cody turned those lectures into tangible, performative events providing equally simplistic responses of sympathy for heroism and repulsion at villainy. If Turner turned a blind eye to the violence that would necessarily accompany the Americanization of the continent, Cody threw a spotlight on it, reveled in it, and, if his experience in Chicago in 1893 is any gauge, profited from it.[11]

While Cody's application to perform at the exposition had been denied, Cody drew on his showman's chutzpah and set up his show just outside the fairground, in effect, extending the boundary of the exposition to encompass his enormous production. It was, ironically, on this frontier that Cody would perform for nearly six million people, many of whom saw the production numerous times. The 22,000-seat arena was continuously sold out for nearly the entire time Cody was in Chicago, making the Chicago season, with its 186 days of continuous performance from April 26 to October 31, 1893, the most successful one of the tour's run to that point (see Bank 603). To give some perspective, it is worth noting that, as of today, Madison Square Garden in New York City has a seating capacity of more than 2,000 seats fewer than Cody's Wild West entertainment in Chicago in 1893. Moreover, unlike any contemporary performance at Madison Square Garden, Cody's act began as soon as all of the seats were filled, leaving thousands of people still clamoring to get in. One reporter estimated that the crowds spent $150,000 a week at the show and that Cody and his partner, Nate Salsbury, made $1 million in Chicago during the performance (Reddin 118–119).

Turner must have been aware of Buffalo Bill's Wild West as a cultural force. Like the other historians at the American Historical Association meeting, he was invited to attend the Wild West on the afternoon of July 12. There is no historical record that suggests that Turner took Cody up on his invitation, nor is there any mention in Turner's works of why he chose to forgo seeing Buffalo Bill. Joy S. Kasson suggests that Turner skipped the show "since he was hard at work completing the speech he would give that very night" (120). At the same time, there is equally no evidence to suggest that Cody was in the audience for Turner's lecture. One might suppose that at least one reason why Cody would not have attended the lecture was that he was the star attraction of his own production and could not spare the time. However, like Turner, he left no record providing his rationale. In a titillating irony, therefore, the two "master narrators of American westering," as Richard White calls them, were exploring similar themes in virtually the same place at the same time, and yet, even though it would never be easier for them to meet, they never did ("Turner" 7–8).

While it is tantalizing to think about how Buffalo Bill's figurative opening of the frontier would have affected Turner, the man who had just spoken of how the historical frontier was coming to a "close," I am not interested in speculating about what might have happened or what could have been in 1893 or how they became the "master narrators" of the American frontier.[12] What I am interested in, instead, is exploring how American history and performance—the history of American performance, that is, as well as the performance of American history—are inextricably linked by their shared fixation on an idea of the frontier, a space, moreover, that is thematically richer, more diverse, and more radical than has been previously supposed. What the great frontier historian's failure to meet the great frontier performer suggests symbolically, in other words, is that this is not a simple narrative. At this point in the narrative, we see another story waiting to be told, one that is distinct and different from the one leading to Turner's and Cody's. This story is one that demands telling, for it does not smooth the path of empire, as does Turner's and Cody's. Rather, throughout most of the nineteenth century, it interrupted, interrogated, and derailed the stories — those two men told.

Pioneer Performances tells this story, and in doing so, it works in two directions simultaneously. It capitalizes on the legacy of New Western Historians like Patricia Nelson Limerick and Susan Lee Johnson who have deftly problematized the Turner Thesis, while not simply rehearsing their arguments. Rather, as I will demonstrate when discussing the performative history of Cody's contemporary Gowongo Mohawk, this study defines a different version of frontier performance that addresses the shortcomings of New Western History as well as argues for a new historical formation, what I will be calling New Western Genealogy.

Likewise, just as I will use the genealogy of performing the frontier to problematize frontier history, I will use that same genealogy to limn a more multifaceted story of the American theater. By bringing the representation of the frontier in American drama to the surface and analyzing its shifting aesthetic formations, we will discover an American theater that used its critical engagement with the dominant representation of the frontier we see in Buffalo Bill's Wild West and the Turner Thesis to explore alternative constructions of ideology and nationalism. Moreover, it also used the critical energy it generated from tackling the dominant representation of the frontier to move the American performative aesthetic down new avenues, from playwriting to scenic technology to acting stylistics. In the speculative gap that exists between Frederick Jackson Turner's missed meeting with Buffalo Bill Cody, in other words, emerges a new model of the frontier whose genealogical "counter-memory," to use Foucault's term,[13] not only recodes what constitutes frontier history but also reconfigures the political and aesthetic shape of the history of American drama.

GOWONGO MOHAWK'S FREE WEST

As a cultural figure, Gowongo Mohawk's name is as unfamiliar as Buffalo Bill's is commonplace. Yet at exactly the same time that Buffalo Bill's Wild West was at the height of its popularity, this Native American actress, the supposed daughter of the famous Senecan orator and leader, Red Jacket,[14] was incredibly popular, selling out shows from cities like Chicago, Baltimore, and Philadelphia to more rural centers like Wheeling, West Virginia, and Iowa City, Iowa. Cody's fame was firmly established when he took his show to Europe, so that the European audiences might, in Cody's terms, "esteem us better." Mohawk's celebrated play, *Wep-Ton-No-Mah, the Indian Mail Carrier*, also made the similar jump to Europe after a successful American run.[15]

Mohawk's play involved swashbuckling knife fights, sensational physical feats, rodeo tricks during a stampede, and perhaps most intriguing of all, the startling enactment of all of these things by Mohawk, who cross-dressed to star as the Indian youth Wep-ton-no-mah, who participates in a version of the Pony Express. Attracted by this strange mixture of elements, audiences flocked to see her perform. One reviewer noted that the Kensington Theatre in Philadelphia was "crowded and the enthusiastic audience cheered and applauded the star and her company to the echo,"[16] while the *Wheeling Register* in West Virginia, noting that Mohawk was about to give her last local performance, remonstrated with its reading public that "those who have not yet seen her should not fail to do so."[17] There can be little doubt, therefore, that Mohawk's performance was popular, and while I am not suggesting that it was as popular as Buffalo Bill's Wild West—few performative events were—what I am suggesting is that she, too, was staging the frontier for large audiences during nearly the same decades that the Wild West was entertaining them.

One might argue that Mohawk's popularity was generated in the same frontier forge that Buffalo Bill's was, that people flocked to see her spectacular displays of riding, knife play, and physical action for the same reasons that they flocked to see his show. At one level, of course, this is true: Both performers mounted spectacular representations of the frontier in their shows, using real horses and real guns to give an air of verisimilitude to their frontier representations.[18] Yet, if we focus on the ways gender and the body were deployed in both productions, we can see a distinct difference between them, a difference that complicates considerably the history of frontier performance.

One of the most productive ways of gauging the differences between the two pieces is to place the two leading actresses of both productions side by side. In other words, I want to compare Mohawk with the Wild West's most famous actress, Annie Oakley. Annie Oakley's role in Buffalo Bill's Wild West was vitally important, for it offered female audience members a figure with whom to identify—and that, as Cody well knew, meant more profit. Yet, while the lure of lucre drove Cody to include Oakley, the problem of gender identification needed to be managed, for to attract the kind of clientele Cody wanted, he had to counter Oakley's inherent aggressiveness and violence that made her a star by coupling it with a more feminine and "ladylike" demeanor.

Annie Oakley dazzled people by firing shotguns and a .22 caliber rifle, hitting stationary targets, shattering airborne clay pigeons, and, most spectacularly, splitting playing cards length-wise. Nevertheless, her entrance was always a "pretty one." "She never walked," Dexter Fellows, longtime press agent for the Wild West, noted. "She tripped in, bowing, waving, and wafting kisses," and while her shooting in the beginning would often bring forth "a few screams of fright from the women," she quickly "set the audience at ease" (qtd. in Warren 247). She was violent, but her violence was domesticated, cosseted to ease the tension that existed between her conflicting gender figurations. Her domestication was visualized for the audience in the dresses she wore in all of the posters she appeared in and even in the arena itself, where she always performed in women's clothing. Moreover, she underscored her family ties—and her thorough domestication—by traveling and appearing with her husband, Frank Butler, and included their pet dog in her act. Perhaps most telling of all, when she rode and performed feats from horseback, she always rode sidesaddle which was "considered," as Paul Reddin writes, "the right choice for a proper lady of that day" (71). Part of Annie Oakley's allure involved her feats of violence, acts tradition- ally associated with the masculine sphere, but her performance could attract audiences, and especially women, because it demonstrated how completely tamed this "wild" woman of the frontier was. She might be able to fire a rifle, but her petticoats, like her pets, registered how safe she was, how clear and convincing her domestic proclivities were, and while she took up the reins, she was, as Louis Warren maintains, "the Wild West show's most power- ful symbol of domesticity, her combination of marksmanship, femininity, temperance, and frugality a huge marketing asset for a show of border life" (249).

Imagine, then, how audience members might have reacted to Gowongo Mohawk, who did not enter wafting kisses or bowing but made her entrance with "fearless riding," which, it is crucial to note, she executed "without saddle or bridle."[19] While both Oakley and Mohawk performed roles that destabilized gender, Oakley rode sidesaddle during her feats of horseman- ship to insure her audience understood how essentialized her gender was, how a "domestic goddess," in short, was handling that rifle. The cross- dressed Mohawk, by contrast, defied these conventions by not merely giving up the feminized sidesaddle but in forgoing any saddle whatsoever. Rather than manage the threat to gender identity she provided for her audi- ence, as Oakley did, Mohawk deliberately threw out a skein of problematic gender signifiers for her audience.[20] Despite these problematic gender sig- nifiers, audiences nevertheless found her, as one reviewer in Baltimore in 1892 mentions, "an exceedingly captivating character."[21]

The fact that Mohawk performed a murky gender identity and was, at the same time, alluring speaks to the idea that it was exactly her imbricated notion of gender that made her captivating. This is, of course, true of Annie Oakley as well, but what distinguished these two figures is the way they managed the gender anxiety their performances created. Oakley played it down with her dresses, while Mohawk intensified it with her cross-dressing; this is a difference of degree, in other words, rather than a difference in kind. Consider how one reviewer described Mohawk. He begins by noting that "[o]n the stage Miss Mohawk is magnetic in manner, fertile in imagina- tion and quick in giving her imagining expression through the medium of a rich and musical voice—a voice that is deep, thrilling and intense in its tragic utterances, clear and ringing in its mirthful expression, and sweet, low and tender in its pathos." Taken together, these read as traditionally coded feminine traits, particularly the way he notes her "fertile" imagination, her "mirthful expression," and her "tender" voice. In this way, the reviewer seems to be performing some of the domesticating of Gowongo Mohawk that Annie Oakley self-administered. Yet this quickly evaporates when the reviewer notes that the "climax of excitement is in the third act, where *Spanish Joe*, the villain of the play, and *Wep-ton-no-mah* meet and engage in a bowie-knife contest. The fight is a ferocious one, and after several rounds the villain is made to bite the dust."[22] If we isolate just this section, we cannot help but read it as being transparently masculine—the "bowie-knife" fight, the "ferocious" character of the contest, and the fact that at the end of it Mohawk makes the villain "bite the dust": All of these read as masculine traits. Taken together, both of these enjambed sections point to the deliberately opaque nature of Mohawk's own identity politics—a highly energized and provocative mixture of competing gendered gestures. Again and again, attention to Mohawk's performing body attempts to fuse her competing configurations, noting her "attractive countenance" and how "lithe her limbs" are, as the reviewer for the *Philadelphia Inquirer* does in a blazonlike cataloging of female physical beauty, then in the next breath admitting that "she is an expert in handling a horse, a gun, a rod, the oars, and a great admirer of all outdoor sports."[23] Such an attractive, physically alluring figure who can nevertheless also handle a gun, a horse, and—in a bit of late nineteenth-century double entendre—a "rod" was perplexing but, interestingly enough, pleasantly so. It is perhaps for this reason that one reviewer of her performance in Chicago stated that the "[l]overs of the weirdly sensational will find in this entertainment more than enough to satisfy their cravings."[24] If we trace the fetishization of Mohawk's body in newspaper reviews alone, we begin to see that her drag act not only made her performance "weird" but also "sensational."[25]

The play's text amplifies this kind of confusing gender identity, for while the audience would have known that the heroic boy, Wep-ton-no-mah, was played by a woman, the play does not diminish this confusion in the dialogue but, in fact, underscores it. As Spanish Joe notes of Wep-ton-no-mah, he is "not only a dead shot and lightning with the knife, but he is as muscular as a panther and the best horseman for miles around."[26] To suggest that s/he is good with a rifle may seem parallel to Annie Oakley's characterization, but to highlight how "muscular" she is—a characteristic that would necessarily draw the audience's eyes to Mohawk's female body—seems to be flaunting, not mitigating, the gender indeterminacy of her performance.

Perhaps the most extreme example of this kind of gender trouble involves the burgeoning infatuation of the female lead, Nellie, with Wep-ton-no-mah after s/he saves her from the stampede, having rushed between the frightened cattle, "seiz[ed] Nellie round the waist," and "plac[ed] her on the back of his foamy steed" (19). In addition to the clearly sexualized language of putting the young woman on the "back" of his "foamy" horse, what makes this titillating moment all the more sexually charged is that Mohawk does not minimize the growing sexual attraction between white woman and Native American woman. The double subversiveness of this maneuver is, of course, both sexual and racial, entertaining both a potential same-sex encounter and, compounding this, a potential act of racial miscegenation. While this relationship is defused at the end, with Wep-ton-no-mah forgoing Nellie's white culture for a return to a distinctly Native American one, Mohawk does more than simply flirt with racy sexual and racial couplings. In a performance that occurs in the same period as Oscar Wilde's famous trials for homosexuality, Mohawk seems to revel in them.

Mohawk's "weird" politics come into clearer focus if we follow how she characterizes the frontier in the play's text, for in doing so, we see how potentially radical her view of the frontier is in relation to the one imagined by Cody and Turner. On Mohawk's frontier, the paternalistic figure of the Colonel tells his daughter, Nellie, "you must never judge people by appearances" and then goes on to say that although the heroic white figure of Captain Franklin seems "a perfect Apollo Belvedere," he is actually "thoroughly worthless." Likewise, he adds that the Mexican Señor Lopez is, as it turns out, a "fine gentlemanly sort of a fellow" (23–24). Using the benevolent figure of the Colonel as a mouthpiece, Mohawk suggests a less racist, more expansive view of the frontier: On the frontier, stereotypes break down, particularly racial ones, and thus like Nellie, we the audience are taught to read the frontier in a different way.

Building on the fact that she was playing the heroic lead, Mohawk uses some of his dialogue to present an alternative view of the frontier. "The Col. offered me the position of Mail Carrier for the Post," s/he confesses, "but I could not stand being under the control of anyone except the great Manitou. I want to be free—free—like the birds, the eagles and deers—owning *no* master but one" (30). This is a frontier under the rule of the "great Manitou," one that does not value "civilization," in Turner's and Cody's term, but yearns, instead, for freedom. We should also note that Mohawk defines the freedom of the frontier in a way that is particularly opposed to Turner's and Cody's frontier ideology, for this is a frontier where there are "*no* master[s] but one," where there is something other than the master/slave dialectic not to mention the equation of women and property that subtends American imperialism.

Mohawk reinforces this precise idea of the frontier in an interview she gave in 1910. When asked why she chose to cross-dress, she says that she "liked to ride, rope, fire guns, and shoot arrows. She decided to enact a male role, she said, because she wanted to do something 'wild and free'" (qtd. in Hall 159). This combination of qualities—wildness and freedom—strikingly underscores her ideological difference from figures like Turner and Cody. If Buffalo Bill's concept of the Wild West was, indeed, wild, then it was a frontier zone where that wildness was neutralized by white American culture—by the "bullet of civilization," in Cody's terms, or by the encroachment of white civilization for the "new development for that area," to quote Turner (2). For Mohawk, the frontier generates this freedom through precisely the same unruly and unruled wildness that Turner and Cody see as something, like Oakley, needing a petticoat. Through her flirtation with dangerously subversive gender roles, sexual relationships, and racial couplings, Mohawk created a "weird" frontier that neither demanded nor invited the juggernaut of conquest to settle its "unsettled" lands but that worked actively to "unsettle" precisely the ideology popularized and promulgated by Turner and Cody.

THE GOWONGO EFFECT I: A NEW WESTERN GENEALOGY

In contrasting traditional notions of history with what he calls "genealogy," Michel Foucault argues that, unlike history's quest for solid foundations on which to build stable narratives, genealogy "disturbs what was previously considered immobile; it fragments what was thought unified; it shows the heterogeneity of what was imagined consistent with itself" (147). This is more suited to generating knowledge, he argues, because the "world we know is not this ultimately simple configuration where events are reduced to accentuate their essential traits, their final meaning, or their initial and final value. On the contrary, it is a profusion of entangled events" (155). With this idea of genealogy in mind, we can see that Gowongo Mohawk's story exposes two things when it is read against the stories told by the "master narrators," Turner and Cody. First, it reveals that the "history" of the frontier is, indeed, a "profusion of entangled events," and, second, it makes use of some of those entangled events to "disturb what was previously considered immobile." From this perspective, Buffalo Bill's Wild West is not the apotheosis of the frontier, even if it was wildly popular. Complicating the very moment of Cody's triumph in 1893 is a much more variegated and diffuse notion of the frontier that was given shape and texture in Mohawk's performance. Although this performance was a singular attempt to reforge the notion of the frontier, it was not the only one. As the following chapters will demonstrate, this alternative story of the frontier as a "free" space—to use Mohawk's term—has shadowed the master historical narrative of the frontier since its inception. Moreover, as

I will demonstrate, these two stories are mutually constructed, gaining definition and relevancy through their intertwined relationship.

Thanks to Gowongo Mohawk and her predecessors, it should be clear that much of the contemporary post-Turner historiography of the frontier has been telling too tidy a story of this important idea. What has been called New Western History has indeed critiqued the Turner Thesis. As one of its avatars, Patricia Nelson Limerick, argues: "Turner was, to put it mildly, ethnocentric and nationalistic. English-speaking white men were stars of his story; Indians, Hispanics, French Canadians, and Asians were at best supporting actors and at worst invisible. Nearly as invisible were women, of all ethnicities."[27] Not only was Turner ethnocentric, but he was also deliberately blind to the ways in which imperial power was being deployed on the frontier; to recode Turner's historiography in this way is to understand the "history of the West," as Limerick suggests, as "a place undergoing conquest and never fully escaping its consequences" (26).

Limerick represents a new generation of historians who began writing in the 1970s in the wake of Dee Brown's *Bury My Heart at Wounded Knee* (1970), the incisive polemic against U.S. military aggression against Native Americans. As historian Donald Worster tells the story, a

> younger generation, shaken by the experience of Vietnam and other national disgraces—poverty, racism, environmental degradation—could not pretend that the only story that mattered in the West was one of stagecoach lines, treasure hunts, cattle brands, and wildcatters.... What was missing was a frank, hard look at the violent, imperialistic process by which the West was wrested from its original owners and the violence by which it has been secured against the continuing claims of minorities, women, and the forces of nature.[28]

This new generation of historians, the New Western Historians, as they came to be called, have recognized that "minorities not only have always shared in the rising power and affluence of the West but also have in some ways thought differently about the ends of that power and affluence" (Worster 12). Countering Turner's simple definition of the frontier as the meeting point between civilization and savagery, historians like Howard Lamar and Leonard Thompson define it "not as a boundary or line, but a territory or zone of interpenetration between two previously distinct societies." More importantly, they go on to note that the frontier "opens" in a given zone "when the first representatives of the intrusive society arrive" and it "closes" when a single political authority has established hegemony over the zone.[29]

New Western Historians opened the history of the frontier by disabusing us of the notion that "the other" was singular and monolithic, that

Native Americans, for instance, had "a simple, homogenous group identity" (Limerick 215).[30] However, while Limerick warns her readers against making the other monolithic, she shoehorns groups with different beliefs, politics, and ideologies into the notion of the "self." She describes how the frontier came with two sides: "the Anglo-American side and the one labeled 'the other side of the frontier.' Jammed into the second category were Indians of all tribes (often tribes that fought against each other as well as against Anglo-Americans), long-term Hispanic settlers, and more recent Mexican immigrants. In lived reality, the people on this 'other side of the frontier' did not form anything remotely resembling a united team of a homogenous society."[31] Disconcerting in its asymmetry between the Anglo-American on one side and the Indians, Hispanics, and Mexicans on the other side, Limerick's New Western History has told a provocative story about the fundamental role played by racialized and gendered "others," but only at the expense of a kind of critical consolidating, or "homogenizing," to use Limerick's critical term, of what constituted the dominant white culture.

Even Susan Lee Johnson's social history of the Southern Mines in California during the gold rush of the mid-nineteenth century, which tells a dynamic story of the frontier as "a time and place of tremendous contest about maleness and femaleness, about color and culture, and about wealth and power," still works to smooth the tangle of suppliers of cultural energy in the period.[32] The florescence of social and cultural boundlessness in the Southern Mines, Johnson laments, began to "give way to more entrenched forms of dominance rooted in Anglo American constructions of gender, of class position, and of race, ethnicity, and nation—that is, in particular ideas about what it meant to live 'like white folks'" (276). Rehearsing the same kind of asymmetrical attention to the suppliers of culture that permeates Limerick's historiography, Johnson again essentializes all Anglo-Americans, a group whose experience with the frontier, like Turner's and Cody's, worked to dominate all forms of cultural and social "savagery." In a bit of nostalgia, Johnson concludes that, because of the influential reach of these "white folks," the "social change in the Southern Mines would not capture the eastern imagination" (316).

While the Southern Mines, in particular, might not have captured the eastern imagination, what its frontier representation captured—the coursing in and out of customary channels of gender relations, race relations, and labor relations (Johnson 121)—certainly did and did so quite well. As I have shown in analyzing Gowongo Mohawk's performance and as I will show in the chapters in this study, this idea of the frontier fired the imaginations of precisely the same "white folks" that Johnson presents as the agents of cultural hegemony. How else might we explain the fact that, as popular as Buffalo Bill's Wild West was in the East, Gowongo Mohawk's performances were incredibly popular there as well? While it is a fool's errand to attempt to chart what kinds of people went to see the two productions, it is equally clear that, at worst, although Mohawk's and Cody's audiences were distinct, they still lived in the same locales, and, at best, they were the same people, those who were as attracted to the more lenient, less hegemonic conceptualization of the frontier proffered by Mohawk as they were to Cody's imperialistic fantasies.

New Western History has done yeoman's service debunking and denaturalizing the Turner Thesis, analyzing its "legacy of conquest" and the way that legacy has obscured a much more nuanced, multifaceted conceptualization of the frontier. That being said, what Gowongo Mohawk and all of the figures I will take up in the pages that follow reveal is that New Western History has tended to reinforce the inclination to simplify a more complicated story by essentializing certain aspects of it. This is not to dismiss the foundational work of Limerick, Johnson, Lamar, Thompson, and others but rather to argue that if frontier historiography has benefited from the salvage work done by them, it is time to turn that critical inclination toward those seemingly monolithic figures who interpreted the frontier leading up to Turner and Cody. I want to balance the historical ledger by building on the work done by New Western Historicists in the 1980s and 1990s by turning to, in this instance, the performance of the frontier in the very core of the eastern hegemony—in theaters from Boston to New York City to Philadelphia. I want to show the differing and competing conceptualizations of the frontier constructed in the theater and substantiated by its patrons. New Western Genealogy pursues this line of inquiry in order not simply to argue for a more sophisticated idea of who these "white folks" were. Rather, in its reclamation of these texts in all of their complexity, it works to illuminate the ways that the performance of the frontier on the nineteenth-century stage did not simply use the frontier to Americanize the Anglo-American population by rallying them around the idol of Manifest Destiny, it also aimed to undercut the central tenets of Manifest Destiny.

THE GOWONGO EFFECT II: AMERICAN PERFORMANCE

If our exploration of Gowongo Mohawk's performance contributes to overturning the notion of a monolithic Anglo-American population rehearsing the performance of the frontier as Manifest Destiny, it also works to explode the politically flat history of the American theater from the Age of Jackson through the World Columbian Exposition. While there were certainly plays about the frontier before Jackson's 1828 presidential victory, I am beginning to chart the frontier's radical theatrical history with the Age of Jackson for three reasons.

First, westward expansion rapidly increased under Jackson's policies to extend the United States' "area of freedom." He facilitated the sale of public lands and eliminated Indian preserves in the South (with the exception, notably, of the Florida Seminoles) to make way for cotton (Stephanson 31). With the rapid increase in the modes and speed of communication between the western frontier and the East—the telegraph, steamboats, newspapers, trains, and so forth—citizens living on the eastern seaboard during the Age of Jackson would have been privy to a wider range of representations of the frontier than those before them had been.[33]

Moreover, because of the "market revolution" of the period,[34] the eastern metropoles grew exponentially, increasing from representing 7.2 percent of the general population in 1820 to 19.8 percent in 1860: New York City, the fastest-growing city in the United States during this period and then, as now, a center for theatrical activity, increased its population by half during each decade from 1790 to 1860, rising from 33,000 in 1790 to more than 800,000 by the Civil War.[35] In the Age of Jackson, cities like New York became industrial centers with burgeoning populations coming from the interior of the country and from across the Atlantic Ocean as well, and the theater became a nexus for linking varying populations' aesthetic predilections and ideas.

While the hostility to the theater in the prerevolutionary period often sprang from both its moral looseness and, as was more often the case, its economic "wasting" of free capital on British imports (including theater), the postrevolutionary theater attempted to "de-demonize the institution," as Jeffrey H. Richards notes.[36] The nature of antitheatricalism fundamentally shifted after the American Revolution and the actions of the Continental Congress, "transforming it," as Heather Nathans observes, "from a simple matter of religious preference to one of patriotic duty."[37] Thus, even when a religious revivalism that embraced the kind of moral objections to the theater made popular by Puritans and Quakers in the prerevolutionary period blossomed during the Jacksonian period in the "burned-over" regions of the country, and even in urban metropoles, the new urban populations were nevertheless still more inclined to go to the theater starting in the 1820s and 1830s than they had been previously.[38] Theatergoing was seen as an American duty, and the new playwriting competitions in the Jacksonian period, offered by actors like Edwin Forrest and James Hackett, attempted to fulfill this duty even as it gave the actors some of their most lucrative star vehicles. As the historian Robert C. Allen suggests, theaters in the Jacksonian period became more numerous and more financially self-sufficient mostly because they traded the patronage of the elites who attended performances during

pre-Jacksonian America for that of the "shirt-sleeve crowd," as Fanny Trollope called the urban artisan and managerial class of the 1830s. This is not
to say that the theater in the United States did not also cater to the elite but
rather to suggest that, starting in the late 1820s, the theater offered a quickly
diversifying range of cultural spaces that could address the multiplying host
of interests, desires, and predilections evinced by the changing population. In this way, as Allen suggests, the theaters maintained their roles as
a cultural formation that policed social roles even as they simultaneously
obtained the leeway to explore other racier and even bawdier material as
well as less established modes, from the minstrel show to burlesque (55),
in an attempt to outline and construct an American theatrical experience.
The Age of Jackson, in short, saw not only a rapid industrialization of the
urban centers but a booming population both more familiar with what was
happening on the frontier and more willing, even eager, to explore new aesthetic ways of representing it in the theater.[39]

One of the most trenchant illustrations of this shift in the American theater during the Jacksonian period comes not from within the nation but
from outside it. In his famous *Democracy in America* (1835–1840), the
French historian and lay anthropologist Alexis de Tocqueville explored a
range of American institutions with the careful eye of the critic: One of the
institutions he devoted time to was the American theater. "Of all forms of
literature it is generally the drama," he observes, "that is first affected by the
social and political revolutions upsetting an aristocratic order, and its influence is always conspicuous there."[40] De Tocqueville is, of course, responding
to exactly the kind of populist upsurge spearheaded by Jackson's Democratic victory in 1828—for the elite de Tocqueville, it was indeed a "social
and political revolution." This concept of the theater was less inclined simply to mimic elite forms, a place where the "pit often lays down the law for
the boxes" (490), and even when these American theaters chose to perform something like a play by William Shakespeare, as Lawrence Levine
has famously demonstrated, they reworked it for their own more egalitarian
ends.[41] For de Tocqueville, the theater was not just another medium for
seeing this democratic uptick but the very testing ground for democracy,
so much so that "[i]f you want advance knowledge of the literature of a
people which is turning toward democracy," he urged, "pay attention to the
theater" (489).

Moreover, the theater was not just a well-calibrated index of the turn
toward democracy, or to put it another way, the vectors of influence did not
simply point one way. If the theater is useful as a place for seeing the desider-
ata of the American citizenry, it was also a key player in shaping them; it was
a "theatrical formation," to borrow Bruce McConachie's term, "the mutual
elaboration over time of historically specific audience groups and theatre

practitioners participating in certain shared patterns of dramatic and theatrical action" (xii). Part of the perspicacity of de Tocqueville's analysis of the American theater is the way he argues this exact idea: "When democratic audiences rule the stage they introduce as much license in the manner of treating subjects as in the choice of them" (491). Democratic audiences, as de Tocqueville calls them, not only participated in the theater from the sidelines but also shifted the way the theater functioned, from seating practices to acting styles to dramatic content. The kind of democratic theater de Tocqueville witnessed was, in many ways, a radically unstable institution. "All literary rules and conventions are shaken by the impact of democracy," he concludes, "leaving only the caprice of each author and each audience" (491). To be sure, we can easily read the French critic's elitist patronizing of the American theater's lack of shape or consistency in his insistence on the "caprice" of the author and audience, but even in de Tocqueville's dismay at the unstable quality of the theater, we sense a critical aspect of the American theater in the Jacksonian period. If de Tocqueville laments the theater's lack of shape, he leavens this by revealing its potency as a cultural institution that was tremendously popular among the burgeoning middle- and underclass and that embraced an aesthetic unmoored from established "literary rules and conventions." It was lightning caught in a bottle, the turbulent aesthetic energy of the Jacksonian period channeled onto the American stage from Boston to New York to Charleston.

While this contemporary commentator on the Jacksonian theater saw it as a radically unstable aesthetic institution interested in challenging rules and conventions, our current histories of this theater have tended to understand the frontier play and its theatrical history as, instead, an uninflected aestheticization of hegemonic ideology. This is not to say, of course, that all critics have treated the aesthetic turn to the frontier as merely reflecting dominant ideology, for as Philip J. Deloria suggests, the "indeterminacy" of portraying Indians in terms of the role it served in codifying national identity opened a representational space for complicating what counted as national identity.[42] Similarly, as Gordon M. Sayre argues, by emplotting the literary Indian as a "tragic hero" in drama, these plays make the catharsis generated by such representations anxious reflections of American political dominance.[43] Yet, for all of their attention to the subtlety of frontier representation, even of performance, both Deloria and Sayre also suggest how uninflected the theatrical representation of Indians and thus of the frontier was. Deloria reads a play I will take up in the first chapter, *Metamora; or, The Last of the Wampanoags*, for instance, as one of the "best examples of the ideological force of the vanishing Indian" (64) and insists that the play's ending had the Indians offering up "their land, their blessings, their traditions, and their republican history to those who were, in real life, violent, conquering interlopers" (65), thus cementing the play's ideological hegemony. Sayre likewise argues that *Metamora* "staged this ritual of the capture and sacrifice of an Indian leader as a symbolic means for securing a social compact that would replace frontier violence and the bitter racial and political factions behind it with a new civil one," one consonant with the vision and mechanisms of American imperialism (8). Sayre concludes that plays featuring Indians "worked to reconcile political and ethnic differences in the interests of a hegemonic U. S. national purpose" (26). What we see in this set of examples, therefore, is that no matter how radically charged the representation of the frontier has become in our critical history, it has tended to remain a conservative organ for the promotion of the "hegemonic U. S. national purpose" in its theatrical history. The frontier has become a way of restaging the politics of Manifest Destiny, while the frontier stage has remained an aesthetic space for performing the tenets of U.S. imperialism. For all of its revolutionary potential, in other words, we have tended to see the nineteenth-century theater as a charmingly strange, yet ultimately toothless apparatus for reinforcing the dominant cultural ideology. Yet if we understand Gowongo Mohawk's performance and see how complicated it makes the nineteenth-century theatrical formation—at least in relation to the concept of the frontier—it makes sense that even during the Jacksonian period, when Manifest Destiny was on its meteoric rise as a guiding national philosophy, the theater's radical aesthetics would not simply echo the call for empire.

This is not to say, of course, that theater never functioned in that way. The Jacksonian theater, like any other art form, produced its own rallying cry for expansionism, and one story I might easily tell in the chapters that follow concerns the way the nineteenth-century theater simply laid the groundwork for the rise of Cody and Turner. Yet Gowongo Mohawk's performance represents a different, more provocative end point for an alternative theatrical tradition. Consequently, to insist, as theater critics have done, that nineteenth-century representations of the frontier worked along only one trajectory seems to be telling just one part of the multifaceted story of the American theater. By arguing, as Roger Hall does, for instance, that nineteenth-century theatrical representations of the frontier merely "reinforced popular but misleading images of white settlers as victims of native populations, responding with violence only when provoked by savage atrocities" (3), thus helping to reinforce the audience's "own sense of righteousness and destiny" (228), we miss seeing how theatrical performances like Gowongo Mohawk's worked assiduously against such images, upending rather than reinforcing the audience's sense of Manifest Destiny.

Critics seem to have ignored this rich theatrical history because they have internalized the theatrical historian David Grimsted's seminal assessment of the nineteenth-century American theater, his argument that the stage was merely compliant with dominant ideas of the frontier and that no "alternative way of constructing 'democratic' plays" existed.[44] This might explain why there have been virtually no critical explorations of the frontier play in the past half century,[45] for, like Grimsted, scholars have tended to (mis)read Lawrence Levine's assessment of antebellum American audiences as being naïve or unsophisticated. For Hall and Grimsted, among others, this lack of aesthetic and critical sophistication was synonymous with a lack of political savvy: American audiences, in other words, would and could only stomach the kind of theatrical entertainments that staged Jacksonian imperialism. Against this idea of a feckless American audience and a listless theatrical endeavor, I will levy a series of popular plays from the Jacksonian period to the World Columbian Exposition that, taken together, underscore not only how provocative a fantasia the frontier was onstage in both cementing and dissolving the formation of ideology, but because of this, how complicated the American theatergoing population also was in its tastes, predilections, and tolerances.

Essentially, I am arguing that the theater's representation of the frontier galvanized the revolutionary aesthetic that de Tocqueville has described, thus revising our understanding of nineteenth-century theater and of American theatrical history more generally. By tracing how Gowongo Mohawk's predecessors drove acting aesthetics toward more realistic characterizations, helped displace the dramaturgical techniques of melodrama, problematized the performance of racial difference, and realigned theater technology from creating stage pictures to staging politically invested spectacles, I will show that the origins of American drama are found precisely at the moments when the theater turned the more abstract fantasy of the frontier into a tactile, textured performance of what it meant to be American.

In this way, finally, we can use the genealogy of American frontier performance—these pioneer performances, as I call them—to offer another definition of the frontier. Like the New Western Historicist's problematizing of Turner's definition of the frontier as a "process" where Americans are forged as a result of conquest, I also want to complicate Turner's idea. However, unlike the historians, I do not want to suggest that we should only think about the frontier as a place undergoing conquest, or a place where there is not enough rain to grow eastern crops, or a place in the western United States where racially diverse populations met.[46] Some of the most radical political performances of the frontier occurred far from the West, in fact, right at the center of urban zones like New York, Philadelphia and Boston. If Turner's notion of process seems purposely to sidestep even as it promotes a kind of rampant power grabbing, then the alternative definitions of the frontier have seemed to suggest that the authentic frontier could only occur in a place far distant from the eastern seaboard—a place that was not the east, to put it simply. Yet, this fetishization of place misses seeing how the frontier is always already a representation, one that creates the notion of place textually and aesthetically. Thus, the idea of a frontier that supercedes or predates its representation in letters, books, posters, diaries, and so forth is itself a fantasy, the fantasy of an "untouched" or "pristine" wilderness that participates in, rather than dismantles, the kind of representational colonialism that we see in figures like Turner or Cody.[47]

This book opens a space for a different definition of the frontier that situates it between process and place at the site of performance. By tending to the historical context of these theatrical productions, as well as to their formal and aesthetic aspects, I show how the American frontier operated not just as a historically or geographically delimited entity but also as a set of performative practices conditioned by history and geography. In recasting the frontier in this way, we get out of the dangerous mindset of thinking that there ever was an authentic frontier distinct from its performance on numerous stages, an idea that is dangerous in the ways that its legerdemain involving what counted as the "true West" necessarily foreclosed other versions of frontier experience. By defining the frontier as a set of performative practices, therefore, we can resituate the frontier from the Wild West to the urban Northeast, revealing that for the majority of the American population who would not travel outside the metropole, the frontier was created as much on the footboards of New York City as it was on the plains of the West. Likewise, in defining the frontier in this way, we simultaneously understand how fluid this notion of the frontier was, how it could circulate as easily among Penobscot Indians, the white working class, mulatto slaves, and mining camp "ladies" as it could among white, privileged men, how it could as easily lead to Gowongo Mohawk's performative event as it could to Cody's or Turner's.

Since the frontier has always been performed, therefore, it was never really closed, as Turner insists, nor has it ever been simply about the reproduction of dominant ideology. While it might be easy for contemporary audiences to point to George W. Bush's brush-clearing "performance" at his Crawford, Texas, ranch in 2005 as just another link in a long chain of frontier performances leading back to Cody and beyond, one must see the way Ang Lee's *Brokeback Mountain* (2005), with its pitch-perfect evocation of frontier tropes as a way of exploring queer aesthetics, also reaches back, this time to Gowongo Mohawk and beyond. The story I tell about this frontier is, therefore, about the mutually constituted and tightly intertwined interplay between both lineages, which creates a genealogy of American frontier performance—and American theatrical history, more generally—that was constructed not only in the different performative practices associated with the frontier but also through their competing ideologies of performance. For every Dubya, in short, there is a Jack Twist, the queer cowboy from *Brokeback Mountain*; for every Buffalo Bill there is a Gowongo Mohawk. Thus, to understand why the frontier has proved to be such an enduring American obsession, we must tell both stories not to the exclusion of each other but in the ways they generated cultural energy through their heated scrimmages over ideology and aesthetics.

The first chapter begins telling these intertwined stories of the theater by exploring the actor Edwin Forrest's "redding up" in 1829, at the beginning of the Jacksonian era, when playing the title role in John Augustus Stone's *Metamora; or, The Last of the Wampanoags*. Unlike the broad-brushstrokes categorization of the Indian play as a tool of Manifest Destiny that critics have advanced, this chapter discovers the foundational role that Forrest had in crystallizing the transgressive genealogy of the frontier, which he articulated, in this instance, as "savage" passion and social formlessness. He implicitly opposed this to the sterile reason and social policing inherent in what Jay Fliegelman has called the European "elocution revolution," which attempted to codify the rules of rhetoric in the early nineteenth century. Forrest's "savage" performative practices were witnessed by Native Americans when the play was put on in Boston, Massachusetts, and Augusta, Georgia. Their rescripting of these practices demonstrates how this idea of the frontier could be redeployed both to bolster and disrupt hegemonic Anglo-American culture.

At the same time as Forrest's Metamora, the frontiersman Wildfire in James Kirke Paulding's drama *The Lion of the West* (1829) also played a key role in interrogating the performative theatricality that led to Cody's imperialist melodramas. Chapter Two reveals how Wildfire's embodiment of the frontier challenged the dominant conception of the frontier as sublime, a notion inherited from Edmund Burke, by defining it instead as wondrous. Paulding represents this aesthetic rift in his play between the wondrous and the sublime through the opposition of his two main characters, the suggestively named Wildfire and the European aesthete, Amelia Wollope. Much to the latter's dismay, Wildfire's performance of the frontier does not identify as the sublime, which uses its reliance on terror and rules to reinforce an imperial hierarchy of power. Rather, Wildfire's performance draws from what Philip Fisher calls "the neglected emotion of wonder," an emotion whose reliance on delight and play is inherently destabilizing. In this area of encounter and exchange between Europe and the United States, Paulding brings his audience into contact with a frontier that frustrated rather than facilitated imperialism.

In Chapter Three, the history of blackface minstrelsy, particularly T. D. Rice's successful farce, *The Virginia Mummy* (1837), gets interpolated as a part of the history of frontier performance. Rice's performance explodes the politics of Paulding's melodrama of wonder in *The Lion of the West*. By charting the two works' shared, if unexplored, performative histories, I argue that Rice's Jim Crow character does not exploit or expropriate black culture, nor is its rebelliousness merely derived from black cultural sources. Rather, by mapping the places where Rice performed his minstrel character across the United States, I demonstrate how those performances sharpened their racial satire by lampooning the frontiersman, a character who purposely mimics Paulding's Wildfire. Restaging the frontier, the minstrel show eliminated the tidy line dividing whiteness from racial otherness and created in its place a zone of racial cross-pollination. The minstrel show thus generated some of its most acute political critiques and aesthetic innovations by manipulating a set of performative practices associated with the frontier. By mining the rich imagery associated with minstrelsy's frontier history—particularly its black and Indian bodies—I suggest the key role that the frontier played in minstrelsy's attempts both to question American racial stereotypes and to imagine a theatrical zone and social space beyond prescriptive notions of race.

All these performances reveal a frontier that worked to highlight the theatricality of Manifest Destiny, as opposed to its factuality, and derived its aesthetic energy from interrogating the ideology undergirding Cody's and Turner's imperialistic fantasies. Nowhere is this dismantling more evident than in the way Dion Boucicault uses the two plots of his "tragic mulatta" melodrama *The Octoroon* (1859) to dispute the frontier's "legacy of conquest." In Chapter Four, I argue, first, that Boucicault employs the play's main plot to critique the theatrical practice of performing the frontier melodramatically, that is, as a "black-or-white" dialectic that reinforces the ideology of American imperialism, insofar as that ideology depended on a clear division between the white, civilized self and the racial, savage other. More important, by then focusing on the play's largely ignored subplot, centered on an Indian played by Boucicault, I develop the idea that Boucicault emplots the frontier as a necessarily blurred, "black-and-white" set of performative practices whose alternate modality challenged the black-or-white opposition that defines both melodrama and imperialism.

In the next chapter, I contrast two plays, Augustin Daly's *Horizon* (1871) and Joaquin Miller's *The Danites of the Sierras* (1881), both successful and vital plays staging the frontier after the Civil War. In the plays examined in preceding chapters, the frontier was both the place where civilization conquered savagery and an area of fundamental wildness that critiqued America's imperialist ideology. These two visions, which had already become separated in the competing plots of *The Octoroon*, veer even farther apart in Daly's and Miller's plays. For Daly, the frontier was a site of memory that needed to be regulated theatrically, and thus he concretized a set of performative practices that systematically erased the other in support of imperialism—the same set of practices that helped Cody mythologize the Wild West. Daly's memory of the frontier was, however, already just a memory of the frontier, for at the moment of its articulation, it was being challenged by Miller's play, which used what Miller referred to as the frontier's unsettled, "plastic" qualities to disrupt the script of an imperialism that consolidated its power by insisting on rigid social categories.

In my afterword, I consider the contemporary legacies of the double genealogies of frontier performance that I have been charting in this project—Daly's frontier leading to Cody and Miller's frontier leading to Gowongo Mohawk—suggesting that these two strands of performance have continued to animate recent representations of the frontier. To illustrate this long history, I explore briefly two recent frontier "performances": the much vilified, political firestorm of George W. Bush's brush clearing in Crawford, Texas, and the much celebrated, cultural touchstone of *Brokeback Mountain* (2005). Bush's hacking away cedar was protested by other Crawford ranchers, who criticized it for its staginess and for the harm it was doing the environment. They rejected one mode of performing the frontier in favor of another, less theatricalized, and less reckless one. These juxtaposed pioneer performances are thematized in Ang Lee's film as well, constructing two frontier spaces—one, the idyllic space of queer sensibility at Brokeback Mountain, and the other, the repressive regime of Riverton, Wyoming. Bush's brush clearing and Lee's film suggest that the genealogy of frontier performance has always been a heterogeneous constellation of acts that work both to settle and unsettle American ideologies. Through this give-and-take across aesthetic and political borders, the identity of American performance became the performance of American identity.

CHAPTER ONE

⌒⋁⌒

Edwin Forrest's Redding Up

Elocution, Theater, and the Performance of the Frontier

On a cold New York City night in mid-December 1829, a twenty-two-year-old actor named Edwin Forrest revolutionized both the art of public speaking and the history of American drama. The audience who came to the Park Theatre that night not only witnessed a star being born but also experienced a seismic change in the way words conveyed meaning. Appearing onstage in John Augustus Stone's play, *Metamora; or, The Last of the Wampanoags*, Forrest was costumed in Indian tunic, pants, and moccasins, accoutered with tomahawk, club, and knife, and colored with a burnt umber concoction called Bollamenia.[1] Yet, it was not his costume or his makeup that captivated the audience. Rather, it was his scenery-chewing performance of the Indian, a matrix of acting choices set off by his physical embodiment of the "aboriginal" and—of even more importance aesthetically—his recalibrating of what counted as the American voice.

Forrest's singular performance as Metamora exists at the intersection between two distinct discourses: the discourse surrounding the voice, oratory, and elocution of late eighteenth- and early nineteenth-century America and the discourse of the frontier epitomized by the antebellum American fascination with Indian plays. Forrest's "loud-mouthed, ranting style," as Walt Whitman dubbed it,[2] coupled with the actor's embodiment of a wild "noble savage," does more than conveniently yoke together these two historically disparate discourses, however. Forrest's "redding up"—his merging of a "savage" voice that was more complicated than simply "ranting"[3] with a "savage" performance that enriched the aesthetically thin representation of the Native American—opens up a critical space between these two discourses that helps us read the discursive limitations of both, even as it reveals the critical traction Forrest got from both discourses to redefine the way American culture made, and continues to make, sense of the frontier.

Critical discussions about the public sphere in the early republic have focused almost exclusively on those forms of written expression that articulated the nation. As Larzer Ziff states, "The establishment of the United States and the spread of print culture went hand in hand."[4] It was the written word—the *"res publica* of letters," as Michael Warner puts it[5]—that legitimated the nation and contributed to nation formation. "What was needed for legitimacy," summarizes Warner, "was the derivative afterward of writing rather than the speech of the people" (104). Warner's overt privileging of writing over speech has been challenged by Christopher Looby, who has recently asserted that "there is a distinct countercurrent in the literature of the period that valorizes the grain of the voice in addition to, or instead of, the silence of print."[6] In a pointed reversal of Ziff's proposition, Looby suggests that "vocal utterance has served, in telling instances, as a privileged figure for the making of the United States" (4).

Looby's work has broken the stranglehold that textuality has had in critical discussions of early republican nationalism, revealing the risks that privileging the text can cause. Yet, Looby's attention to the "vox Americana" (14) tends to elide orality and performativity, as is evident in the way figures of the period discuss theatricality. For instance, John Adams lamented to his friend, Benjamin Rush, that

> scenery has often if not commonly in all the business of life, at least of public life, more effect than the characters of the dramatis personae or the ingenuity of the plot. Recollect within your own times. What but the scenery did thus? or that? or the other? Was there ever a *coup de théâtre* that had so great an effect as Jefferson's penmanship of the Declaration of Independence?[7]

Adams's "antitheatrical prejudice"—his insistence that theater is merely scenery—dovetails nicely with the impatient jealousy he felt toward Jefferson's seemingly effortless creativity: Both theater and Jefferson, Adams snipes, deserve our contempt. Adams continued his tirade about the Declaration of Independence, confessing that he always considered it a "theatrical show," and that "Jefferson ran away with all of the stage effect of that... and all the glory of it" (Schutz and Adair 182). More than mere pettiness, Adams's remarks about Jefferson do two things—first, they derogate Jefferson's theatrical predilections, and second, as Looby insists, they anxiously acknowledge "the historical efficacy of such theatricality, performativity, or, as I would prefer to call it, rhetoricity" (Looby 25).

What strikes me as strange is Looby's own discomfort with what is clearly theatricality and performativity, not just rhetoricity. Adams is suggesting how the voice in performance had a power of persuasion that the written word could only partially match. He keenly understood that the Declaration of Independence was a document read out loud as often as it was read silently. It was a theatrical script, in other words, as much as it was a written document, and part of its power lay in the way it worked superbly on both fronts. However, what is revealed in Adams's anxious attack on the theater is his underlying fear that the declaration's performativity, no matter if it was just "scenery," may indeed have meant more and been more effective than its textuality. Adams' concern speaks to the distinction between the *langue* and *parole* of the document and to the fact that although these two aspects often mutually reinforce each other, they need not do so. When a written text is performed, a space can develop between what is said and how it is said. Not all texts, in other words, speak with just one voice.

Looby's discomfort with the way performance functions as a crucial element of "voicing America" (to quote his title) leads him to see the univocality of texts, which obscures the dissonance existing between text and performance. Looby's reluctance to acknowledge the independence of performance is shared, moreover, by all of the recent studies of the voice, orality, and elocution in this period. Performativity makes no appearance in the works by Kenneth Cmiel, Jay Fliegelman, Thomas Gustafson, Michael P. Kramer, or James Perrin Warren,[8] and thus, while most of these critics open the door for an investigation of the way performance articulates nationalism, none of them systematically pursues the relationship between performance and the voice.[9] As with Looby, these studies tend to ignore the performance of national identity in favor of texts of national identity, or, what is more often the case, they tend to assume uncritically that these two things are one and the same.

These texts had a long history in the early nineteenth century as well, and, as I will demonstrate, Edwin Forrest's performance of Metamora points out the limitation in the critical discussions of the voice, orality, and eloquence by productively focusing on the distance between text and performance. By exploring Forrest's "savage" performance as Metamora, I will show how Forrest deployed a fantasy of the frontier as unsettled and unsettling in order to disrupt the antebellum American grammar of the voice.[10] Attending to the performative practices that Forrest constructed when he played the Indian reveals two things. First, as Sandra M. Gustafson has noted, the Indian existed as a representation of "bodily extravagance" in the early republic, a resistant embodiment that in its enactment challenged traditional modes of orality.[11] Second, by redding up, therefore, Forrest's "savage" voice and performance illuminate the range of voices articulating what it meant to be American.

However, if by leveling our attention at Forrest's "savage" performance we encounter the limitations of contemporary discussions of the voice, orality, and elocution, examining the way Forrest developed his "savage" voice will also throw light on the limitations of our own contemporary notion of frontier performance. Forrest's performance cuts both ways, making us reconsider the place of the voice through its recoding of the discourse of frontier performance and making us reevaluate the ideology of frontier performance by focusing on the development of the voice.

John Augustus Stone's play was not the only Indian play in 1829, even if it was the only one with such a vocal actor as its lead. Starting just after Andrew Jackson entered the Oval Office and just before the Indian Removal Act of 1830, the American theater turned to the Native American because of its desire for an aesthetic that was truly "American." Ironically, in the early years of the Jacksonian era, even as real Native Americans were driven off their native soil, this infatuation with the Indian manifested itself in a vogue for plays that took the American stage by storm. The noble savage, a figure inherited from Montaigne and Rousseau and fictionalized by Washington Irving, John Greenleaf Whittier, and James Fenimore Cooper, became the central character in a spate of plays that dominated the scene from 1829 to 1845.

These plays by white playwrights were "the first theatrical form[s] to put a supposedly genuine version of the racial other before the American public,"[12] but in staging the Indian, they were not merely preserving the memory of native peoples. In performing the "genuine savage" in this way, they made the stage Indian a key figure of American "imperialist nostalgia," the nostalgia, argues Renato Rosaldo, involving imperialists' "mourn[ing] the passing of what they themselves have transformed."[13] The notion of imperialist nostalgia thus helps explain why so many Indian plays were produced during this time period, for in assuming a pose of nostalgia, these plays and playwrights attempted not only to titillate the audience but also to mask their own "complicity with often brutal domination" of Native Americans (Rosaldo 108).[14]

As Werner Sollors suggests, by positioning Indians as pseudoancestors of American characters while simultaneously villainizing British characters onstage, Indian plays "assured rather than merely intimidated white theatergoers" and thus became effective ideological tools for American expansionism.[15] Gordon M. Sayre has extended this argument, suggesting that, rather than nostalgia, *Metamora*'s tragic emplotment created a catharsis at the end of the play and therefore does the work of empire building by "replacing frontier violence and the bitter racial and political factions behind it with a

new civil order" consonant with the politics of expansionism.[16] This catharsis became a way of championing the construction of American identity
based on consent, to use Sollors's terms, rather than on the British value of
descent. For critics like Theresa Strouth Gaul, Mariyln J. Anderson, Susan
Scheckel, Shari M. Huhndorf, Gordon M. Sayre, and especially Sollors,
Metamora was an Indian play that worked, in Sayre's words, "to reconcile
political and ethnic difference in the interests of a hegemonic U.S. national
purpose" (26) with Forrest being the voice for American imperial expansion across the continent.

Yet, however accurate this argument may be for the majority of Indian
plays, these critics have not read Forrest's provocative performance of
Metamora closely enough. This is not to say that they have misread the text
of *Metamora*. Rather, they have misread *Metamora* by reading it only as text.
Most people in the nineteenth century would have encountered *Metamora*
not as a text but as a performance, and what intrigued these audiences,
I would argue, is the productive space existing between the play's textuality and its performativity. By exploring the way Forrest constructed his
"savage" voice, we see that in performance the play had a much more quali-
fied and resistant relationship to the juggernaut of American imperialism
than these critics have allowed it. Attending to the way Forrest negotiated
the culture of the voice and orality when he deployed his particular
construction of Indianness in Augusta, Georgia, in 1831 and Boston,
Massachusetts, in 1833 will allow us to see how the performance of the
frontier in the nineteenth century both facilitated and frustrated American
imperialist nostalgia's attempts to make the frontier into a key element of
what Lauren Berlant calls our "national symbolic."[17]

THE GRAMMAR OF THE PASSIONS

In an era of many theatrical stagings, when the best of productions often
barely lasted two weeks, Forrest's redding up as Metamora was a blockbuster, running at least fifty-eight years until 1887.[18] This unimaginable
success attests to the fact that Forrest's embodiment of the Wampanoag
chieftain did more than appeal to an ever-changing audience; it created that
American audience, one that could appreciate this Indian character as well
as Forrest's dynamic acting style.[19] Like the audience he was playing to, Forrest was searching for an American dramatic style distinct from European
models—those of actors like Charles Kemble, Junius Brutus Booth, and
especially Edmund Kean, whom Forrest both admired and envied—and
in turning to his own country and choosing to play an "aboriginal," Forrest
found what he had been searching for.

Forrest chose to identify himself completely with the Indian—a kind of method acting *avant la lettre*—and to transform his performance style entirely. The result of such a change was that the "very boys in the streets were seen trying to imitate his posture and looks, swelling their little throats to make the words sound big, as they repeated, 'Metamora cannot lie.' "[20] "Many of the little speeches which the great actor pronounced as from the lips of the Indian king," remembers Gabriel Harrison from a performance in Brooklyn, "were...as familiar upon the public's tongue as the name of Washington."[21] Forrest's performance as Metamora was therefore transformed from an impressive stage act to a popular cultural phenomenon, from a mere theatrical entertainment to a performance of national identity equaling, at least for Gabriel Harrison, that of the "great father" of the country, George Washington.

Yet, the congratulatory reviews of Forrest as Metamora still leave us with only a vague idea of what exactly his acting choices were and why they were so popular. In order to understand Forrest's dramatic decisions, we must examine the ways in which his performance was inflected by the conceptions and conventions of acting in his time, notions that were the culmination of what Jay Fliegelman calls the period's "elocution revolution." Starting as early as the mid-eighteenth century, intellectuals and political luminaries had expressed their "desire for something beyond the people to give law to language: a natural law that would provide a standard appeal to decide questions of usage" (T. Gustafson 183). The late eighteenth-century cultural landscape was, in fact, revolutionized by "an intensified quest to discover (or theorize into existence) a natural spoken language that would be a corollary to natural law, a language that would permit universal recognition and understanding" (Fliegelman 1). In searching for this natural law and accompanying natural language, these same people came to see that the body could articulate ideas. In other words, conveying information effectively and powerfully—and naturally—involved both mind and body.[22]

What made this "elocution revolution" revolutionary, however, was precisely the way it attempted to displace the rather stilted forms of elocution spelled out in Cicero and Quintilian. "The eighteenth century," insists Fliegelman, "witnessed the culmination of a movement away from a circumscribed, ceremonial view of rhetoric as but figures and tropes serving as handmaidens charged with the artful presentation of ideas determined by a master logic and expressed through the conventions of grammar" (28). In its stead, elocution theorists of the late eighteenth and early nineteenth century demanded that public speakers invest their orations with passion. Thomas Sheridan, one of the avatars of this renaissance in elocution, summarizes the difference between classical and modern forms of expression when he states that all "writers seem to be under the influence of one common delusion, that by the help of words alone, they can communicate all that passes in their minds. They forget that the passions and the fancy have a language of their own, utterly independent of words, by which only their exertions can be manifested and communicated."[23]

Yet, if theorists like Sheridan wanted to focus on the synthesis of voice, physiognomy, and physicality in an effort to reanimate vocal communication, they were also interested in controlling this animation by taking it down certain carefully laid-out avenues. Sheridan certainly believed that such a revival of oratory would contribute to the national good, but like his godfather, Jonathan Swift, he also thought that it would be an excellent means for "refining the English tongue" (T. Gustafson 189).[24] Ironically, the effort to achieve a "natural language" involved refining those articulations of nature, and thus systematically controlling the inherently uncontrollable passions as they erupted from the speaker. Drawing on Foucault's notion of the classic episteme in *The Order of Things*, we can see how these elocutionists, by attempting to control the body, voice, and the communication of affect, were helping to fuel a form of cultural policing that extended well beyond the arena of elocution.

As Kenneth Cmiel has argued, this effort at refining language in the late eighteenth and early nineteenth century fed into the "traditional division between the few and the many, a division that excluded 'the many' from any systematic contribution to public debate" (15). Not only was the effort to control the passions a mode of policing society along class and racial lines, as Cmiel insists, but it was also a mode of rhetorical imperialism, according to Eric Cheyfitz. "The scene in which an orator through the power of eloquence 'civilizes' 'savage' humanity," argues Cheyfitz, "is the driving force of Anglo-American imperialism in the New World."[25] Nowhere is this notion of rhetorical imperialism more clearly illuminated than in Benjamin Rush's comments in his "Of the Mode of Education Proper in a Republic," which were aimed at an audience of newly American readers in 1798. An eminent physician and political theorist, Rush states:

> Connected with the study of languages is the study of eloquence. It is well known how great a part it constituted of the Roman education. It is the first accomplishment in a republic, and often sets the whole machine of government in motion. Let our youths, therefore, be instructed in this art. We do not extol it too highly when we attribute as much to the power of eloquence as to the sword, in bringing about the American Revolution.[26]

Rush's recognition of the power that was possessed by a savvy rhetorician who could "elocute" well echoes James Burgh's pronouncements on the same aspect of public speaking. Burgh states in *The Art of Speaking* that "under the popular government of ancient times...the tongue of an orator could do more than the *sceptre* of a monarch, or the *sword* of a warrior" (7). Both Rush and Burgh, therefore, suggest that eloquence is a powerful tool for creating and governing a new republic, on par with the sword of a warrior or the musket of a revolutionary in shaping national identity. More importantly, the concerted effort to refine the contours of communication—to control this newfound florescence of affect—became synonymous with the institutionalized maneuverings of national power. To be a descendent of the American Revolution, to be a true American, in short, meant speaking powerfully, speaking eloquently, but most of all, speaking nationalistically.

The newfound emphasis on elocution was a product of a culture, therefore, that was trying to do two distinct things simultaneously: first, to animate what was felt to have become a cold, impoverished mode of communication and, second, to regulate the dynamic product of that animation. Thus, the elocutionary movement blended rhetoric and science, passionate utterances and rational discourse in an effort to construct what I will call a grammar of the passions. Informing the genres of the elocution revolution, the grammar of the passions attempted to systematize the passions, to regulate the passionate eruptions of affect by classifying them, ordering them, and making them immediately recognizable. As James Burgh put it, "Nature has given to every emotion of the mind its *proper* outward expression, in such a manner, that what suits *one,* cannot by any means be accommodated to *another*" (17). For all of its mustering of strong emotions and vehement passions, the revitalization of elocution aimed to parse those emotions, distinguishing one from another, fixing each emotion's facial expression and detailing the gestures that would accompany it.

The clearest example of the ideological nature of the grammar of the passions is Gilbert Austin's incredibly popular *Chironomia; or a Treatise on Rhetorical Delivery.*[27] Published in 1806, this work presents—in agonizing detail—the facial and corporeal moves necessary to "elocute" the various emotions correctly. Not only does Austin describe the elements of good elocution in writing, but at the back of the work, he also offers a series of illustrations that physicalize this grammar of the passions.

Focusing on one such diagram of an orator's movements illustrates how *Chironomia,* like the fervor for elocution more generally, was invested in detailing the infinite possibilities of rhetorical action as well as the decidedly finite boundaries of emotive expression. In an image called the "Imaginary Circles for Determining the Place of the Direction of the Gesture" (Figure 1.1), Austin reveals the nearly limitless number of radii to which a trained speaker can align his arms to convey meaning. The illustration even hints at its own insufficiency through its inclusion of a narrow oval going

Figure 1.1   Imaginary Circles for Determining the Place of the Direction of the Gesture.
Source: Gilbert Austin, *Chironomia; or a Treatise on Rhetorical Delivery*, 1806.

around the chest, indicating the way this two-dimensional rendering cannot fully illuminate the range of expressions available in three dimensions. At the same time, the gestural axes are clearly delimited, and as if to reinforce this notion of regulated limitation rather than unregulated limitlessness, Austin literally circumscribes the orator. Unlike the other axes, this circle does not correspond to the body of the orator but, rather, controls the space around the speaker in a measured way. It is not that the speaker cannot emote, this figure suggests, but that the speaker's emotions have boundaries that cannot be transgressed, even if the orator were to stretch his arms out to their limits. This invisible sphere supplied by Austin surrounding the speaker on every side seems cognate with the invisible sphere supplied by the dominant culture that, in its elocutionary fervor, attempted to encircle and control the potentially limitless freedoms afforded individual citizens who could elocute well.

Austin thus promotes what Joseph R. Roach sees as a mainstay of the science of acting and rhetoric starting as early as the sixteenth century and continuing well through the 1830s.

> Rhetoric thus imbibed from physiology two contrasting, even contradictory interpretations of the body. Learned opinion viewed the body as an instantly malleable, highly volatile concoction of dangerous essences: like a spirited horse, it responds swiftly to firm commands but can easily get out of control. Learned opinion, however, also regarded

the body as a mass of sludge, inclining to dissolution and decay. The actor's art, therefore, requires him to discover a *via media* between the Scylla of spirit and the Charybdis of humours. His art requires him to set his bodily instrument in expressive motion, not by freeing his actions, but by confining them in direction, purpose, and shape. He has to keep his flammable inner mixture stable even in the heat of passion…. Emotion, passion, transport, ecstasy—these he can take for granted—like mercy, they rain down from heaven; but to attain restraint, control over these copious and powerful energies, represents both artistic challenge and preventive medicine. Alumni of modern-day acting classes have a difficult time grasping this essential fact, though all the best evidence we have points toward it: the actor/orator of the seventeenth century sought to acquire inhibitions. (50–51)

ACTING NATURAL

Considering Austin's interest in regulating the performance of emotion and of "acquir[ing] inhibitions" against the overflow of passion when speaking to an audience, it should not be surprising that, when he addresses acting in the theater, he evinces a marked hostility toward drama and its effects on the speaker. In his very short chapter "Of Acting," Austin warns that the orator must guard against "imitation" of the actor: "[T]he limits allowed to such indulgence are very narrow; and if he transgresses them in the smallest degree, he at once loses his dignity and his credit with his audience…. [T]he liberty of the theatre would be licentiousness in the orator, and he is to guard himself carefully against it" (240). For Austin, theater is a zone of license, an area of liberty that could undermine the speaker's carefully maintained credit with the audience. Acting, as Austin makes clear, is a transgressive indulgence. Recalling standard tropes of the "antitheatrical prejudice," Austin derogates the theater for all of the ways it refuses to articulate itself through the grammar of the passions; theater as both a site of bodily display and a flashpoint for potentially passionate disruptions was too problematic to regulate, and without the regulation the grammar of the passions provided, it could, as Roach argues, lead to "anarchy" (54–55).[28]

When Edwin Forrest took the stage, therefore, he had already chosen a venue that was particularly fraught to those writers and thinkers, like Austin, involved in the "elocution revolution." As Forrest's performance in *King Lear* later in his career reveals, his performative style did not so much articulate the elocution revolution as articulate itself through—and against—it. At a moment in the play when Forrest was galvanizing the language of a curse, a spectator, who later wrote a life of Forrest, recalls how he and a friend in the audience "heard a strange sound proceeding from a gentleman sitting beside us—a sound so strange and unnatural, which induced us to turn suddenly round. The fearful words of the curse were ringing in his ears as uttered by the only living actor capable of giving it with that fierceness and rapid vehemence so essential to render it effective." The man, reeling from the power of Forrest's curse, was in a state of shock, with his eyes "fixed, his mouth open and a death-like paleness overspreading his face. His hands were clenched together, and it was evident that all voluntary motion was suspended." Fearing for the life of the man, the narrator and his friend shook him, causing him to awaken with a gasp. The man turned to them, thanking them, and saying, "One moment more ... and I should have been a dead man."[29]

Forrest's performance was, in short, a passionate one. Yet to deliver one's lines passionately was one thing, but to nearly kill someone with your voice was quite another. While it seems likely that this anecdote is an exaggeration, it nevertheless underscores the way Forrest's performance, separate from the text he was quoting, could work against the ideology of the elocution revolution. If the newly energized mode of communication was supposed to animate but still control the passions, Forrest's performance seems only to have achieved half of the goal: Forrest galvanized his speech, sharpened his voice, recoded his gestures, but he did not do this in an effort to stabilize the transmission of meaning. Forrest's "fierceness and rapid vehemence" purposely outstripped the elocution revolution's efforts at control. His was a new language, in short, that went beyond the grammar of the passions to find its voice.

Moving beyond the grammar of the passions meant discovering a new discursive source, and Forrest found this source in the frontier. While Forrest came to maturity during the height of the elocutionary fervor and learned much from European actors trained in its associated methods,[30] it was his time spent as a strolling player in New Orleans that was one of the most formative periods of his life, as his nineteenth-century biographer, William Rounesville Alger, recounts. At that time, Forrest was conversing with the likes of James Bowie, and he was also "going native" with the Choctaws of southern Louisiana. The "fine chance here offered him," argues Alger, "of getting an accurate knowledge of the American Indian, alike in his exterior and his interior personality, he carefully improved, and when he came to enact the part of Metamora it stood him in good stead" (138). Like an extended exercise in acting, Alger maintains, Forrest's sojourn among the Choctaws and his willingness to don their garb and sing their songs helped give his performance of Metamora the patina of "verisimilitude" for the urban northeastern audience for which he performed most of his life.

Whether Forrest's utilization of Choctaw ceremonial and social customs was truly authentic, or whether what he did was just exotic enough to fit into his audience's fantasy of the Indian, seems of little importance. What needs underscoring is the fact that Forrest spent a significant amount of time getting to know Push-ma-ta-ha, the young Choctaw chieftain who was both the specific model for Forrest's characterization of Metamora and the figure in whom Forrest witnessed and from whom he appropriated the basic "language" of the Indian he would represent onstage. Forrest's encounter with Push-ma-ta-ha did nothing less than impel the young actor to articulate a new grammar of performance that in his characterization of Metamora transcended the kind of elocutionary training he had received. Forrest recalls how "Push-ma-ta-ha was a natural orator of a high order" (Alger 127), and the actor illustrated this fact by recounting that when he asked about the identity of Push-ma-ta-ha's grandparents, the young chief sprang up, his

> nostrils curling with a superbly beautiful disdain, and, stretching forth his arms with a lofty grace which the proudest Roman orator could not have surpassed, he replied, "My father was never born. The Great Spirit shivered an oak with one of his thunderbolts and my father came out, a perfect man, with his bow and arrows in hand!" (Alger 139)

Alger's depiction of this event, as supplied by Forrest, creates a dialectic between classic oratory, represented by the Quintilian-like Roman orator, and a performative rhetoric, represented by Push-ma-ta-ha.

While Forrest had certainly studied classical oratory and had internalized the tenets of the elocutionary turn at the beginning of the nineteenth century, his predilections lay with Push-ma-ta-ha's performative rhetoric. The Choctaw's performance transcended his elocutionary background, connecting with something novel and "wondrous" in Forrest's mind. The actor's "wondering admiration" (139) speaks volumes about how distinct his encounter with Push-ma-ta-ha was from anything spelled out in the acting manuals of the Northeast. Drawing on René Descartes's influential *Les passions de l'âme*, the modern critic Philip Fisher defines wonder as an experience "located at that promising line between what we already know—the familiar world—and all that it would be pointless to think about because we personally lack, or our historical moment as a whole lacks, the skills and framework of knowledge that would let us profitably spend time thinking here and now at this location." "Wonder," in other words, "occurs at the horizon line of what is potentially knowable, but not yet known."[31] Alger's noting that Forrest was in a state of wonder, a fact that Forrest supplied his biographer, suggests that his experience during this oratorical performance of the chief was completely unlike anything he had ever seen, heard, or felt before.[32] For Forrest, Push-ma-ta-ha's speech drew attention to the "horizon line" separating what he had already known, the prominence of the passions in the newly galvanized elocutionary movement, and what was just beyond it—the "natural" power demonstrated by the chieftain's pronunciation and gestures, physiognomy and intonation. What the dialectic between Quintilian and Push-ma-ta-ha revealed was that there were numerous "natural languages" circulating through antebellum American culture, available to whoever could access them: One language was the elocutionary movement's and its efforts at "refining nature"; another language—the one that piqued Forrest's interest—was the Native American's language that unsettled nature. For Forrest, Push-ma-ta-ha's language was a fantastic frontier dialect that traded in "shivered oaks" and "thunderbolts" and, in doing so, was a far cry from the "tall oaks" and "sunny skies" under which his biographer, James Rees, recalls that Forrest "first tried his voice in 'public speaking'" (402–403). Distinct from Forrest's earlier oratorical efforts, Push-ma-ta-ha's "wondrous" performance became the basis for Forrest's performance of Metamora, and it was this performance's production of a fantasy of the frontier as wild and unsettled that revolutionized the elocution revolution that dominated Forrest's culture.[33]

As we saw earlier, the newfound emphasis on elocution depended on the grammar of the passions, and this grammar functioned as a tool for bolstering American nationalism, marking the ideological energy used to refine the voice as a strategic form of nation building. By challenging this grammar, therefore, Forrest's performance also necessarily challenged the nationalism it shaped. That performance was aided considerably by Stone's script, which had been solicited by Forrest and was written specifically for him.[34] Consider the scene after Metamora has killed Annawandah, the Indian betrayer of the Wampanoags, and is rallying his warriors to wage war on the English colonists. In an attempt to assert his power, the chief declares, "I started to my feet and shouted the shrill battle cry of the Wampanoags. The high hills sent back the echo, and rock, hill and ocean, earth and air opened their giant throats and cried with me, 'Red man, arouse! Freedom! Revenge or death!' (*Thunder and lightning. All quail but Metamora.*) Hark, warriors! The Great Spirit hears me and pours forth his mighty voice with mine."[35] This scene of Metamora urging his council to act neatly summarizes what Forrest was after in redding up, and the playwright's script contributed to his success. The "natural language" that the elocutionary movement prized so highly is identified by Stone as being coarse and crude, voluminous and vast; it is rocks, thunder, and lightning, as well as being "giant" and "mighty." Thus it evokes exactly the same set of values, values so inimical to nineteenth-century elocution's insistence on order, that Push-ma-ta-ha's performance evoked for Forrest. Furthermore, through its repeated use of exclamation points, Stone's script demands that Forrest invest his speech with passion, for exclamation points are rhetorical figures, we might note, that in their very nature chafe at grammar's ordered and measured rationality. Finally, Stone's drama punctuates his lead actor's emotional eruption with thunder and lightning, making sure his audience understands—through nothing less than a startling stage effect—how the actor's declamation transcends the "natural" codes for evoking the passions detailed in the tracts of the elocution revolution.

The punctuation of Metamora's speech by the flash of lightning and the clap of thunder not only emphasizes the connection between the chief and a fantasy of nature that empowers the individual, but it also casts this natural power in defiantly American terms. Metamora's rousing cry, "Freedom! Revenge or death!" closely echoes American revolutionary language of the sort that the audience at the Park Theatre would have recognized. By putting an amalgamation of Patrick Henry's famous declaration, "Give me liberty or give me death!" and the motto from the New Hampshire state seal, "Live Free or Die," in the mouth of an Indian, Stone constructs Metamora, with the audience's imaginative participation, as patriotically American.[36] Yet, this "thunder and lightning" construction of American identity, peppered with exclamation points and rife with images of natural power, is not the same American identity that the elocution revolution calls for—this is passionate exclamation, not a grammar of the passions.

This notion of America, evident to the members of Forrest's audience every time he redded up, struck one of them, Gabriel Harrison, as being not merely a set of acting choices but—and here he deploys some of the crucial terms of the elocutionary movement—"a new human nature; a nature I had failed to discover the slightest likeness to in any other character I had seen him perform" (36). When Harrison describes what this new human nature looked like, moreover, we do not see the rhetorical stability demanded by people like Sheridan, Burgh, Caldwell, and Webster but rather the inherently unstable rhetoric of Push-ma-ta-ha. "Forrest had frequently startled me," Harrison remembers, "by *unexpected* tones and inflections of voice" (42; my emphasis), and this unexpected quality is apparent to Harrison in Metamora's exchange with his wife, Nahmeokee. As the Indian chief relates his troubling dream of the Indians' eradication at the hands of the white colonists, "[Forrest] raised his figure to an additional height," recalls Harrison. Then, he

> lifted his right arm to the level of his shoulder, grasping his bow, [and] looked directly into the eyes of Nahmeokee, and listened for her answer which did not please him and slightly ruffled his temper, and then with a clear, orotund voice, which in the *change and quality was so unexpected* that it resembled the sudden sweep of the wind when it stirs the crisp leaves and hums through the leafless branches of the forest, he said: "Yes, when our fires are out..." (42–43; my emphasis)

As Harrison indicates, it is the unexpected quality of Forrest's performance of Metamora that disrupts the elocution revolution's policing of the voice. However, Harrison's description indexes not only how far Forrest's performance was from the tenets of the elocutionary movement but also how distinct his fantasy of the frontier was from what Harrison had been accustomed to. Harrison compares Forrest's acting here not to unsettled land, rich with the possibilities of civilization, but rather to an unsettling and sudden wind whipping through a barren landscape that refuses to be civilized. Like Push-ma-ta-ha's "thunderbolt" performance, Forrest's performance drew on a vision of nature on the frontier—wild, untutored, potent—that challenged the notion of natural language and, importantly, the fantasy of nature undergirding the numerous elocution tracts in the eighteenth and nineteenth century as that thing that could be ordered.

Forrest's challenging of the elocution revolution and his promotion of a fantasy of the frontier as unsettling drew a popular following. It must be remembered that in the same year that Stone's *Metamora* opened uptown at the Park Theatre, Five Points, that infamous nineteenth-century neighborhood of sin and vice, first earned its reputation downtown as "the most dangerous place in our city." In general, the 1820s and 1830s in New York City were a time of increased congestion, commerce, and conflict. It was during this time that the first tenement houses were constructed to accommodate the burgeoning number of working-class poor—mostly Irish and Catholic—who swelled the little island of Manhattan, leading to riots by the 1830s and 1840s; and it was but a few years after Forrest first performed Metamora that a devastating cholera outbreak swept through the city, started because of the crush of unwashed masses in the same neighborhood from which Forrest drew his audience.[37] Invited to imagine a geography free from this, free from the city's rigidly ordered landscape of streets and avenues and from even more severe markers of class and race, the theater audience surely saw Forrest's representation of the frontier as appealing precisely because of its unsettled and indeterminate quality.

While appealing, Forrest's performance, however, also singled him out for ridicule. Consider the following satiric depiction of Forrest acting Metamora (Figure 1.2), a widely circulated cartoon that reveals in its humor, ironically, Forrest's real artistic achievement. The cartoonist's slightly corpulent representation of this "Histrionic Savage" decked out in peacock feathers and grass skirt, wielding a tomahawk, satirizes the actor's pride. Only an egomaniac, it suggests, so self-involved that he cannot see how poorly he represents a lithe, sinewy savage, would contemplate acting such a role, and it brilliantly mocks Forrest's decision by crowning him with what clearly are peacock feathers, a bird associated with pride and ostentation. While the artist uses the peacock crown to mock Forrest for

Figure 1.2 Cartoon of Edwin Forrest as a "Histrionic Savage."
Source: Portrait Prints (Forrest, Edwin), Harvard Theatre Collection, Houghton Library, Harvard University.

his pride and self-righteousness, crowning him in this sense as a dunce, he also inadvertently suggests how entirely appropriate a peacock crown is for this "king" of a new acting style. While the cartoonist demonstrates how self-absorbed Forrest was, he also reinforces how ostentatious Forrest was as an actor, how over the top he was in his emotions, and how frenetic he was in his action. This cartoon stands in stark contrast to Gilbert Austin's measured, rational diagrams at the back of *Chironomia* (Figure 1.1), which map out the boundaries of the grammar of the passions. Arms akimbo, legs astride, this representation of Forrest breaks through the fourth wall and gesticulates grandly to his audience while in the midst of one of his staggering curses. It was precisely this kind of outburst, an outburst fueled by the savage fantasy of the frontier, that was at the core of Forrest's changing the way Americans "acted." The satiric cartoon thus captures in a way that few words can how successful Forrest was as an actor and how he had distanced his acting aesthetic from the dominant elocutionary culture, for if he had not been so staggeringly successful, this cartoon would not have been so staggeringly accurate.

"THAT D—D INDIAN SPEECH"

When Forrest applied the first dab of Bollamenia to his cheek, he not only used an unsettling performance of a Native American on the frontier to challenge the regulating impulses of the elocution revolution, he also used his unsettling rhetoric to challenge the ideological position of the Indian play in American culture. As Sollors has argued, though Indian plays are rife with curses on the white colonists, "the structural position of the chieftain as that of a better parent or substitute ancestor may have assured rather than merely intimidated white theatergoers" (124). As in most Indian plays, Metamora's cursing is leveled against British colonists who trap and destroy him while the young American figures, Oceana and Walter, are kept offstage when the curse is being hurled. In this way, Metamora's curse authorizes an American vision of social experience or, in Gordon M. Sayre's terms, "a new civil order" (8) in which the tragic Indian hero acts as the legitimating figure, replacing Oceana's altogether English father, Mordaunt, and sanctioning the union of Oceana and Walter. As Sollors suggests, "Indians were...metaphorically portrayed as pseudo-ancestors, yet nonetheless as advocates of spouses against parents, of consent against descent, and blessed not only the new principles of marriage based on love but also young America as the rebellious daughter of Europe" (129).[38] Metamora's position as the substitute ancestor, argues Sollors, makes his curse against the British a benison on "the new form of postrevolutionary citizenship based on [a] doctrine of consent" that Oceana and Walter represent (129). In this way, the standard melodramatic figure of the blocking father, whom Mordaunt embodies perfectly, is staged in order to make the eventual death of the "tragic" Indian and his fiery curse, according to Sayre, a political strategy for authorizing through the tragic catharsis a "new civil order" embodied in the young couple.

   Yet, by paying particular attention to the way Forrest acted in a production of *Metamora* in Augusta, Georgia, in 1831, we can see that his performance actually worked against the standard dynamic of the Indian play that Sollors has described and, in this way, problematized the theater's use as an imperial tool. From what we know of it from Forrest's fellow actor, James E.

Murdoch, who was in Georgia at the time with Forrest,[39] the Augusta performance went smoothly until the celebrated council scene where Metamora
"upbraids the elders of the council for their unjust and cruel treatment of
his tribe, and denounces war and vengeance upon them until the land they
had stolen from his people should blaze with their burning dwellings and
reek with the blood of their wives and children." Metamora then throws his
tomahawk down into the floor and escapes. To Forrest's surprise, the Georgian audience responded with hostility: "[H]e was followed by loud yells
and a perfect storm of hisses from the excited audience, who seemed ready
in a fury to tear everything to pieces." Although the performance continued, the closing curtain was greeted with "unqualified evidences of disap-
probation," for the "sentiment of the play was a positive protest against the
policy which had deprived the Indians of Georgia of their natural rights and
driven them from their homes."[40] In the same year, therefore, that the Cherokees took their case to the Supreme Court in *Cherokee Nation v. Georgia*,
Forrest's performance in a play that seemed to sympathize with the Indians
caused an audience in need of justification to respond with fury.

For Sayre, this contradictory response from a proremoval Georgian
audience to an ostensibly proremoval play can be resolved if we understand
Metamora as being "not simply [about] the removal controversy of 1829–
1830 but [about] the historiography of sovereignty and revolution in both
England and America" (81). As Sayre argues, the "death of Metamora is
not that of a vanishing Indian who is forced to abandon his sovereignty and
remove beyond the western horizon but that of a revolutionary stoic and
lawgiver bestowing his sovereignty on a republic that he has nurtured in the
body of his foster daughter, the heroine, Oceana" (122–123). While Sayre's
reading offers a nuanced view of the typological, rather than topical, structure of the play, I want to refocus our attention on the audience's strongly
topical reaction to the play, the way, in particular, Forrest's performance, his
acting stylistics, enraged an audience distinctly and fervently invested in
the Cherokee removal controversy of 1829–1830. What is striking about
this moment in American theater history, in other words, is not the way
Stone was pilloried or the way his script was blamed but, rather, the way
Forrest's performance incensed the audience so powerfully. By focusing on
Forrest's reconceptualization of what elocution entailed, in other words, a
space opens between the text that Sollors and Sayre read and the performance that the audience in Georgia experienced. As Murdoch reports, one
citizen attempted to explain that an actor did not express his own opinions
when he played a character but rather mouthed the words the playwright
had penned—that what they were seeing was a matter of textuality, not
performativity. An eminent lawyer, Judge Shannon, however, dismissed
this, arguing, "Any actor who could utter such scathing language, and with

such vehemence, must have the whole matter at heart. Why... his eyes shot fire and his breath was hot with the hissing of his ferocious declamation. I insist upon it, Forrest believes in that d—d Indian speech, and it is an insult to the whole community" (Murdoch 299–300). As Shannon's reading of Forrest's performance suggests, the line between impersonation and incarnation was rather slight, something critics such as Lawrence Levine have made abundantly clear was the case for nineteenth-century audiences in general (26–27). At a more significant level, Shannon's response to the production testifies to the critical space existing between what Forrest said and how he said it. Rather than the words themselves, it was Forrest's animated, fiery, and passionate elocution—the way his "eyes shot fire," the way his "breath was hot with the hissing of his ferocious declamation"—that made audience members like Shannon so indignant at Metamora's "bitter threats" (Murdoch 299). By focusing on Forrest's dynamic and "unsettling" performance, we see how Forrest's redding up subverted not only the dictates of the elocution revolution but also the deployment of the Indian play in nineteenth-century theater as an agent of American imperial expansion. Shannon's anger reveals, if nothing else, that Forrest's performance—not the text of the play—was out of step with what Sollors, Sayre, and others have argued was the nature of the Indian play's imperial dynamic.

What we have discovered in exploring the dynamics of Edwin Forrest's performance is the discursive limitations of critical discussions of orality, eloquence, and the voice in antebellum America—the way these discussions have turned a blind eye to what happens when we move from page to stage. Likewise, we have seen the limitations of Sollors's and others' arguments about the Indian play between 1829 and 1845—the way these arguments have tended to forget the subversive potential of vocal communication. What Forrest's redding up shows is that as Forrest exposed the limitations of one discourse, he simultaneously highlighted the limitations of the other, gaining traction from his challenge to the elocution revolution for a challenge to the imperial ideology informing Indian plays.

A NIGHT OF INDIAN PERFORMANCE

Two years after Forrest pulled up stakes and left Augusta, sneaking out of town to avoid being pilloried, he again was donning Indian costume and redding up as Metamora at the Tremont Theatre in Boston, Massachusetts. Far from the hostile crowds of the South, Forrest no doubt thought that the audience would thrill to his by then famous enactment of the Indian chief. Yet on the night of November 6, 1833, the audience at the Tremont was anticipating more than Forrest's passionate portraiture of Metamora, for

Metamora was to be attended not only by the usual Jacksonian Democrats of the urban Northeast but also by a delegation of Penobscot Indians from Maine.

The visit from the Penobscots was not, in and of itself, particularly novel, for Indians had been spectators of and spectacles themselves for white audiences at the American theater since the eighteenth century.[41] This practice continued through the eighteenth century and accelerated in the nineteenth century—a fact Forrest would have been aware of more than a decade before his performance in Boston. As George C. D. Odell recalls, at the same performance of Mordecai M. Noah's *She Would Be a Soldier* on December 14, 1821, in which Forrest first played an Indian, there was a "great novelty": the visit of the Indian chiefs from Council Bluffs in their "national costume."[42] Yet, the presence of the Penobscot Indians at *Metamora* that night in Boston promised to be more than just another group of Indians attending a play, for the Penobscots were witnessing the premiere performance of the Indian by the premier actor of antebellum America in the premier Indian play of the era. By focusing on the Penobscots' complicated relationship to *Metamora*, therefore, I am heeding Rosemarie K. Bank's advice of not simply reading the play "as an extension of U.S. government Indian removal policy," for by doing so, this reading "empties out 'the Indian,' reinscribes the myth of the omnipotent state, and reinserts the white man as the center of the reading."[43] My reading of this play has already put pressure on what this "white man" was enacting politically and aesthetically, but in reading the Penobscots as also at the center of the performative space, we can see more fully the complicated, heterogeneous performative text called *Metamora*.

The Tremont Theatre that evening was packed to the rafters, and as the *Boston Morning Post* indicates, when the time for the play began to approach and the Indians had still not arrived, the audience grew anxious that they would not show up at all. Finally, much to everyone's relief, the Indians filed in, and when the eager crowd had been quieted, Forrest began his performance of Metamora while the Penobscot Indians sat in the boxes—on full display themselves—taking in the spectacle, and through their presence, argues Sayre, adding a "stamp of authenticity from 'real' Indians" (16). The play went well, although to the dismay of the audience, the Indians attending it were noticeably silent. At the end, however, according to William Rounseville Alger, as Metamora died after delivering his curse, strange voices and stranger words erupted from the Penobscots' boxes. As Alger relates it, the Penobscots "were so excited by the performance, that in the closing scene they rose and chanted a dirge in honor of the death of the great chief" (240).

For Jill Lepore, through this "naïve" act, the Penobscots solidified the play's crucial role in justifying Manifest Destiny to white audiences, for Indians who could not understand such a simple thing as the fiction of a play surely could not understand a much more complicated issue like self-governance. Echoing this point, Theresa Strouth Gaul argues that the "naïveté" of the Penobscots witnessing the performance "could be contrasted...with the sophistication of the white spectators who surely knew that Forrest was only impersonating an Indian and that the death scene on stage was a theatrical illusion. By positioning American Indians as more naïve, even childlike, spectators, the whites could confirm their own superiority of development over them" (17). Both Lepore and Gaul draw attention to the way the Penobscots were being manipulated by the white audience watching the play: they had been invited to add their approbation to a play that justified the imperial "march of civilization" across the continent and through the Indians' native land, something they also did with their seemingly naive eruption of sorrow at the death of Metamora.

Yet the reviewer for the *Boston Morning Post*, who had been anxious that the Penobscots might not show up, makes no mention of a dirge at all; nor, in fact, do any of the newspapers of that day. Searching editions from that and succeeding nights of all of the major Boston newspapers—*Boston Daily Advertiser, Boston Daily Advocate, Boston Daily Atlas, Boston Daily Courier, Boston Evening Mercantile Journal, Boston Post,* and *Boston Evening Transcript*—one finds no mention of the Penobscots being at the performance and certainly no mention of their chanting a dirge at the end of the show.

By broadening the scope of the search, however, one finds one review that may help illustrate the dynamics at play on that night in Boston. In an extraillustrated volume on Forrest, there is a review from a Portland, Maine, performance of *Metamora* on July 22, 1831, which was attended by six Penobscots, with their names capitalized and italicized in the account: Micknell Lewise, Polsosef Ossone, Etienna Lola, Jo Sawkikks, Jone Nicolalaw, and Saul Ninepence. Clearly, the naming is meant to lend credibility and authenticity to the idea that the Penobscots were there—presumably, one might have been able to ask the Penobscots named if they had seen the performance.

Curiously, though, the mention of the Penobscots in attendance also works to add them to the cast list. Nineteenth-century broadsides and reviews tended to give the roles and actors for a given performance, an attempt to sell the performance by highlighting the actors and actresses playing the roles. Unlike modern examples of promoting theatrical or filmic productions based on acting performances, though, nineteenth-century producers tended to publicize all of the roles and all of the actors. The fact, therefore, that the Penobscot names are not only all capitalized and italicized—second in size only to Forrest's own name—indicates that the Penobscots were not only part of the draw but were also actors in the play. This is highlighted by the way they are described. These six Indians, reports the advertisement, have been "engaged" to come. They will "appear in their native costume and dance the WAR DANCE of their tribe. They will also perform as attendants on Metamora during the evening." The Penobscots, as it turns out, were canny actors and manipulators of public sentiment.[44] Within their own tribal culture, they often engaged in war dances and the "game of barter," both highly ritualized and, as I want to underscore, highly theatricalized forms of cultural practice,[45] and by the mid-nineteenth century, Penobscots, in particular, "started offering Indian-show performances designed for urban audiences."[46] It would not have been out of keeping for the Penobscots to embrace and excel at the kind of playacting that went on in the antebellum American theater.[47]

This returns us to the Tremont Theatre in Boston on the night of November 6, 1833, and to the account of the Penobscots singing a dirge at the death of Metamora, as reported by William Rounesville Alger. By contextualizing this theatrical production, I want to suggest that, while it seems clear that Alger did not imagine the idea that there were Indians at this performance, it seems equally clear that those Indians certainly did not sing the kind of dirge he recounts at the death of Forrest's Metamora. To be generous, we might say that Alger is transposing the theatrical event from Portland, Maine, to the Tremont Theatre performance, but even that Portland performance does not mention the kind of dirge Alger seems to want there to be. What is troubling, therefore, about reading the text without situating it within its performative context, balancing what was said with how it was said and what audience members said (or did not say) about it, is that this critical evaluation then becomes a kind of political programming. I am not suggesting that Sollors's analysis of *Metamora* or Lepore's reading of Forrest were efforts at misrepresenting the facts or misdirecting the reader. Rather, I want to suggest how these strong textual readings of *Metamora* and Forrest can work unintentionally, but insidiously, to smooth the path of empire by failing to imagine a play as something other than words on the page.

If *Metamora* is situated carefully within its performative context, then one can, I am suggesting, discover another vital aspect of this theatrical moment. If we read Forrest's Portland performance of 1831 and the theatricalized culture of the Penobscots against the Tremont Theatre performance of 1833, we see several vital issues illuminated. We see how the Penobscots were active and agile performers, actors with skills springing from their theatricalized culture of ritual and from their willing performances with Forrest in the Portland production of *Metamora*. With this, we therefore understand how critics have too eagerly suggested that the Penobscots' dirge at the death of Forrest's Metamora bespeaks their own innocence and naivety about the function of white imperial power. For such a theatrically savvy set of performers, it seems highly unlikely that they would have naively misread what was happening onstage, that they would have been unable to puzzle out what was being enacted before them at the death of the stage Indian, Metamora.

Yet, Alger was not given to fabricating events completely any more than the reviewer for the *Boston Morning Post* was given to forgetting about them completely. If the Penobscots were there, however, as the *Morning Post* notes, and they chanted a dirge, as Alger suggests, then why do sources besides Alger not say anything about it? This kind of reaction would have doubtless accomplished exactly what Lepore seems to want it to: It would have justified the continued expansion and domination of Native Americans by the burgeoning white empire, for, as Michael Paul Rogin has suggested, Indians were often imagined as "children" needing their white "father" to help them see more smartly how, in this example, the theater works.[48] The Boston newspapers, it seems, had every reason to fail to report this vocal protest, for this would have acknowledged that Native Americans were self-aware enough to know that their objections and rights were being suppressed.

Likewise, as the Penobscots were canny manipulators of white opinion, their outburst could be read as protesting the applauded death of the stage Indian with a kind of mock dirge. The court records at the Massachusetts Supreme Court note that on the same day the Penobscots went to the theater, their petition to block the transfer of ownership of four principal Penobscot land holdings—Shad, Nicatow, Smith's, and Pine Islands in Maine—to the state had been denied by the court (MacDougall 126–127). In the two years that had passed from Forrest's performance in Portland to the Boston performance, therefore, the Penobscots' situation had gotten worse to such an extent that it is counterintuitive to think that they would have been anything other than hostile to the politics of manifest destiny.

There is no piece of evidence that unequivocally illuminates what happened that night, and I would not want to suggest otherwise. Yet, even as we speculate about what might or might not have happened, we can still draw some tacit conclusions. First, we can see how the Penobscots—and Indian populations generally—were savvy performers, ones who might use the theater to stage ideology as easily and palpably as did white performers like Forrest. In this way, unlike the textuality of the novel, poem, or essay of the antebellum period, the theater's give-and-take between textuality and performativity helped make it a privileged site for seeing how ideology was performed, resisted, and reperformed. Second, by concentrating on this performative moment—how Forrest acted Metamora and how the Penobscots literally reacted his performance—I want to suggest how the play in performance, far from being a set piece justifying imperial expansion, could both facilitate and frustrate it. Lastly, if Forrest's acting aesthetic was formed in the crucible of his enactment of the frontier figure of Metamora, then this theater lets us see how his acting aesthetics were deployed and redeployed by both the white and the Native American subjects. In this way, *Metamora*, with both Forrest and the Penobscots as actors, helps rescript what it meant to "act" American both before and behind the footlights.

If the theater helps us fill out the edges of a cultural moment more fully, focusing on how the American theater staged the frontier complicates the sets of values and political configurations undergirding American culture, creating a richer, more nuanced cultural picture. Rather than buy into the idea that all nineteenth-century theatrical representations of the frontier lead inexorably to Buffalo Bill's Wild West and its imperial fantasies in the 1890s, as critics have suggested they do, I think we can use Forrest's and the Penobscots' performances in Boston in the 1830s, among others, to begin to lay out a much more filigreed genealogy of the American theater, a theater that just as deftly problematized the politics of empire as it did promote them. Moreover, if we note how theatrical practice was crafted in its aesthetic reaction to the practice of politics, we can also see how the theater's resistant politics moved drama itself in new directions, pushing Forrest to restructure his acting and the Penobscots to recode their own performances both in the theater and outside it. In conclusion, by focusing on this "pioneer performance," we begin to see not only the codification of the politics of domination, but also the formation of an aesthetics of resistance, a socially invested and innovative theatrical enterprise—what Walt Whitman called an "American style of acting" (69).

CHAPTER TWO

⌘

The Swamp Aesthetic

James Kirke Paulding's Frontiersman and the

American Melodrama of Wonder

In a 1931 article in *American Literature*, Nelson F. Adkins wrote that James Kirke Paulding's successful play, *The Lion of the West*, was of "especial interest to students of the American theater as the first drama to introduce a raw and uncouth frontiersman as its leading character."[1] Adkins was basing his proclamation on a summary of the play printed in the April 27, 1831, edition of *The Morning Courier and New-York Enquirer*, not on the text itself, which had been missing for nearly a hundred years.[2] Through careful archival work, Adkins could extrapolate on the nature of the play, its shape, and its effects on audience members from Chicago to New York to London, locales where it was staged with some degree of regularity from 1831 to early 1865. Adkins's claim that Wildfire is the first staged frontiersman was taken up by James N. Tidwell when he found the manuscript of the play in the British Museum in 1951.[3] "Even though the play itself was not available," Tidwell relates,

> it was known to be the first American comedy to use an uncouth frontiersman as its central character. Before it was produced in 1831, there had been plays about Down-East Yankees, but here was a new, tall-talking, Southwestern type of humor, and here too was reputedly one of the most successful characters in any of the nineteenth-century American plays—Nimrod Wildfire, "The Lion of the West."[4]

Like Adkins before him and like critics such as Larry J. Reynolds and Lorman Ratner after him,[5] Tidwell thus celebrates the figure of Nimrod Wildfire as the first example of one of the most important stage types in the history of the American theater, distinguishing it from another important type in American culture in the same period: the stage Yankee.

Adkins and Tidwell thus framed the debate about the frontiersman around his difference from the stage Yankee, and, yet, defining the values that have concentrated around these two figures—much less how these two sets of values differ—has been more intuitively delineated than rigorously distinguished in the theatrical history of the frontiersman and Yankee. For instance, citing the actor Dan Marble's staging of Sam Patch, a "western Yankee," Tice L. Miller suggests that "[a]s the country moved westward, the Yankee took on the shadings and color of western life,"[6] an idea that builds on Francis Hodge's seminal study of the stage Yankee, where he claims that Dan Marble "brought to the Yankee...the openness, the freshness, and a good deal of the bombast and rugged individualism of the frontier."[7] Hodge and Miller thus suggest that the aesthetic physique of the Yankee changed with Marble's frontier inflections, but the nature of this frontier's "shadings" and "colors" and what counted as its "freshness" are too vague to prove useful in articulating what made the frontiersman different from his previous iterations as the Yankee.

While I am not interested in codifying a schema of difference between these two figures, I do think it is vital to specify the aesthetic as well as cultural differences between them, for in doing so we gain a more robust idea of what made Paulding's frontiersman so "originary," as Adkins and Tidwell suggest he was. Starting with Jonathan from Royall Tyler's *The Contrast* (1787), continuing through Marble to the actor Joshua Silsbee's characterization of the Yankee in 1849, the Yankee became a repository of distinct values; he was offered to the audience as "independent, self-assertive, rural, uncouth, and witty."[8] Miller emphasizes that he was also "honest" and "hard-dealing but fair" (45), and Hodge adds that "uniqueness in dress, substandard speech, and country dialect" came to characterize the Yankee (44). The frontiersman also embodied a number of these traits: He was honest, good-hearted, unrefined, and a specimen of homegrown wit. It thus seems unsurprising that the stage Yankee mixed with the frontiersman in the 1840s; they seemed to have been plucked from the same family tree.

Yet if there is some familial resemblance between them, then the frontiersman is the red-headed stepchild in this family. Jonathan was pragmatic and business minded, a shrewd embodiment of bourgeois common sense. While ridiculous because of his uncanny country innocence, the Yankee was nevertheless an object of good-natured humor—he was, to put it succinctly, safe. His frontier cousin, by contrast, for all of his humor, was extravagant, violent, and, at times, dangerous. While the audience chuckles at Jonathan's misunderstandings as a way of reinforcing the order that structures the audience members' lives, we can never erase the idea that Wildfire is laughing at us, aggressively puncturing our own sense of superiority and upending our own sense of order. As an embodiment of the frontier, therefore, Wildfire reveals a cultural and aesthetic formation quite distinct from Jonathan's New England, itself a lingering placeholder for a European-infused eastern establishment, a "structure of feeling," to use Raymond Williams's term, "*in solution,* as distinct from other social semantic formations which [had] been *precipitated* and [were] more evidently and more readily available."[9] The frontiersman is thus not originary because he is first but rather because the fantasy of the frontier that he both evokes and embodies inflects an aesthetic formation that can be used to interrogate—aggressively, even dangerously, at times—the aesthetic and cultural formations structuring the hegemonic establishment.

By exploring the way Wildfire dynamically interacts with the snobbish European critic in *The Lion of the West,* Amelia Wollope, I will demonstrate how the play mobilizes this fantasy of the frontier, embodied in the aptly named Wildfire, to overturn the European aesthetic principles for which Wollope stands, principles that were incarnated in the idea of the sublime. More than mere satire, however, Wildfire's provocation and abuse of Wollope reveal the play's investment in reformulating—indeed, its reterritorializing of—the melodramatic mode, making it less a province of the Old World and more an aesthetic for the New World. By monitoring how the play's frontier investments help articulate a new mode of melodrama that operates not at the level of the Burkean sublime but at the level of Cartesian wonder, I will demonstrate how the play's frontiersman complicates the trenchant arguments made by critics like David Grimsted and Peter Brooks about the seeming uniformity of the ubiquitous melodramatic imagination.[10]

Finally, I will demonstrate that *The Lion of the West* succeeds in articulating this reterritorialized dramatic aesthetic—what I call the American melodrama of wonder—through the deployment of a fantasy of the frontier that depicts it as wondrous in order to erase the memory of a Europe whose attempts to negotiate the landscape were overwhelmingly conservative, middlebrow, and hierarchical. In doing so, this frontiersman distances himself from the stage Yankee even as he amplifies the political and aesthetic work done by Forrest's redding up in *Metamora,* for these contemporary pioneer performances reveal that, at the dawn of the Age of Jackson, dramatic productions imagined the frontier not simply as an unoccupied space ripe for imperial ordering but also as a challenge to that very idea.

THE GOOD, THE BAD, AND THE FRONTIERSMAN

James Kirke Paulding was the son of the American northeastern frontier, the same New York frontier that influenced and became the setting for James Fenimore Cooper's masterpieces and Washington Irving's locally colored fictions. Unlike the cosmopolitan Irving, Paulding's life-long friend, Paulding was born to a family of struggling Dutch farm-ers and spent most of his informative years not in Knickerbocker New York society, but in the Sleepy Hollow country that Irving would make famous. Accordingly, his well-received novel, *The Dutchman's Fireside* (1831), as well as some of his best-remembered short stories, such as "The Little Dutch Sentinel of the Manhadoes" (1827) and "Cobus Yerks" (1828), show a flair for local color and a keen knowledge of the region—a region whose natural wonders he saw reflecting the true American character.[11]

The idea of America's novelty deriving from its natural landscape and indigenous characters became the hallmark of Paulding's work. Evert A. Duyckinck, the editor and champion of authors such as Herman Melville, was one of the first critics to point out this particular nationalism evident in Paulding's writing. He noted that Paulding

> found his inspiration at home at a time when American woods and fields, and American traits of society, were generally supposed to furnish little if any materials for originality. He not merely drew his nourishment from his native soil, but whenever "that mother of a mighty race" was assailed from abroad by accumulated injuries and insults, stood up manfully in defense of her rights and her honor. He has never on any occasion bowed to the supremacy of European example or European criticism; he is a stern republican in all his writings (qtd. in Reynolds 39)

Paulding drew his "nourishment from his native soil," Duyckinck wants us to believe, and used this nourishment to formulate an original national fan-tasy. Edgar Allan Poe thrilled to Paulding's nativism, calling him "an author in whom America has the greatest reason to rejoice" and praising him as a "writer of pure and vigorous English, as a clear thinker, as a patriot, and as a man."[12] And Cooper, Paulding's friend and sympathizer, ranked Paulding third behind Bryant and Irving on a list of American writers who had cre-ated fictions that "cannot be put down" (qtd. in Reynolds 138). Cooper's assessment, like Poe's and Duyckinck's, thus highlights American patrio-tism as the bedrock of Paulding's "republican" literature.

Turning his pen to the composition of plays, Paulding attempted in form as well as theme to sketch out such a republican character. His first oppor-tunity to do so came in early 1830 when the American comedian, James H. Hackett, offered a $300 prize for "an original comedy whereof an American should be the leading character." Hackett contacted Paulding and asked if he would submit a piece: Paulding responded with *The Lion of the West; or a Trip to Washington*. By December 1830, the panel, which included William

Cullen Bryant and Fitz-Greene Halleck, among others, chose Paulding's play, awarded it the prize, and had it staged.

A drama critic for the December 4, 1830, *New-York Mirror* focused on Paulding's nativism, his efforts, as the reviewer said, to "lay the foundation for a national drama." Yet the reviewer did not seem to notice—or did not want to mention—that this effort at constructing a national drama was based on melodrama, a mode of performance that was inherited from France and Germany even as it was restaged in the United States. Melodrama was *the* dominant genre of the nineteenth century.[13] As Rosemarie K. Bank notes: "[I]n the repertories during these decades [1820s and 1830s]," there was a shift "from a dominance of comedy and tragedy to two-thirds melodrama and one-third comedy (and the near disappearance of tragedy)."[14] Rousseau used the word *mélodrame* for his attempt to enhance the emotional effervescence of the play *Pygmalion* in 1770 by adding a musical accompaniment to the soliloquy and pantomime of the plot, what he called the *scène lyrique*. As Daniel Gerould recalls, drawing on theater historian Boris Tomashevsky, melodrama as a genre was derived from two distinct sources: the *drame* of Denis Diderot, Michel-Jean Sedaine, Louis-Sebastien Mercier, and Pierre-Augustin Caron de Beaumarchais and the heroic pantomime of the small Parisian theaters in the 1780s. "From the *drame* melodrama took its basic method of constructing a play and from pantomime its complex staging, each act having a different setting."[15]

Although the settings differed from scene to scene, the forms of this French melodrama—and thus, the formal aspects of melodrama as a genre—were quickly schematized and laid out on a grid of sentimental coordinates. Underlying this formulaic drama was the reliance on and bolstering of what Peter Brooks calls the "moral occult," the "domain of operative spiritual values which is both indicated within and masked by the surface of reality" (5). Brooks continues: "The moral occult is not a metaphysical system; it is rather the repository of the fragmentary and desacrilized remnants of sacred myth. ... The melodramatic mode in large measure exists to locate and to articulate the moral occult" (5). As a balm to the psychically bruised French citizen, melodrama attempted to make whole what had been so recently splintered, to provide a sense of moral coherence and living virtue. As theater historian Daniel Gerould remarks, all of the elements in melodrama are subordinate to its raison d'être: "the calling forth of 'pure,' 'vivid' emotions" (154), and virtuous emotions at that. The melodrama's trajectory—its initial mise-en-scène, the problem that generates the plot, its varied peripeteias, and its denouement—all contribute to the play's ultimate salvation of morality, and the tension driving the play's action stems from the villain's threats to this salvation. The melodrama's teleology is circular: It ends where it begins, with the assertion of the moral occult made stronger by its temporary encounter with and triumph over villainy.[16]

Russian critics such as Aleksandr Blok, Anatoly Lunacharsky, and Maxim Gorky have "argued that the strong didactic and theatrical values inherent in melodrama made it the ideal popular theatre for mass audiences in a new revolutionary society" (Gerould 153), and it was precisely the French Revolution's emotional violence that, in Matthew S. Buckley's argument, defines melodrama's central dramatic and psychological function: "its capability to produce affective and emotional sensations of great intensity."[17] While the French Revolution provided just such a context for the birth of melodrama, the American Revolution and the more recent War of 1812 provided another version of a revolutionary society in which a fledgling American melodrama could "grow up." If the French Revolution and the Terror made Parisian culture an unstable mix of conflicting ideologies, the cultural upheavals of the nascent United States created an equally rocky moment. No amount of braggadocio, backslapping, or "holding these truths to be self-evident" could ease the fear that the world had become unglued. Nevertheless, although a quest for ordering principles lay at the heart of the development of American melodrama, as I shall demonstrate, the ordering principles activated by the frontier were very different from those traditionally encoded as melodramatic virtue. Thus, while Buckley suggests that European melodrama's "lofty moralism" was less crucial that its emotional effervescence (188), I will mobilize *The Lion of the West* to suggest how the self-reflexivity of this emotional effervescence was integral to American melodrama's recoding of its moralism in a new context.

We can see this recoding of the traditional melodramatic formation in its American version by sketching out the relationship between the brusque, ranting frontiersman, Nimrod Wildfire, and his love interest and the play's snob, Amelia Wollope. In the middle of the play, having finally understood that Wildfire intends to marry her, Wollope, the play's social critic, relates her terror to her assistant, Mary.

MRS. WOLLOPE:	But you don't mean to say that I am *alone* in this house?
SERVANT:	Oh, no, ma'am. There's two of us to wait on you—me and another nigger wench.
MRS. WOLLOPE:	Mary!
MARY:	Ma'am?
MRS. WOLLOPE:	Do you hear that? I'm betrayed—there's not a soul here that can defend me. This savage will marry me main force, thrust me into his covered waggon [sic], and then—
MARY:	La, ma'am, don't think of it! (47)

What exactly does Wollope think that Wildfire is going to do with her in his covered wagon? As Mary's breathless reply makes clear, it will not be ameliorating the domestic manners of this American, as her name suggests she is involved in. Part of Wollope's terror, I suggest, stems from the wagon's coveredness. When Wollope speaks of how she fears that Wildfire, the "savage," would "thrust" her with "force" into a covered wagon, the act becomes readable as a matter of sexual violation. Wollope fears that this covered wagon—out of sight of a watchful society, beyond the gaze of civilized men—would become a zone of depravity in which her worst nightmares of violation would be actualized.

The play stages her fear even more stridently later when Wollope encounters her brother, Jenkins, and pleads for his help, citing Wildfire's "love letter":

> MRS. WOLLOPE: Pitying the savage's condition, I asked him to subscribe to my academy. He in his ignorance of English interprets this with—but read, read!
>
> JENKINS: Ha, ha! An amusing mistake.
>
> MRS. WOLLOPE: Do you call it amusing? Do you know that this man prides himself on his being half an alligator ... ?
>
> JENKINS: Is that your only danger?
>
> MRS. WOLLOPE: A great deal more.
>
> JENKINS: What?
>
> MRS. WOLLOPE: A covered waggon [sic] (48)

As in the previous scene, the issue here is not so much what Wildfire is doing or who he is, but rather what Wildfire might do and what his character implies—the interpretation of action is at stake, in other words, not the realization of action. Again, we see Wollope's fetishizing of the "covered waggon," that space of unregulated sexuality, but her fears are brought to a point by her implications about the Colonel. While Jenkins finds the miscommunication amusing, Wollope balks at this comic dismissal: "Do you call it amusing? Do you know that this man prides himself on his being half an alligator ... ?" Jenkins asks her if this fact—Wildfire's ferocious animal side—is Wollope's only danger, and in this way, the coordinates become clearer. Wollope fears Wildfire because this man is not a man but a beast, and because as such, he represents for her an unstoppable, unflagging sexuality.

Both the scene between Wollope and Mary and the one between Wollope and her brother hinge, however, on the unutterable, that which is at the edge of articulation. The source of her fears being unmentionable, she cannot speak about it to her brother but can only gesture to it weakly. The scene's drama, therefore, balances quite delicately on misinformation, on particular knowledge to which most characters are not privy or—to invoke melodramatic formulations—are secret. In delineating the various formal elements of melodrama, theater critic Daniel Gerould posits that most often "melodrama makes dynamic use of a *secret*. The secret is the most powerful factor in the play's dynamics, permitting the melodramatist to hold the spectator's interest uninterruptedly throughout the performance" (158). The secret's ability to capture the audience's attention makes it a key mechanism in melodrama's effect, according to Carolyn Williams. For Williams, the melodramatic form "should be understood as the oscillation between introversion and extroversion in dramatic representation."[18] Wollope's secret—the unmentionable violation and abuse that she would surely suffer at the hands of Wildfire outside the surveillance of society—draws Jenkins into her psychological inner space, which then motivates his outward movement of challenging Wildfire to a duel. Jenkins's reluctant agreement to challenge Wildfire then ultimately unmasks the true villain in the play.

Yet if we understand Wollope's scene with Mary as a titillating piece of melodrama, we must also understand it as, in Jenkins's phrase, "an amusing mistake." After all, Wollope recognizes that Wildfire is a "generous" man, not a monster (42) and, throughout the drama, Paulding reinforces the initial proclamation made by Freeman, Wildfire's uncle, that his nephew "overbalances" his unconventional action with a "heart which would scorn to do a mean or a dishonest action" (22). Regardless of this, however, when Wollope hears that the house is empty except for a few maids to protect her, she starts to anticipate her violation in a mode typical of European melodrama. Wildfire, the villain, will violate her virgin purity in the dark of the covered wagon, thus depriving her of the virtue that melodrama prized.[19] Wollope, essentially, casts herself as the pure melodramatic heroine endangered by the devilish villain, a half-savage frontiersman preying on her innocent virtue. If Wildfire is no villain—and Jenkins's chortle at Wollope's supposed danger certainly suggests as much—then her hysteria puts the elements of her interpretation into question. Jenkins laughs at her precisely because she is painting Wildfire and herself in broad melodramatic hues, because her interpretation is out of sync with the realities of the play's action.

When we examine Wollope's comic secret, in other words, what is revealed is the rather comic exaggeration of melodrama itself. Williams underscores a similar moment of self-reflexivity in the European melodrama *The Bells* (1867). "The revelation of a secret is of course a stock melodramatic plot device; but I want to focus our attention on the fact that within the stage conventions of the melodramatic theater, this plot device takes on a generic or metatheatrical resonance" (108). Williams's noting of the metatheatrical moment, however, draws attention to the way the play highlights its own emotional modality, while I am suggesting that Paulding's play uses its metatheatricality to draw attention to melodrama's overwrought, overblown sentimentality. The playwright uses the melodramatic investment in the secret to point to the histrionic excess that would be the proper "interpretation" in a typical European melodrama, like *The Bells*, but makes Wollope's melodramatic sensibility the butt of the joke in Paulding's play. And Wildfire is the character who creates this humor.

While Wildfire's boorish interactions with Wollope certainly border on abuse, he is no villain. He is no purely virtuous hero either. He falls in between the good and the bad, the play giving voice to both aspects of his character—a position that results from a series of artistic changes that were made to Paulding's text during its production history in the nineteenth century. For, while *The Lion of the West* met with great success when it opened in April 1831,[20] it did not stay in this successful, prizewinning form for long. The play went through two separate versions: The first was John Augustus Stone's rewriting of the piece at the behest of Hackett to make it more "stage worthy," and the second was Bayard Bernard's, which he prepared for the play's productions in England. Although the play now exists only in the Bernard version, we can use summaries of the earlier versions in newspapers and stage histories to see how its melodramatic elements were retooled from one to the other.

The initial version of the play by Paulding, as reported in the April 27, 1831, edition of *The Morning Courier and New-York Enquirer*, involves "Cecilia Bramble, daughter of Governor Bramble, a senator" and her dangerous affection for the Count de Crillon, "a noted swindler and impostor at that time in Washington," who is inveigling Cecilia to elope. Also vying for the hand of Cecilia is her other suitor, the heroic Roebuck, "an ardent and sincere admirer of the lass."[21] Through a farcical duel and a humorous turn of events managed by Nimrod Wildfire, Cecilia eventually rids herself of the foreign villain and promises herself to Roebuck.

John Augustus Stone, who, as we have seen, had achieved popular success with *Metamora*, was asked by James Hackett to rewrite Paulding's play. Stone's version of the play is the most traditionally melodramatic: He utilizes a long-lost-daughter set piece and has an actual duel between the heroic suitor and the foreign villain, now named Trueman Casual and Lord Luminary, respectively. The daughter, rechristened Fredonia, is guarded over by Peter Bonnybrown, a member of the gentry, whose cousin Wildfire saves the day through his ingenuity.[22]

Among the myriad alterations that were made to the play, two significant developments stand out that help us to chart its relationship to the European melodramatic mode. First, the play's sympathies became more and more bourgeois as the text is transformed. The play's patriarch begins as Senator Bramble, shifts to Bonnybrown, a member of the gentry, and finally, in the only version to survive, becomes Freeman, a merchant in

New York City. This funneling of the characters from elite to bourgeois is, however, in keeping with the predilections of the melodramatic mode. As Bruce McConachie argues, "Americans worked through their political anxieties and desires at the melodramatic theatre, not by listening to speeches on political philosophy but by applauding heroes, scapegoating villains, and weeping for victims. The theatre of yeoman independence facilitated the transition from paternalistic to bourgeois forms of cultural authority."[23] This shift in the class of the play's patriarch in *The Lion of the West* may be correlated with melodrama's faith in bourgeois morality—that the good shall be rewarded, the bad punished, and that everything will turn out well in the end.[24]

The second major development in the play as it goes through various versions is the increasing importance given to Wildfire in the plot. We can see this change if we focus on Wildfire's role in the duel between the rivals for Cecilia's hand. In the initial version of the play, Wildfire "proffers battle" to the Count de Crillon, and in Stone's version, there is an actual duel between the dastardly villain Luminary and the virtuous merchant Casual. In the final version of the play, however, the duel is rendered absurd, thus undercutting the climactic moment of the play and facilitating Wildfire's discovery of the kidnapping of Wollope and his effecting its comic remediation. In a sense, the duel between good and evil, between virtue and infamy, is reduced to a minor incident whose function is to further the action of the plot. Since it is no longer a grand contest, Jenkins's position as a villain is impoverished; he does not get the respect allotted to a genuine villain, as he did in Paulding's original version, any more than he is able to actually fight his opponent and wound him, as he did in Stone's version. As a result, the character of Wildfire becomes more central to the play, and thereby one of the major elements of European melodrama, the "interplay of virtue and villainy,"[25] is diminished, as is the possibility that the staging of this conflict could make some part of the traditional moral universe visible to the audience.[26]

Although David Grimsted has argued that the "low-comedy man who represented some sectional or national type" in American melodrama of the nineteenth century did not detract from the melodramatic nature of the plays, he has also noted that in many plays "the central hero-heroine-villain situation became increasingly superfluous" (186). Essentially, Grimsted wants to force figures like Wildfire to fit the classic pattern of melodrama in a play like *The Lion of the West*, disregarding what he himself has observed, namely that this melodrama was now dominated by a figure who did not feel beholden to the genre's traditional sense of morality. Moreover, Grimsted suggests that this melodrama made its moralistic lessons perfectly clear by denying "a mixture of good and bad traits [in] the same person" (221), that, as Mason insists, the "essential action of melodrama is to polarize its constituents, whatever they might be—male and female, East and West, civilization and wilderness, and, most typically, good and evil" (16). Yet we encounter just such a mixture in *The Lion of the West*, which allows the good and bad traits of Wildfire to bleed into one another. The play actually violates what Robert B. Heilman argues is the key trait of melodrama, namely the characters' "monopathic" construction as singularly minded types.[27] Wildfire assumes the mantle of virtue even as he continues to chafe at this same virtuous representation, thus keeping him safe from the Manichean morality of European melodrama.

While the different versions of the play helped reinforce its traditional melodramatic character by making it more and more bourgeois, Wildfire's increasing importance as a disruptive agent in the melodramatic plot underscores the complicated relationship *The Lion of the West* had to the melodramatic mode.

THE MELODRAMA OF WONDER

While I have begun to suggest how the frontiersman's increasing importance in *The Lion of the West* challenged the rules of classic, European melodrama, I want to turn to Paulding's own reflections on theater and theatrical form to develop what he thought this new mode of melodrama might look like and how it might function. As the first author of the text, Paulding's views on melodrama offer a vital understanding of how and why he constructed the play as we did. Like his protagonist, Paulding also tended to critique European melodrama in his writing, jabbing at its simplistic vision as inadequate for the United States. "From the city on the sea-side, to the frontier settler," Paulding writes,

> there are continual gradations in the characters and situations of mankind; and every state in the Union is a little world by itself, exhibiting almost the same degrees of difference that we observe in the English, the Scotch, and the Irish. Their manners, habits, occupations, prejudices, and opinions, are equally various and dissimilar. For these reasons, we believe that there is no want of sufficient varieties of character in the United States to afford ample material for a diversified drama.[28]

Paulding's attention to and infatuation with the "gradations of character" available in the United States is consistent with his belittlement of the British national character. After all, for Paulding, while the British have only "the English, the Scotch, and the Irish" in their nation as native populations, America has a comparable diversity in every one of its states.

Paulding goes out of his way to criticize the melodrama coming from Europe in this same essay. He writes that the chief characteristic of the European melodramatic style "consists in a total departure from nature and possibility." He goes on to lament this facet of the genre, asking: "Does it never occur to a particular class of dramatic writers, that people ought sometimes to talk common sense, even in a melo-drama?" ("American" 344). Paulding's question, according to David Grimsted, is misguided. "Common sense was not wanted in the highest level of melodrama, but rather something stylized, refined, elevated above the level of ordinary existence" (232). Grimsted may be right in asserting that common sense was not needed in traditional melodrama, for it was invested in a simplistic moral universe, but Paulding's question constitutes a major criticism of this established mode and, through this criticism, opens up other possibilities for melodrama.

Just because an audience wanted the melodramatic "attractions of a menagerie and a puppet show combined, and will relish nothing living, but horses, dogs, dromedaries, and elephants, prancing in the midst of pasteboard pageantry," Paulding argued, "it is alleged that there is no help for it" ("American" 333–334). As this statement implies, Paulding's mission became to move beyond the "pasteboard pageantry" of European melodrama and to establish something that "talked common sense." Indeed, Paulding argued that dramatists need not rely on fantastic aspects of our "nursery horrors" to create entertaining and enriching drama since "[r]eal life," as he wrote in another essay, "is fraught with adventures, to which the wildest fictions scarcely afford a parallel."[29] Paulding's celebration of real life might sound like a realistic manifesto of fiction, and indeed there is much about Paulding's theories of drama that seems a clarion call for a literary form of realistic "common sense." Yet, as I shall argue, Paulding really sought a kind of "wondrous" realism in the theater in a movement that consciously veered away from traditional melodrama, with its insistence on man's subservience to higher moral codes. In a sense, Paulding's investment in common sense highlights how common he wanted our understanding of the forms of expression to be. Rather than use the theater to suggest that there was a "moral occult" that citizens needed to have reconfirmed, Paulding wants the theater to articulate the "common" sense of virtue shared by all the citizens, a republican recasting of the melodramatic mode. If done correctly, American dramatists would thus be able to conceive of true pieces of theatrical art, which he proclaimed as "domestic wonders" ("American" 332).

Paulding's reliance here and elsewhere on the notion of wonder speaks to the complexity of the playwright's attempts to imagine an American melodrama that talked common sense, for while both the stage Yankee and the frontiersman speak common sense, as we saw earlier, only the frontiersman is "wondrous." Throughout Paulding's critical writings, he insists on *wonder* as the operative term for energizing American drama. In a statement that anticipates Ralph Waldo Emerson's calling for the "poet" and Walt Whitman's cheering of the "divine literatus," Paulding prognosticates that this pioneer spirit in American drama will eventually be realized. "The time will assuredly come," Paulding declares,

> when the same freedom of thought and action which has given such a spur to our genius in other respects, will achieve similar *wonders* in literature ... and that those who led the way in the rugged discouraging path will be honoured, as we begin to honour the adventurous spirits who first sought, explored, and cleared this western wilderness.
> ("National" 271, my emphasis)

Paulding wants literature, as an aesthetic experience, to be wondrous; the pioneering spirit that has "cleared the western wilderness" will likewise clear the American aesthetic scene of the infectious influences of foreign ideas, and in its stead, there will spring up "wonders in literature." Paulding's mobilization here and throughout his writings of the notion of wonder is not accidental. His word puts in play a collection of ideas regarding the aesthetic experience of wonder that helps clarify what Paulding wanted the American theatrical aesthetic to entail.

The term *wonder* began to develop a life of its own in the mid-seventeenth century with René Descartes's influential *Les passions de l'âme* (1649), or *The Passions of the Soul*. Descartes defines wonder (*l'admiration*) as "a sudden surprise of the soul, which makes it inclined to carefully consider objects which it finds rare and extraordinary."[30] Wonder moves us because of its novelty and its freshness, not because we have any inkling of its possible benefit for ourselves. This fact makes Descartes rank wonder as the first of all the passions ("*la première de toutes les passions*" [723–724]): It is a pure, unadulterated, direct experience of the soul itself. For Descartes, wonder strikes the brain through the impressions garnered by the senses that code them as extraordinary. Then, "by the movement, or motion, of the spirits which are disposed by this impression to advance with great force toward the place in the brain where it is lodged, in order to strengthen and preserve it" (729).[31] Wonder begins in the senses—by means of what we gather through our eyes especially—and then this sensory experience moves to the mind, where it is strengthened by rumination. In this way, wonder is more than merely astonishment (*l'étonnement*) since astonishment "makes the whole body become immobile like a statue, and renders one unable either to perceive anything about the object other than the first face presented, or, subsequently, to acquire a more detailed, or particular, knowledge of it" (729).[32] Wonder may begin as a form of astonishment, but it then moves to thought.

In Philip Fisher's contemporary account of wonder, this Cartesian moment in the history of the aesthetic experience of wonder was a "Copernican revolution," for in "setting out its features [Descartes] sets out a new template for the passions in general, and grounds human nature in its capacity for wonder rather than in its capacity for anger."[33] The aesthetics of wonder involves "the feeling of radical singularity of means and purpose..., the idea of incomparable experiences..., the self-consciously fresh or first work in a technical direction where preparation for seeing it breaks down and gives few clues" (6). Importantly, though, it also banks on the fact that this feeling of "radical singularity" will make its way to the brain. "Wonder begins," summarizes Fisher, "with something imposed on us for thought" (40).

Paulding makes the aesthetic experience of wonder the telos of his artistic project—he wants to create works that are, as he said, "domestic wonders." The "dramatic exhibitions" he wishes to see dazzling us before the footlights should "address themselves both to the understanding and the senses, and carry with them the force of precept and example." In witnessing them, we are "excited by the passions of others," and it is "by this mode of giving play and excitement to the mind, by mimic representations" that the theater earns its reputation as a "humanizing and refining agent" ("American" 332–333). Paulding's aesthetic formulation echoes the Cartesian understanding of the passions and their movement in the soul leading to thought: We first see something extraordinary of which we have no preconceived notions. Then, with our "passions" thus "excited," we are led to "understanding," and to a larger more encompassing view of "humanity." Although we cannot know for sure whether Paulding was drawing on Descartes's idea of *l'admiration*, we do see, without a doubt, the ways in which this American dramatist internalized and vehemently defended a form of artistic expression that used the "natural resources" of the nascent republic to create a theatrical aesthetic that traffics in the currency of wondrous stage events.

THE MELODRAMATIC SUBLIME AND WONDROUS MELODRAMA

Just as Emerson's and Whitman's prognoses about the future of American art discursively underpin their actual aesthetic endeavors, Paulding's attempts to implement his aesthetic theories inflected his theatrical endeavors. If Paulding characterizes Wildfire as dangerous and uses him to punch through the "pasteboard pageantry" of European melodrama, he also uses the fantasy of the frontier embodied in Wildfire to articulate what the "melodrama of wonder" might look like. Moreover, as the play was reworked, *The Lion of the West* clarified what this melodrama of wonder is by juxtaposing it with what we might call the melodrama of the sublime, the classic European melodrama identified in the play with the character of Amelia Wollope. When Wildfire is being interviewed by Wollope about the peculiarities of the United States, for instance, he declares that "Old Kaintuck's the spot. There the world's made upon a large scale." Still enchanted with the frontiersman at this point in the plot, Wollope notes, "A region of superior cultivation—in what branch of science do its gentlemen excel?" Bemused, Wildfire responds: "Why, madam, of all the fellers either side of the Alleghany hills, I myself can jump higher—squat lower—dive deeper—stay longer under and come out drier" (35). This exchange epitomizes the dialectic between competing aesthetic modes. While Wollope attempts rhetorically to limit the "large scale" of Wildfire's Kentucky by calling for detail, for specificity in terms of the branch of science in which the people of Kentucky excel, Wildfire sidesteps Wollope's move. First, he avoids the question directly, and then, he breaks apart and thus opens up her attempted funneling down of possibility and spatial freedom. Wildfire's bouncing from boast to boast—his breathless heaping of superiority upon superiority—pays tribute to the play's own sense of him as virtuous and villainous. Virtue, as Wildfire's language and form exemplify, involves breaking apart a constricting unification of action, language, and rhetoric that would not allow Americans to live "upon a large scale."

The play's notion of virtue does not rest on European melodrama's appeal to the "moral occult" and thus the reinforcement of hegemonic values for the audience. Wildfire's description of Kentucky figuratively as an unsettled frontier zone whose wildness is reflected discursively in his unsettled rhetoric, disrupts Wollope's attempts to tame it. For Wollope, with her European sensibilities, the fantasy of the frontier is supposed to be sublime, not wondrous. Her interpretation of the frontier is conditioned by European modes of engaging with the natural landscape that would see it in such a way. The notion of the sublime, as outlined by Edmund Burke in *Philosophical Inquiry into the Origins of Our Ideas of the Sublime and the Beautiful* (1757–1759), exerted a profound influence on literature and art in the late eighteenth and early nineteenth centuries. Burke's sublime was characteristically "harsh, antisocial, and masculine. Unlike the sunny, accommodating world of the beautiful, the sublime was a realm of obscurity and brute force."[34] Burke defines the sublime as "[w]hatever is fitted in any sort to excite the ideas of pain, and danger, that is to say, whatever is in any sort terrible, or is conversant about terrible objects, or operates in a manner analogous to terror." Because it assails our desire for self-preservation, this phenomenon, Burke continues, is "productive of the strongest emotion which the mind is capable of feeling."[35]

Yet, as Burke makes clear in his section on power, this "astonishing" experience of fear leads inexorably to the reinforcement of existing social power structures in the individual. "If we rejoice, we cannot but shudder at a power which can confer benefits of such mighty importance" (111). The sublime exists to recement the potentially fractured lines of power, propping up the moral and ideological order by generating fear and reverence in the subject. As Burke makes plain, the experience must be astonishing to count as sublime, but this extraordinary quality must then lead to a newly activated appreciation for and reinvestment in the hierarchy of power, specifically in God's power, evinced by his ability to control the seemingly limitless energy of natural forces, like oceans or storms. It also confirms our own subordinated relationship to that power, often highlighted in eighteenth- and nineteenth-century landscape painting by scaling down the size of humans and enlarging the natural worlds that engulf and threaten them.[36] As recent critics have suggested, therefore, Burke's depiction of the sublime as an engrossing experience is a move that ultimately reinforces the power of the bourgeoisie and its capitalist ideology, even as it entertains, albeit only fleetingly, their dissolution.[37] The sublime thus evinces and trades on a conservative politics, and for this reason, the Burkean sublime is ultimately an experience that strengthens, rather than challenges, ideological structures.

The ideological function of the sublime clearly informs the aesthetics of late eighteenth- and early nineteenth-century melodrama. The classic melodramatic mode imperils the protagonist, heightening our emotions by triggering our fear. We fear for the heroine tied to the train tracks, to cite one of melodrama's weariest tropes, but her rescue just in the nick of time and the subsequent righting of the moral order through the punishment of the villain for his deeds help reestablish the hierarchy of power relations that has been destabilized before then. In terms of its political and ideological emplotting, therefore, both the melodramatic mode and the sublime experience parallel each other. They are both manifestations of the aestheticization of fear, and in both cases, they end by confirming the hegemonic order.

It is not surprising, therefore, that Wollope is associated with the traditional melodrama and the sublime. As we have seen already, she fears she might be violated by Wildfire, and her typically melodramatic hysteria mobilizes exactly the same kind of trope of imperiled femininity typical of the genre. Moreover, her attempts to order the landscape in her relations with Wildfire—to record and document it, in particular—underscore the way she stands as the avatar of the sublime's attempt to reveal the ordering power of hierarchy in the face of unordered wildness.

For Philip Fisher, the sublime and the wondrous are the antipodal aesthetics of rare experiences. "In the sublime," Fisher writes, "fear and surprise, power and danger occur in a rich blend. The sublime could be called the aestheticization of fear. Wonder, the more neglected of primary aesthetic experiences within modernity, involves the aestheticization of delight, or of the pleasure principle rather than the death principle, whose agent within aesthetic experience is the sublime" (2). If Wollope stands for the sublime, then Wildfire acts out the aesthetics of delight. His gleeful boasts about what he can do are not meant to strike fear into Wollope, they are impish attempts to sidestep her effort to burden the wondrous with the ordered. The virtue in this movement is that it drives us to question our own melodramatic—and moral—expectations. Descartes says as much when he adds to his definition of wonder that

> one can say in particular that wonder is useful in making us learn and keep in our memory the things that we have been ignorant of before, because we only wonder at that which we find rare and extraordinary. Nothing can appear to us that way unless we were ignorant of it, or, as well, just because it is different from the things which we have known, for it is only this difference that can make something extraordinary. (730)[38]

Cartesian wonder uses the extraordinary quality of the aesthetic experience to challenge our preconceived notions, just as Wildfire's "wild" characterization—the way he pushes at the boundaries of what we see as rational and reasonable—demands in a real sense that Amelia and the audience reimagine the aesthetics of melodrama so as to make room for the expansive notions of Kentucky.

As Wildfire's privileging of Kentucky's grand natural landscape and his own physical, exuberant nature make clear, Paulding's sense of wondrous virtue is also tied to the land from which Wildfire's character springs, so that the frontier becomes a privileged space for negotiating aesthetic values. The metaphors that give shape to Wildfire's character and even to his name stress the natural. Within the space of two pages, both of the Freemans introduce their nephew: Mrs. Freeman, in a curt conceit, declares that he is a "pleasing specimen of unrestrained nature" (22); and, Mr. Freeman counsels Percival, Cecilia's English suitor, that upon his return to England, he should rank Wildfire "next to the wonders of Niagara. He's a human cataract from Kentucky!" (23). An American wonder, Wildfire is a waterfall from Kentucky, a piece of American geography parallel to, if not surpassing, that great tourist site of the nineteenth century, Niagara Falls.[39] To engage in an American aesthetic, Paulding wants us to understand, means representing as wondrous the fantasy of the frontier, a Kentucky frontier whose unsettled and unsettling pleasure undercuts the European notion of the sublime.

Paulding's most striking illustration of Wildfire's "unrestrained nature" occurs at the end of the first act when Wildfire subverts the melodramatic tradition of the tableau. The party that draws the cast of characters together is the motivating event behind the first act, and all the action converges at this point in the play. As the party progresses, Wildfire bursts in and calls for a dance. Apparently drunk, he demands

> something strong—some music of about 300 horse power. Here, stranger (*To a musician*), I'll trouble you to play "When Wild War's Deadly Blast Was Blown" and bear pretty considerable hard upon the treble. Oh, don't know it? Then play what you like, only let it go quick on the thunder and lightning principle. (*Music commences a jig. He dances furiously, kisses a girl and exclaims*) Ain't I a horse! (*Pulls off his coat and recommences dancing. Servant enters with refreshments. Wildfire kicks them over, pulls out dollars.*) Hullo! What's the damage? (*Mr. and Mrs. Freeman importune Wildfire to desist. He throws down dollars. Mrs. Wollope sits sketching in a corner and the curtain falls. End of 1st Act*). (40)

Even in his first demand, we sense Wildfire's lack of restraint. He wants to hear some music, but he wants it at "300 horse power," an ecstatic, wild dance that will galvanize the civilized soiree. What makes this particular instance so important is the way the play's language, form, and action all point to the same end. As with his association with nature through his name, his command that the song "go quick on the thunder and lightning principle" rehearses this same point: The language he uses draws a connection between his identity as "wild" "fire" and "unrestrained nature." Paulding's crafting of this concluding moment also contributes to this same "cataract" pattern, for the words themselves gush from his mouth in an uncontrollable stream. He moves from demands to advice to excuses to a disregard for everything within a few short lines. His actions, moreover, punctuate his energized proclamations. Like Nora's dance nearly half a century later in Henrik Ibsen's *A Doll's House* (1879), Wildfire's jig here is a dance of freedom and rebellion. His action mimics the force and power of the cataract, or of the "300 horse power" he insists on, for it drives him to upset the tray of drinks the servant is bringing in. His frontier dance, full of wildness and power, figuratively upsets the rules of melodrama, and even when the curtain drops, he does not stop dancing.

The tableau at the end of an act was one of the key features of classic melodrama that drew its connection to the world of visual art directly. It was by using a "pictorial dramaturgy," dramatizing the text "as a series of achieved situations," that melodrama made its name.[40] In the tableau, the actors would "strike an expressive stance in a legible symbolic configuration that crystallizes a stage of the narrative as a situation or summarizes and punctuates it" (Meisel 58).[41] In this way, if the use of the tableau is not only typical but also essential to the dynamics of European melodrama, a "pictorial dramaturgy," as Meisel puts it (58), then Wildfire's violent dance in *The Lion of the West* undoes this key feature of melodrama. Like Paulding's deflation of melodramatic tension in relation to Amelia Wollope's fear of the covered wagon, Wildfire's jig violates the conventions of melodrama; his overturning of the tray effectively overturns one of the devices in melodrama used to make meaning readable. After all, as the curtain goes down, Wildfire does not stop dancing—he does not play by the rules of melodrama and freeze in position—making Wollope's attempt to sketch him as part of a tableau utterly impossible. Wildfire's action thus works in two ways. First, his refusal to stop dancing, which makes it impossible for him to be inscribed by Wollope's pencil, signals his—and the play's—rejection of European melodrama and its conventions. Second, and dependent on the first, his refusal to stop dancing, to have his energies diminished and contained in Wollope's tableau, makes his rebellious over-the-top dance an experience that exposes the conservative ideology of the Burkean sublime for all to see: If this were truly a sublime experience, Wollope would doubtless be able to capture it on paper and thus would be able to immobilize its energies. The anxiety felt by the partygoers when faced with the uncontrollable frontiersman is, however, translated into delight on the other side of the footlights. Just as we laugh at Amelia Wollope's overblown, clunky attempts at playing the melodramatic victim, we equally delight in Wildfire's overturning of the gentry's aesthetics. Delight trumps fear; wonder triumphs over the sublime.

THE MIGHTY, MUDDY MISSISSIPPI

Just as Wildfire resists Amelia's inscribing pencil, the playwright, Paulding, also resists the pointed and dismissive critique of American customs leveled at figures like Wildfire by such foreigners as Fanny Trollope in her well-known *Domestic Manners of the Americans*. Enormously successful, Trollope's social critique of the United States went through five editions by the end of the 1830s.[42] While it dismissed the American theater as being amateurish and boorish, its real critical energy was focused on belittling the American landscape's ability to inspire wonder, an ability, as we have seen, that Paulding highlighted as distinctly American. By reading Trollope's interpretation of one of the great symbols of the American frontier, the Mississippi River, against Paulding's interpretation, recalled in his son's biography of his father that appeared after *Domestic Manners* was published, we can see the terms of Paulding's disagreement with Trollope. To be sure, both interpretations of the American frontier were not written until after the play had been first staged, but they are nevertheless useful in revealing the development and trajectory of the ideological and aesthetic tensions structuring *The Lion of the West*, and for this reason, help us decode more clearly the nature of this tension.

Near the beginning of *Domestic Manners of the Americans*, Trollope writes: "I never beheld a scene so utterly desolate as this entrance of the Mississippi." As her boat makes its way up the river to Cincinnati, she muses, "Had Dante seen it, he might have drawn images of another Bolgia from its horrors. One only object rears itself above the eddying waters; this is the mast of a vessel long since wrecked in attempting to cross the bar, and it still stands, a dismal witness of the destruction that has been, and a boding prophet of that which is to come."[43] "For several miles above its mouth," Trollope continues,

> the Mississippi presents no objects more interesting than mud banks, monstrous bulrushes, and now and then a huge crocodile luxuriating in the slime. Another circumstance that gives to this dreary scene an aspect of desolation, is the incessant appearance of vast quantities of driftwood, which is ever finding its way to the different mouths of the Mississippi. Trees of enormous length, sometimes still bearing their branches, and still oftener their uptorn roots entire, the victims of the frequent hurricanes, come floating down the stream. Some times several of these, entangled together, collect among their boughs a quality of floating rubbish, that gives the appearance of a moving island, bearing a forest, with its roots mocking the heavens; while the dishonoured branches lash the tide in idle vengeance: this, as it approaches the vessel, and glides swiftly past, looks like the fragment of a world in ruins. (26)

Trollope's personification of floating islands of driftwood lashing the river in "idle vengeance" and her emphasis on the unending, unfathomable mystery of the river suggests an idea of hell. More pointedly, Trollope's acerbic critique of the Mississippi registers her own disappointment with how this "desolate scene," which might have risen to the level of the sublime, fails even to be "interesting." Trollope approaches the Mississippi, a key symbol of American grandeur in the antebellum period, with the eye of the European aesthete. She expects a vertiginous, roaring river, an American version of the Nile, not the muddy, dreary waterway she actually encounters. What she records, in other words, is not only her description of the river but also the ways in which seeing the Mississippi fails to constitute a sublime experience.

Paulding's description of the same river also aestheticizes it, but he uses a different set of descriptors that frame it as a wondrous creation. He begins: "'The Father of Rivers,' as it was called by the Indians, whose names of places persons and things are so apt and expressive, is assuredly one of the wonders of nature" (qtd. in W. Paulding 290).[44] Whereas the Mississippi makes Trollope recollect Dante, Paulding highlights the Indian origin of the river's name and elevates the river to one of the wonders of the world. He is jubilant in describing exactly the same phenomenon that makes Trollope feel despair, namely that the

> formation of new points of land, and islands, is constantly going on in this river. ... A great tree grounds at some projecting point, or some shallow, of the river, and intercepts frag-ments of drift wood, vast quantities of which come floating down during the high stage of the waters. Here the sand and sediment gather rapidly, until a bank appears above the surface. Sometimes these accumulations are caused in the current, and it is quite surpris-ing in how short a time they become clothed with trees. (291–292)

While Trollope sees the "fragment of a world in ruins," Paulding sees one of the wonders of nature in action; he does not find it terrifying and "des-olate," as Trollope does, but instead calls it "surprising." While Trollope sees the floating tree islands as "mocking heaven," Paulding thrills to the speed with which these floating pieces of land are "clothed" with trees, a word connoting the positive, progressive aspect of this river phenomenon. What Paulding admires so much about the Mississippi is the way it fires the imagination, the way it "is yet a mystery." He understands it "as the great artery into which flow all the rivers, that, like the veins of the human body, permeate that vast undefined world justly styled 'The Great West,' wind-ing its majestic course a distance of three thousand miles, and forming the connecting link between the rough winter of the North and the abode of perpetual spring and summer" (290).

Paulding saw in the "Great West" the "depository in which is to be cher-ished and preserved, the genuine characteristicks [sic] of Americans."[45] What draws Paulding to the frontier specifically, however, as he records it in his naming of the Mississippi River, is its capacity to inspire wonder. Paulding's vision of the frontier draws on the same qualities that charac-terize the Mississippi: its constantly changing character; its electrifying fecundity; and its paradoxical ability to connect two seemingly antipodal zones of meaning, the wintry North and the vernal spaces of the South and West. In a letter to Daniel Drake, Paulding cherishes the Mississippi, as he does the "Great West," because they are "undefined worlds ... far distant from the shores of the Atlantic where every gale comes tainted with the moral, political, and intellectual corruption of European degen-eracy, and where the imitative faculty seems exercised to the exclusion of all others." As Paulding goes on to say, those writers who "explore the region of the West discover an unexhausted world, as rich in its intellectual Spoils, as in its natural productions."[46] Like Cartesian wonder's enticement to thought, the West prods those who witness it to pursue its "intellectual Spoils," treasures connected in Paulding's statement with its "natural productions."

This stark contrast between Trollope and Paulding's aesthetic responses to the frontier landscape is staged in its nascent form in the interactions between Amelia and Wildfire in *The Lion of the West*. Amelia asks about the soil of Kentucky, to which Wildfire robustly responds: "The soil—oh, the soil's so rich you may travel under it." Shocked and perhaps a bit skeptical, Amelia says, "Travel under ground, sir? I must put this down." Wildfire then narrates a scene to illustrate his claim.

> Yes, madam, particularly after the spring rains. Look you here now, tother day, I was a horseback paddling away pretty comfortably through No-bottom swamp, when suddenly—I wish I may be curry-comb'd to death by 50,000 tom cats, if I didn't see a white hat getting along in mighty considerable style all alone by itself on the top of the mud—so up I rid, and being a bit jubus, I lifted it with the butt end of my whip when a feller sung out from under it, Hullo, stranger, who told you to knock my hat off? Why, says I, what sort of a sample of a white man are you? What's come of the rest of you? Oh, says he, I'm not far off—only in the next county. I'm doing beautifully—got one of the best horses under me that ever burrowed—claws like a mole—no stop in him—but here's a waggon [sic] and horses right under me in a mighty bad fix, I reckon, for I heard the driver say a spell ago one of the team was getting a leetal tired. (35–36)

Wildfire's world is one of muddy and swampy uncertainty. Like the Mississippi, this swamp is a mystery because it has no bottom and allows an entire world to exist in the effluvium: Wildfire is at one level, the man with the hat at the next, and a whole team of horses and wagons under him farther below. It is a mixed-up world, and the crucial point is that Wildfire, like his author, thrills to its possibilities.[47]

This novel vision of the frontier was exactly what was picked up on by the critical reviews of *The Lion of the West* when it first opened in 1831. In a long and generous April 27, 1831, review of the play, the anonymous critic for the *Morning Courier and New-York Enquirer* wrote that the

> author has made this character (i.e., Wildfire) an extremely racy representation of western blood, a perfect *non-pareil*—half steam-boat half alligator, &c. It possesses many original traits, which never before have appeared on the stage. ... Occasionally, there were a few allusions and expressions that might be thought to border a little on the taste of the East, but the body and soul of Col. Wildfire was Kentuckian—ardent, generous, daring, witty, blunt and original. The amusing extravagance and strange features of character which have grown up in the western states are perhaps *unique* in the world itself. There

is nothing in the English varieties of national character which have the least resemblance to the "Western Dasher."

Wildfire is called the "perfect *non-pareil*" of the West, a term that nicely captures Paulding's aesthetic achievement. Wildfire is not only the "first" staged frontiersman and thus "unique," but he is also untranslatable. Like Paulding's lauding of the mysterious Mississippi, his activation of the trope of the swamp and his description of his character's uncontrollable jig, being extravagant and strange in this way uses the frontier's wildness and its fluidity—its wondrous qualities—to create a pleasurable form of theatrical experience that resists the European rules of aesthetic engagement.

Simultaneously, Wildfire's particular embodiment of the frontier also creates the frontier itself as an always already performed fantasy: The frontier is nothing more than a stylized performance rather than a historical entity referenced by the play. In this sense, calling the frontier a performed fantasy aligns it with the way Judith Butler defines fantasy: "fantasy is not equated with what is not real, but rather with what is not *yet* real, what is possible or futural, or what belongs to a different version of the real."[48] The tension between the wondrous frontier and the sublime frontier, between Wildfire's and Wollope's versions, stands as a testament to the way the frontier functions as a fantasy of possible ideological and aesthetic formations not yet realized in the 1820s and 1830s. It is a space that can stage new possibilities of social relationships and alignments as easily as it can retrench American imperialist mandates and visions. By representing the fantasy of the frontier in this way, *The Lion of the West*, like *Metamora*, staged not just a space for the enactment of Manifest Destiny but one that also attempted to articulate a different future for the American aesthetic and national project.

CHAPTER THREE

✧

The Blackface Pioneer

Thomas Dartmouth Rice and
Minstrelsy's Frontier History

"To black up was an act of wildness in the antebellum U.S."[1]

Blackface minstrelsy was one the most famous forms of American performance in the nineteenth century, and Thomas Dartmouth Rice—Jim Crow Rice or Daddy Rice, as he was also known—was its avatar. As an anonymous commentator remarked in a retrospective on blackface minstrelsy at the beginning of the twentieth century, "Had we never a Jim Crow Rice, or had he been less of an actor, the present profession might not be of the importance it is. It was he who first created this *furore*."[2] While Rice was a key figure in the rise of minstrelsy, it seems overblown to suggest he also fundamentally accelerated the growth of the art of acting in the United States. Nevertheless, it is important to note how Rice's accomplishments as an actor in blackface minstrel shows helped align the history of blackface minstrelsy with the history of the American theater, an alignment that suggests his vital role in nurturing the theatrical genealogy of the American theater in the nineteenth century. In his own time, Rice's performance of the character of Jim Crow was immensely popular, as we can see in one New York editor's contemporary reaction to Rice in the 1840s: "Entering the theatre, we found it crammed from pit to dome, and the best representative of our American Negro that we ever saw was stretching every mouth in the house to its utmost tension."[3] Audiences flocked to see Rice black up as Jim Crow; he at once "filled the bill and the theaters, too, wherever he appeared, and sustained his success for thirty years afterwards" (*Negro Minstrelsy*). When he played at the Bowery Theatre among a panoply of stars such as the acting powerhouses Edwin Forrest and Junius Brutus Booth, the crowd favorites Frank Chanfrau as the b'hoy hero Mose, and the pantomime mainstays George L. Fox as Humpty Dumpty, it was Rice's blackface performance that "brought more money into the Bowery treasury than any other American performer during the same period" (*Negro Minstrelsy*).

The Bowery Theatre, moreover, was a flashpoint for measuring working-class sentiments and taste, and thus, as Eric Lott has argued, its successful staging of blackface minstrelsy spoke to the way class and blackface were coupled in the antebellum imagination. Lott suggests that performers like Rice turned to and experimented with blackness as a way of both managing class anxiety and critiquing underclass alienation and disenfranchisement.[4] W. T. Lhamon, Jr. suggests even more, arguing that minstrelsy is an unqualified act of subversion, a repository of revolutionary gestures aimed at tearing down the edifice of racism in the antebellum period.[5]

Countering these critics' views of Rice's blackface minstrelsy as subversive, however, a number of other critics have argued that Rice's enormous popularity merely went to popularize an all-too-prevalent kind of racist degradation.[6] As Saidiya V. Hartman explains, it was the very pleasure afforded by the continually objectified and punished black body onstage—the "spectacularization of black pain" onstage, as she puts it—that at least partially explains minstrelsy's popularity in the white communities.[7] In particular, Hartman suggests that as much as the minstrel stage lampooned bourgeois cultures and interrogated class hierarchies, it could only do so by "reproducing the abject status of blackness" (29).

These critical interventions have framed the debate around the political ramifications and cultural effects of minstrelsy's relationship to the production of racial subjectivity, to the question of how race is constructed, manipulated, and performed—by the "social relations of 'racial' production," to use Lott's terms (39). Because of this focus, these critics have concentrated on the political gestures of racial performance in minstrelsy rather than on the performative and generic history of these gestures and their political effects. Yet the theater was not just one more place to witness race being constructed; rather it was a privileged site, both spatially and discursively, for seeing how race was also articulated through theatrical formations. It is not that racial construction was not integral to minstrelsy's performative history—for certainly it was—but rather that mining minstrelsy's theatrical influences unearths a vital, dynamic aesthetic investment by the minstrel performers that enriches our own assessments of blackface's role in racial construction. I shed light, therefore, on how race was articulated through the discursive interplay between aesthetic modes and theatrical genre. In the improvisational back and forth between the kind of competing theatrical experiences that nineteenth-century audiences would have been both acquainted with and fluent in, I suggest that the theater did not so much stage racial construction as it actually theatricalized the construction of race. For this reason, I want to unpack not minstrelsy's theatrical history but rather its "genealogy of performance" that can address both its racial and theatrical engagements.[8]

While the scope of this project does not allow me to detail every moment of this genealogy, I want to offer a productive starting point for witnessing it by limning the intertwined and mutually sustaining developments of blackface minstrelsy and what might seem an odd pairing: the performance of the frontier in antebellum America. By reading the theatrical history of the avatar of blackface minstrelsy, Rice, and his enormously popular farce *The Virginia Mummy* (1835) against the work I discussed in the last chapter, James Kirke Paulding's *The Lion of the West* (1831), I will demonstrate that this odd couple is not, as it turns out, odd at all. By mapping not only how this minstrel show shared a performative genealogy with a key frontier play but also how minstrelsy, in this example, articulated itself through the (re)presentation of the frontier, I want to add to our assessment of this cultural and aesthetic formation by laying out both minstrelsy's theatrical development and its racial investments and the ways they get interpolated. Through exploring one of the most popular minstrel shows by the preeminent antebellum minstrel performer, I want to suggest how Rice's minstrelsy was as invested in its theatrical identity as it was in its racial identity. By not displacing race as the central question of minstrelsy anymore than I am subordinating its importance in antebellum theater culture, I will show how this minstrel show's continual figuring and disfiguring of the idea of the frontier moved in two directions simultaneously. Along one trajectory, this minstrel performance's engagement with the frontier disrupts the critical assessment of minstrelsy's supposed objectification of blackness through violence and, at the same time, uncouples minstrelsy from its role as white working-class commodity. Along the other trajectory, we can trace how this minstrel performance's imagining of an unsettled and unsettling performance of the frontier becomes identical to its crafting of a nuanced political aesthetic that troubles the idea, as Robert Toll and William J. Mahar suggest, that minstrelsy was an instrument for transmitting the ideology of manifest destiny.[9] Instead, by looking at the way *The Lion of the West* and *The Virginia Mummy* resonate with each other, one can see how the minstrel show used the shifting terrain of the performative frontier to envision a more flexible understanding of racial identity, one that could avoid the enervating effects of operating in a public sphere that demanded, and still demands, clear and legible identity formation. It was precisely the theater's centrality to antebellum American life, as well as minstrelsy's foundational and vital role in that theater, that energized minstrelsy's aesthetic of strategic illegibility, one that gestures to a much more complicated and multifaceted idea of theater than has been historically outlined previously.

MINSTRELSY'S FRONTIER

Narratives of "beginnings," as Edward Said suggests, have little to do with essentializing identities or histories and much more to do with the principles of difference, or differentiation, which provide the possibilities for and the end results of the "knowledge" they intend.[10] The narrative of the beginning of blackface minstrelsy, of its origins and identity in the early nineteenth century, has a similar function, for as one of Rice's contemporary historians, Edmon S. Conner, points out, Rice "discovered" blackface through a complex act of appropriation and differentiation. Conner recounts that

> Rice found his prototype in Louisville, and that while playing there in the company of Samuel Drake the elder he made the great hit which resulted in an enduring fortune and in temporary affluence. Standing at the stage door of the theatre Rice observed a curiously deformed negro singing and dancing while at his work in a stable yard. With that quickness at developing suggestions from real life which characterizes all intelligent comedians, he immediately availed himself of this hint. Gaining the reluctant consent of his manager, he introduced the character of Jim Crow as a Kentucky cornfield negro into a play called "The Rifle," and made an instantaneous success, being recalled twenty times at the opening performance.[11]

This much-quoted story of the origins of blackface minstrelsy depends for its rhetorical effectiveness on the utter and complete difference between the two performers, here the black figure of the slave and the white figure of the actor. While the "curiously deformed" black performer does not possess the intelligence to capitalize on his own performance, the implicitly undeformed white performer, with the "quickness" and "intelligence" of a savvy actor, immediately cashes in on this kind of black performance. This story both reinforces the "authentic" roots of minstrelsy (it was the mimicking of an actual black slave) and works to differentiate the white performer with his power of the gaze from the clueless, happy-go-lucky black subject. With its political utility as an origin story, this is an anecdote that in a number of subtle variations made its way into a range of authoritative histories of minstrelsy.[12]

Recently, however, this story, and stories like it, have been criticized for the disenfranchising politics they contain, leading critics like W. T. Lhamon, Jr. to insist that "there are many reasons *not* to consider this the beginning either of minstrelsy in general or the formulaic minstrel show in particular" (*Raising* 57). Lhamon argues instead that Rice "rejected the British black stage talk that had...carried over to U.S. theatres," and as he went about constructing a new black American voice, he "absorbed and shaped what he could from the emerging North American conventions for representing black acts—speech, steps, and songs" (*Raising* 156). While conventions like Calathumpian bands, Pinkster, the circus, and so on have been abundantly outlined in a number of different histories,[13] minstrelsy's theatrical influences have been given little attention.[14] However, it was this theatrical relationship, I will argue, that played a vital role in minstrelsy's cultural construction, in its beginnings as an aesthetic that attempted to differentiate itself from some kinds of racialized frontier performance. "The minstrel show," Eric Lott notes, "is one instance in American commercial culture of an outland form exported to the northeastern city, rather than vice versa" (47). While Rice was born in New York City's notorious Seventh Ward, he cut his teeth as an actor playing on the frontier. At the start of his career, from 1827 to 1830, he was a traveling player in the gulf states and the Ohio River valley, and it was somewhere between December 1828 in Mobile, Alabama, and May 1830 in Louisville, Kentucky, that Rice constructed and popularized his Jim Crow songs and persona. From a stretch of geography that defined the frontier in the nineteenth century, in other words, Rice perfected the Jim Crow characterization he took to New York City's Bowery Theatre.[15]

This intertwined relationship between the minstrel show and the performance of the frontier can be seen most clearly if we understand how completely de rigueur it was at a performance in Philadelphia on February 8, 1833, for instance, for Rice to play both a minstrel character and a frontiersman not in succession but rather simultaneously. As the broadside for the theater relates, after the main performance of *Rent Day*, "Mr. RICE will appear as JIM CROW [a]nd sing: The last of DAVY CROCKETT[,] De Nigger Ball [,] Mr. Crockett and the Coon [,] De Callaboose [, and] Louisiana Alligator."[16] What is notable here is the way that Rice does double duty, both blacking up and thus appearing as the character of Jim Crow even as he chooses to perform songs and skits associated with that prototypical frontiersman, Davy Crockett. Not only were the frontiersman and the minstrel the backbones of American popular culture and humor during this period, as Constance Rourke has famously argued,[17] they also tended to impersonate each other without hesitation or interruption.

If we turn our attention to *The Lion of the West* and *The Virginia Mummy*, we see exactly how complex this relationship between blackface minstrelsy and the frontiersman was. As a matter of theatrical history, we should note that, in addition to the fact that the plays were produced just four years apart, the lead actors in both shows knew each other; Rice had actually appeared as the black servant, Caesar, in *The Lion of the West* with James Hackett, who played Wildfire, at the Adelphi Theatre in London when Paulding's play was beginning its European tour (Lhamon *Jump* 408). Not only did Rice feel comfortable performing the frontier through Davy Crockett songs, in other words, but his performative investment in stage blackness was at least partially formed in the crucible of one of the most famous representations of the frontier in antebellum America. Crockett himself had an intimate relationship to Rice. "He informed us yesterday," writes the *Eastern Argus* of Crockett's trip to Boston in 1834, "that during the five or six winters that he has spent at Washington he was never inside of the theatre in that place but twice. He don't like acting—but has a discriminating musical ear. Speaking of Fanny Kemble he said he *seed the kritter* at the Park theatre in New York, on Friday evening, but that he had rather hear Mr. Rice sing Jim Crow once, than see Fanny Kemble a dozen times."[18]

More than merely preferring Jim Crow to Fanny Kemble, however, Crockett actually seemed to perform with Crow at times. On two occasions, the *Boston Morning Post* noted that Colonel Crockett and Rice were friends and even that Crockett was Rice's "partner, and shared with Crow the profits of the theatre wherever they appeared together."[19] While this might exaggerate the relationship, it does seem to be substantiated, at least partially, by Crockett's visit to the Walnut Street Theatre to see Jim Crow in 1834. "The house was full," reports the *Philadelphia Sun* of the theater, "and peal after peal of applause greeted the city's guest. Jim Crow bowed to Crockett, and Crockett bowed to Crow. Nothing could be more dignified, yet cordial & pathetic, than was the exchange of civilities."[20] While it seems clear from this account that Jim Crow and Crockett were not working together per se, they did benefit from their mutual performances, symbolically highlighted by the bit of stage business involving their bowing to each other.

Moreover, just as Rice and Crockett shared theatrical spaces, their characterizations as Ginger Blue and Nimrod Wildfire respectively shared a performative and linguistic vernacular as well. Consider one of Wildfire's most famous monologues from *The Lion of the West* where he begins:

> I was riding along the Mississippi one day when I came across a fellow floating down
> the stream sitting cock'd up in the starn of his boat fast asleep. Well, I hadn't had a fight

for as much as ten days—felt as though I must kiver myself up in a salt bin to keep—'so wolfy' about the head and shoulders. So, says I, hullo stranger, if you don't take keer your boat will run away wi' you. So he looked up at me 'slantindickular,' and I looked down on him 'slanchwise.' He took out a chaw of tobacco from his mouth and, says he, I don't value you tantamount to that, and then he slopp'd his wings and crowed like a cock. I ris up, shook my mane, crooked my neck, and neighed like a horse. Well, he run his boat foremost ashore. I stopped my wagon and set my triggers. Mister, says he, I'm the best man—if I ain't, I wish I may be tetotaciously exflunctified! I can whip my weight in wild cats and ride strait through a crab apple orchard on a flash of lightning—clear meat axe disposition! And what's more, I once back'd a bull off a bridge. Poh, says I, what do I keer for that? I can tote a steam boat up the Mississippi and over the Alleghany mountains. My father can whip the best man in old Kaintuck, and I can whip my father.[21]

Wildfire's stylized frontier idiom springs not only from the fact that he is from "Kaintuck" but also from his verbal markers. The monologue is rife with frontier slang—"cock'd up in the starn of his boat," "slantidickular," "slopp'd his wings," and so on—but the slang is perhaps best exemplified in the boast Wildfire recalls: "I can whip my weight in wild cats and ride strait through a crab apple orchard on a flash of lightning." This phrase is imbued with the slang and figures of speech typical of the frontier idiom, words like *whip* and *strait*, as well as being inflected with the kind of "violence" and "disorder" that typified the frontier idiom of Davy Crockett as popularized in his songbooks and almanacs, according to Carroll Smith-Rosenberg.[22]

Wildfire also strategically invokes an unsettling kind of liminal identity as a way of challenging melodrama's moral mapping. His statement that he "shook [his] mane, crooked [his] neck, and neighed like a horse" blends the civilized and natural worlds by insisting on his own liminality, his being both "the best man" and, at the same time, a horse. As Smith-Rosenberg suggests of Crockett's similar claim, he had lost "part of his humanity" and had thus become "superhuman." "But," she continues, "he had also become uncontrollably violent—that is, uncivilized" (97).

Taken altogether, Wildfire's monologue rehearses exactly the kind of frontier braggadocio that characterized Davy Crockett in the popular imagination,[23] making Wildfire an intriguing "surrogate" for Crockett in antebellum American culture.[24] Although Paulding denied publicly that he had Crockett in mind,[25] and even went so far as to write Crockett himself in an attempt to evade the threat of a suit for libel,[26] the opening night of Paulding's *The Lion of the West* in Washington, D.C., seems to suggest otherwise. At Crockett's request, the play was staged in Washington in one of its first versions, and the congressman was seated near the front of the apron. As Tidwell relates, "[U]pon his entrance the audience, recognizing the famed Colonel, burst into unrestrained cheers and hurrahs.

James H. Hackett then appeared on stage in the character of Wildfire and bowed first to the audience and then to Crockett. The redoubtable Davy returned the compliment; to the amusement and gratification of the spectators."[27] The mutual recognition between Hackett and Crockett suggests, in many ways, that the two figures mirrored each other, Hackett playing Wildfire and Crockett playing himself. Both Wildfire and Crockett, therefore, crafted images of themselves as frontiersmen straddling the frontier between the natural and civilized world, and in the process of doing so, blended frontier slang with violent boasting to create what antebellum American audiences would have recognized as the characteristic idiom of the frontier.

What is equally important, however, is the fact that exactly the same theatrical scene occurs four years later when Crockett and Rice bow to each other on the Philadelphia stage. If, therefore, Wildfire can be read as a surrogate for Crockett, then Jim Crow's discursive performance of blackness can also be read as a surrogate not just for Calathumpian bands or Pinkster dances but for Wildfire's frontier lingo. This is borne out not only by the similarity of the events taking place in the theater but also by the language of the characters. Accompanying his first entrance in the play, Wildfire barks: "I'm half horse, half alligator, and a touch of the airth-quake, with a sprinkling of the steamboat" (21). As in the monologue, Paulding thus announces his character's liminality, breaking down identity into "natural" and "wild" factions and fusing them through the energetic boasting of the frontiersman. This is exactly the frontier idiom that Jim Crow speaks when, as a preamble to his "jumping Jim Crow" in the song "Jim Crow, Still Alive!!" he defines himself in the following way: "I'm a touch of the snapping turtle, / Nine-tenths of a bull dog. / I've turned the Mississippy, / All for a pint of grog." As with Wildfire, Jim Crow defines himself as a liminal figure, both man and animal, adopting Wildfire's fractionalization of identity. Wildfire's frontier braggadocio is also rehearsed by Rice's character, for in a statement that sounds like vintage Wildfire, Jim Crow announces, "I sit upon a hornet's nest, / I dance upon my head, / I tie a wiper round my neck, / And den I goes to bed. / Wheel about, &c."[28] The figure who is tough enough to "tote a steamboat" over the Alleganies, in other words, is synonymous with the figure tough enough to sit on a hornet's nest.

Perhaps the clearest similarity in the performative surrogacy of Wildfire and Jim Crow comes in the moments of violent bragging of the two figures. Wildfire's boast that he can "whip [his] weight in wild cats and ride strait through a crab apple orchard on a flash of lightning" performs its frontier qualities in all of the ways that we mentioned above. Full of images of wild nature and violent, swaggering masculinity, statements like this become the signatures of frontiersmen like Wildfire. In a similar vein, Rice's Jim Crow boldly sings, "I wip my weight in wild cats / I eat an Alligator, / And tear up more ground / Dan kiver 50 load of tater."[29] Here, we see a kind of performative lifting going on, a displacing of the frontier idiom from the frontier play to the minstrel show. While the figurative terrain of both statements echoes each other, achieving the same boastful tone and trading in the same kinds of violent images, the fact that they exactly mimic each other's first lines—"I w(h)ip my weight in wild cats"—highlights the performative surrogacy between the frontiersman and the minstrel.

While I have isolated this moment of discursive flickering between the frontiersman and the minstrel, this example of symbiosis is far from unique. Even as figures like Wildfire were constructing the frontier as a set of performative practices, these same practices were being repossessed, reimagined, and redeployed within the blackface tradition. Rather that treating the frontier play and the minstrel show as involving mutually exclusive performative traditions, the kind of discursive flickering going on here between the two traditions suggests that we read them as being constructed through each other. While drawing on a range of contextual sources for its construction, from Calathumpian bands to Pinkster dances to the American circus, blackface minstrelsy exists as well as a kind of frontier performance.

PERFORMING THE FRONTIER IN BLACK AND WHITE

If blackface minstrel players like Rice drew on both his own experience with the frontier and his interactions with the performance of the frontier envisioned by Hackett, Paulding, and others, his theatrical endeavor did not simply mimic these performative practices. In one particular version of "Jump Jim Crow," Rice manipulates the language, dropping out the line that mimics Wildfire's boast—"I wip my weight in wild cats"—and substituting the following: "I wip de lion ob de west, / I eat de Alligator; / I put more water in my mouf, / Den boil ten load ob tator."[30] What makes this iteration of Rice's famous song remarkable is not the way it substitutes yet another set of the frontiersman's vernacular talk or violent boasts but rather the way it (mis)quotes Wildfire's famous statement in such a way that the frontiersman himself becomes the object of rhetorical violation. In a pointed reference to Paulding's play and Hackett's character, Rice mocks exactly the figure from whom he borrowed his blackface persona. This is a moment of dramatic surrogation or "ghosting," to use Marvin Carlson's term,[31] but it is also ghosting with a difference, for it works to construct minstrelsy by self-consciously highlighting how it is targeting its predecessor. By "whipping" the "Lion of the West," and not "wild cats," Jim Crow is highlighting that, no matter how consonant Wildfire's and Jim Crow's idioms might sound, their racial and political investments were discordant. Moreover, it was precisely this discord, trumpeted loudly across a range of stages from the United States to Europe, that helped blackface minstrel figures like Rice construct their own performative practices. More importantly, it was these practices that envisioned the frontier not as a space to enact the pantomimes of power but rather as an unsettled—and unsettling—space for critiquing the repressive racial logic of antebellum America.

To discover why Jim Crow would want to "wip the lion ob de west," we need to recall how Paulding mapped out Wildfire's performative practices associated with the frontier. If Wildfire's frontier characterization worked to undercut the European conceptions of the sublime and of melodrama, then it also shored up its resulting fragile sense of American identity by objectifying black subjectivity. After proposing marriage to Amelia Wollope, the symbolic figure for Europe, and seeing Caesar, the stereotypical black servant, Wildfire exclaims, "Hullo! skulk, you black snake!" To this disparaging comment about Casear, Wollope counters, "What, sir, is a free citizen of America averse to freemen of a different skin?" to which Wildfire snorts, "The Niggers! why no, madam, but they're such lazy varmints. I had one myself, he caught the fever and the ague—the fever he kept, but the ague wouldn't stay with him, for he was too lazy to shake!" (37). This exchange highlights Wildfire's virulent racial discourse, for not only does he objectify black subjects by turning them into "varmints," ironically disparaging black figures of the underclass for not being as hale and hearty as he is, but he also does so as an American corrective to the European misreading of the nation's racism. After all, by having a laugh at the expense of the character who most directly voices a critique of racist ideology, Wildfire—and Paulding through him—is creating this American character by levying his racist standpoint against the European critique of racial inequality.

Paulding creates Wildfire's frontier idiom not in relation to racial invective but actually through mouthing the language of racism typical of Jacksonian Democrats. Consider Wildfire's reaction to the "tariff question." Written as a contemporary color piece, Wildfire's soliloquy on the "tariff of abominations"—the 1828 attempt by the federal government to stymie the flow of capital to the slave state of South Carolina—is a masterpiece of political balderdash. Wildfire admits that he is "clear for reducing all duties. Only let me gain my election and I'll settle the whole in a simple speech" (27). Freeman, his audience here, is entranced with the thought of Wildfire settling this tense debate with a single speech and so encourages Wildfire to continue. The frontiersman does:

The moment the Tariff Bill comes upon the floor I'll jump upon the table and I shall say to the speaker, Look here, Mr. Cheerman, just stop your steam! Now about these Tariff

duties—warn't my father the first man that ever lopp'd a tree in old Kaintuck? warn't
he the first to float down Kentucky river with a hogshead of tobacco, when the Ingens
stood so thick upon the banks you couldn't see the trees for em? I say, Mr. Cheerman,
about this here Tariff—there's no mistaken in men; of all the fellers on this side of
the Alleghany mountains, I can jump higher—squat lower—dive deeper—stay longer
under and come our drier! There's no back out in my breed—I go the whole hog. I've
got the prettiest sister, fastest horse, and ugliest dog in the deestrict—in short, to sum
up all in one word on these here Tariff duties, Mr. Cheerman—I'm a horse (27).

Brimming with the same kind of frontier slang, violent boasting, and
liminal constructions that we have seen Wildfire use, this monologue is
yet another perfect encapsulation of Wildfire's idiom. However, we need
to understand that Wildfire's discursive spasm works here not only to
help construct his identity but also to obscure the real politics of slavery
associated with the "tariff of abominations." After all, while this monologue addresses the Tariff and might have been used to critique its support of chattel slavery, it instead manages to heap frontier language on
top of more frontier language to such an extent that the question of slavery gets buried under the cumbersome weight of frontier rhetoric. The
frontier self-fashioning here enables racist retrenchment. Like Wildfire's
exchange with Amelia, therefore, the frontiersman's racism stems from
his embodiment of the frontier—Wildfire's racial degradation goes hand
in hand with his jingoistic self-creation as the American figure of the
frontier.

Davy Crockett, Wildfire's ghostly original, certainly embodies this kind
of rampant racial degradation. In the same visit to Boston, New York, and
Philadelphia where he encountered Rice, he likewise gave vent to his own
racist sentiments, arguing that he was not a "party man" and that he "had
rather be a 'coon dog and belong to a nigger, than be tied to any party, or
any man's party.'"[32] Crockett's own virulent racism was mythologized in
his almanacs and songs so much so that the "Crockett myth," as Smith-
Rosenberg calls it, emerges as "violence directed toward women but
more overtly toward the inhabitants of the wilderness—toward Indians,
Mexicans, and escaped slaves. Racism is central to the Crockett myth—a
racism whose objective is to justify barbarism and cannibalism against non-
whites" (108). It is not surprising, therefore, that Wildfire's racist discourse
was coterminous with his endeavor at creating a frontier character akin to
Crockett's.

Moreover, if Crockett's racism can be seen as inflecting the characterization of Wildfire, Paulding's own ideological engagement with
the American South helped him frame his character's relationship to
race. In addition to being a playwright, Paulding was also an amateur

historian and sensational journalist, and his reactions to the South, and particularly to the institution of slavery, help us understand more fully Wildfire's sympathies. In his *Slavery in the United States* (1836), Paulding remarks:

> But history will be searched in vain for similar triumphs of the wooly-headed race. They seem equally wanting in powers of the mind and in energy to exert them; and not all the discouragements under which they labour can account for this contrast, without the aid of a radical inferiority. It is therefore not without ample reason, that anatomists and physiologists have classed the negro as the lowest in the scale of rational beings.[33]

For Paulding, the "wooly-headed race" is not simply inferior intellectually because of its unceasing labor but actually from its "radical inferiority," a kind of aggressive racism substantiated, as was so often the case in antebellum America, by recourse to those avatars of scientific "objectivism"—anatomy and physiology—popularized by figures like Samuel Morton, Josiah Nott, and Louis Agassiz.[34] Backed by a kind of quasiscientific discourse, Paulding's fiery espousal of racism led him to excoriate "the advocates of immediate emancipation" and to "term all abolitionists dangerous enemies of religion, morals, liberty, patriotism, and all the social relations of life."[35] Because of the obvious inferiority of black subjects, Paulding insists, only someone completely naive would entertain the idea of having them included in the citizenry. This desire to have the races separated distinctly crystallizes in Paulding's hostility to "amalgamation," for as he argued in *Slavery in the United States*, amalgamation would "debase the whites and destroy the homogeneity of the American people because of the inferiority of the Negro, mentally and racially."[36]

That Rice, in his performance, would want to "w(h)ip the lion of the west" speaks to his own racial politics, to his resistance to Paulding's racist political programming and to his hostility to Paulding's anxiety about racial mixing. Rice provides a perfect vehicle for his critique in the figure of Rifle, whom he introduces in *The Virginia Mummy*. Like Wildfire who arrives in the city at the beginning of *The Lion of the West* from the frontier, Rifle is a white frontiersman who, at the beginning of the play, comes to the city from the frontier. Moreover, just as Wildfire's name denotes the wildness of his frontier persona, Rifle's name similarly denotes an aggressive, masculine persona associated with the frontier. Rifle thus seems a surrogate for Wildfire in Rice's play, a frontiersman who somehow managed to wander into a blackface minstrel show. Still, while we have explored how this kind of generic porosity is not unique, the treatment of this Wildfire-like frontiersman within the confines of Rice's blackface performance deserves some careful unfolding of his meanings, identities, and ideologies.

Within three lines after the beginning of the play, Rifle soliloquizes that he hopes that his paramour—Lucy—will recognize him, for, as he says, "a two years' campaign on our western frontier changes a man's complexion, as a chameleon does its color."[37] Rifle gives voice here to his anxiety surrounding skin color and by extension, to his racial anxiety, for he is afraid that Lucy will not recognize him as white because he has darkened up under the sun of the frontier. While Wildfire neither evinces any signs of a less-than-pure racial identity nor fixates on how his racial identity is being performed, Rifle fetishizes both ideas, so much so that this is virtually the first thing we hear from him. While *The Lion of the West* easily distinguishes enfeebled "niggers" from robust (and white) frontiersmen, *The Virginia Mummy* begins on a note of racial ambiguity, where the markers of racial identity are blurred and unfixed. By moving racial identity to the foreground through the figure of the frontiersman, Rice is not only announcing it as the subject of his performance, he is also critiquing Paulding's racist politics in two ways. While Paulding and Hackett both ardently dismissed the politics of amalgamation—the productivity, even feasibility, of the blending of racial categories—Rice uses Rifle's initial anxiety concerning his own racial legibility to cast the frontiersman as an amalgamated identity. Paulding used Wildfire's frontier idiom to embed his racist sentiments, creating a white frontier free of the shadow of black subjectivity and thus of amalgamation; Rice inverts this maneuver. In an attack on Paulding's racial politics in regard to the frontier, Rice's initial treatment of Rifle as a frontier figure who is both black and white suggests that one cannot perform the frontiersman without also literally blacking up.

Rifle's anxiety surrounding his blacking up not only suggests the mutual constitution of the frontiersman and the minstrel, but it also makes plain that, for Rice, the frontier is not an aesthetic space for the tidy demarcation of racial categories, the way Wildfire has characterized it. Rather, the frontier exists as an aesthetic space of racial mixing, thus jettisoning the idea of the frontier as an unsettled space ripe for racist retrenchment and offering instead an idea of it as a space that works to unsettle exactly those attempts at racial policing. What produces anxiety in Rifle, in other words, is the way that his racial identity, which, like Wildfire's, was so homogeneous before, has become so heterogeneous, so diffused and diluted on the frontier that his romantic interest, Lucy, may not recognize him as the same person. For Rice, racial identity is not something inherently stable but is rather like a chameleon that changes, morphs, and blurs depending on its context.

CONFRONTING RACE HEAD ON

By changing the context in which he presented the play on certain occasions, Rice also underscored his critical engagement with Paulding's depiction of the frontier. For example, he often included songs and skits on the playbill with *The Virginia Mummy*, and certainly one of the most famous was his song "Such a Getting up Stairs."[38] Like *The Virginia Mummy*, Rice's "Such a Getting up Stairs" also opens with a frontiersman. "There came one night to dis Fancy Ball," Jim Crow begins, "A bone squash Captain handsome and tall / He was a traveller [sic] of high degree / And all his adventures he told to me." Meant to evoke not just Captain Rifle, but also Wildfire's arriving at the Fancy Ball at the end of the first act of *The Lion of the West*, this "captain" also comes to a fête. However, he does not strike up a jig and kick over a serving tray, as Wildfire does, nor does he anxiously fixate on his skin color, as Rifle does. Rather, Rice uses the majority of the song to dismember this frontiersman, literally, piece by piece. He goes on:

> In a fight one day he was cut in two
> He went and got a pound of glue
> He stuck himself togedder so right and tight
> When dry he came back and finish de fight.
> He went to sleep on a berry hot day
> De glue it melted all away
> And when he woke he found vid surprise
> Some tief had carried off both his thighs.
> Dis being de case he saw no fun
> And having no legs he couldn't run
> So he shied a stone at de old tief's head
> And tho' seven miles off he kill him dead.
> A ball one day knock'd of his head
> De people all thought he was quite dead
> But he pick'd up his head and ran way
> And nebber was heard of since dat day.[39]

While we can, of course, recognize the frontier idiom in the frontiersman's ability to throw a stone seven miles and his strength in weathering any number of fantastically fatal moves, what is most remarkable about this song is its zest for dissecting the frontiersman. Verse after verse, the song works meticulously to dismember his body limb by limb, cutting his trunk into halves, taking off his legs, and finally decapitating him. In this theatrical abattoir that accompanied *The Virginia Mummy*, Rice challenges the legitimacy and utility of exactly the kind of authority Paulding and Hackett—

mimicking Nott, Morton, and Agassiz—placed on scientific discussions of race in antebellum America. Rice turns the physiology and anatomy that Paulding relies on for his racist authority into a kind of grotesque mockery, for the only thing the anatomized body of the frontiersman reveals is its own susceptibility to being anatomized. In highlighting how easily, even comically, the integrity of the frontiersman's body is violated, Rice is also literally deconstructing the mythology of the frontier that Wildfire embodies. Part by part, Rice dismantles the frontier's reliance on an autonomously conceived, rigidly demarcated identity until he reveals it is not only fragile and unnatural but also capable of being displaced so it will "nebber" be heard of again.

While Rice literally dismantles the ideology of the frontier embodied in a figure like Rifle, he uses the frontier figure of Jim Crow, called Ginger Blue in *The Virginia Mummy*, to resist this same kind of bodily violation, which, as critics like Hartman and Brooks have argued, characterized the performed black identity in minstrelsy. If minstrel shows were replete with black bodies being cuffed and beaten, violated for the pleasure of white audiences, and if this violence "engendered blackness" (Hartman 26), then it is curious that in Rice's incredibly popular minstrel show black bodies violently resist being violated. In *The Virginia Mummy*, Ginger Blue agrees to pretend to be a mummy so that Rifle can infiltrate the laboratory of his lover's ward, Dr. Galen, a mad scientist type who wants to perform various experiments on the mummified body. This depiction of the mummy, as Scott Trafton has shown, stems from its popularization in the public imagination in the 1830s, for P. T. Barnum began showing mummies just before Rice's play. During the first two decades of the nineteenth century, "mummies were an especially visible part of the early American exhibition culture..., placed alongside other motionless curiosities such as dinosaur bones and Native American artifacts, with very little distinction in status."[40] During the time that Rice was writing *The Virginia Mummy*, mummies were most famously objects of medical attention, "framed very quickly and thoroughly as materials for unwrapping, inspection, and dissection by the newly burgeoning American medical community" (Trafton 125). Much of the humor of the second half of this farce comes when various characters attempt to "unwrap, inspect, and dissect" the black body of the mummy—the very much whole and alive figure of Ginger Blue.

One such attempt occurs when Charles, Galen's assistant, sees Ginger Blue in his sarcophagus and is attracted to the idea of removing a finger. He confesses to the audience,

I would like to touch it; there can be no harm in that. How soft and moist the flesh is, and quite warm. How confoundedly it smells of shoe blacking. I would like to have a finger

to keep as a curiosity. I'll just clip one off. No doubt this hand held a scepter with as firm
a grasp as Sampson did (172).

Charles's monologue jumps from a fascination with touching the black
body to a desire to commodify it in a few sentences, which is deftly
ironized by Rice when Charles admits that the body smells of "shoe
blacking." By drawing the audience's attention to the method Rice would
have used to black up, to the de-essentialized idea of race in this play, the
playwright mocks the notion of commodifying blackness by violating it
in this way.[41]

Yet Rice does more than slyly wink at the audience here, for just as
Charles approaches the body to snip off the finger, Ginger strikes back,
"butt[ing] him on the head" and causing Charles to fall. Charles runs off
screaming, "Murder! Murder! Murder," to which Ginger guffaws, "Yah!
Yah! I guess he won't want anoder finger in a hurry. Dese white folks must
all be crazy. Dey talk like de Indians do when dey don't know what to say"
(172). Ginger Blue's response to Charles's attempt to commodify his black
body is remarkable in two ways. First, in a pointed contest to Hartman's
and Brook's assessment of the politics of blackface minstrelsy, Ginger Blue's
headbutting of the white figure of Charles stages a form of active, dynamic
resistance to being violated. Rather than lose a finger, the black subject
strikes back, not only disabling his attacker but also sending him screaming
out of the room. Even though this black figure is being made to perform for
the white figure of Rifle—as well as for the white audience watching this
scene—what is also notable is the way that Ginger Blue performs this role
rather badly by actively resisting being just a body to be dismembered for
the pleasure and profit of white society.

Second, when Ginger Blue characterizes himself as being someone
familiar with the way "de Indians" talk, he is also performing the frontiersman, and so his violence seems to epitomize exactly the kind of violence
associated with the frontiersman. The minstrel not only sounds like a frontiersman, he also acts like one. Just as Wildfire kicks over trays and threatens
to devour the villain by swallowing him whole (*Lion* 61), Ginger Blue violently strikes his opponent. Yet unlike the kind of white violence associated
with the frontiersman, Ginger Blue's act redirects this violence away from
the black body and toward exactly the white figures who worked to commodify blackness. Ginger Blue is performing the frontier, in other words,
but his frontier is not a space of essentialized racial identities and violated
black bodies. Rather, this minstrel figure understands the frontier as a performative practice that resists essentialization through referencing the staginess of racial identity (smelling of shoe blacking) and violently confronting
"head on" the objectification of the black body.

Rice's articulation of blackface minstrelsy through repositioning and rep-
erforming the frontier occurs again in a similar encounter between Ginger
Blue and a white figure interested in objectifying the body. Unlike Charles,
who goes from fascination with the black body to a desire to commodify it,
Susan moves from disgust with the black body to a desire to violate its integrity. She begins, "Oh, my! What an ugly thing it is [*starts*] I thought it moved
its eye. Pshaw! I won't be afraid. There—I should like to touch it. I will just
put my finger in its mouth" (173). While not desiring to dismember the
black body the way Charles does, Susan's desire to stick her finger in Ginger
Blue's mouth stands as another kind of violation of the integrity of the black
body—symbolically equivalent to a kind of white penetration, or rape, of
the black body. Rice clearly reverses the usual gender roles involved in the
threat of miscegenation in the white imagination, but what is more striking
here is that Rice is drawing our attention to the mode of empowerment. As
Rice stages it, disenfranchised social groups in antebellum America—here,
white women—attempt to empower themselves through the assumption
of a phallic authority that depends for its agency on the violation of objectified bodies—here, the black character of Ginger Blue.[42]

Like the scene with Charles, this encounter also does more than simply
outline the power dynamics of the racial exchange, for as soon as Susan puts
her finger in Ginger's mouth, he bites it. As she "screams and runs round the
room," Ginger pursues her, finally driving her from the stage and boasting to
the audience, "I cocht de finger in de trap like dey do de wolf" (173). Again,
Ginger Blue's reaction resists the kind of violation associated with Susan's
figurative bodily penetration, attempting to dismember the kind of phallic
power Susan is invoking in her performance. As with the previous encounter,
Ginger Blue also fights back by simultaneously performing the frontier, here
by imagining himself as the frontier figure of the trapper who catches Susan's
finger in a trap "like dey do de wolf." The minstrel is performing the frontier
here, but as with the example above, this is not a frontier space for the phallic
violation of black bodies. Rather, Ginger Blue clearly imagines the frontier as
a set of performative practices that are able not only to resist these attempts
at objectifying the body in this way but also to strike back against the figurative rape of the black subject by a phallocentric white society.

The fact that Susan is not only a white woman but also a working-class
subject helps identify the way Rice is deploying the frontier here. As Lott
has suggested, the white working class, like the character of Susan, turned to
blackness to empower itself through a kind of "love and theft" of black culture
(51–52). Yet if Susan desires to try on the "accents" of blackness by, appro-
priately enough, reaching her hand into the mouth of the black subject, then
Rice uses Ginger Blue's biting her white finger to stage blackface minstrelsy's
disruption of the white working-class appropriation of blackness. If Susan

represents the white working class, then her encounter with Ginger Blue does not simply rehearse the expropriation of blackness Lott suggests undergirds the political construction of blackface minstrelsy. Ginger Blue's chomping down on Susan's finger is a direct comment on the abusive, asymmetrical power relationship between the white working class and black subjectivity in antebellum America: The minstrel uncouples it by attempting to bite it off.

THE REVENGE OF THE MUMMY

For Scott Trafton, Rice's Ginger Blue is "a standard blackface coon, an ignorant and unmanageable buffoon, alternatively impetuous and scared, hopping between disposability and dangerousness" (122). Yet Rice's blackface performance deploys the frontier in order to stage a much more complex and richly politicized performative event than Trafton allows. Nothing demonstrates the politically engaged nature of Rice's theater more fully—and minstrelsy's genealogy of performance more generally—than one of the images of Ginger Blue as the mummy that circulated as promotion for the show (Figure 3.1). While images of Jim Crow—and of Rice—were a veritable cottage industry in antebellum America, images depicting Rice as a character other than the lumpenproletariat figure of Jim Crow are rare, and virtually no other images of *The Virginia Mummy* exist in the archives. On its most obvious level, we see incarnated visually what has been described in the play, for Rifle insists that he is going to paint Ginger like a mummy, "white, black, green, blue, and a variety of colors" (165). Ginger here is clearly painted with myriad letters, runes, and glyphs, and so we see Rice as a white man painted to look like a black man painted to look like a mummy.

Like the dialogue from the play that gestures not only to the mutual constitution of the minstrel and the frontiersman but also to the way the frontier is used to articulate a resistant form of racial subjectivity, this image works in a similar way, for its coats of paint function as an animated palimpsest through which we can trace the presence of two aesthetic traditions— one, the representation of the frontier and the other, the representation of black subjectivity on the nineteenth-century stage.

While Ginger's body is clearly meant to recall the hieroglyphics of a mummy, at another level it resonates with the popular white fantasy of the frontier, embodied as it was so often during the nineteenth century in the figure of the Indian. After all, if we remember how Rifle wants to paint Ginger with a range of colors, which might connote the imagery surrounding mummies in the 1830s, we can see how Rice is also invoking images of Native Americans that would have been familiar to his urban audiences.

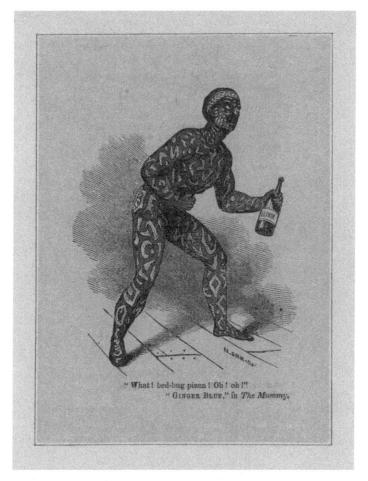

"What! bed-bug pizen! Oh! oh!"
"GINGER BLUE," in *The Mummy.*

Figure 3.1 Ginger Blue as Mummy in T.D. Rice's "The Virginia Mummy."
Source: Harvard Theatre Collection, Houghton Library, Harvard University.

Thanks to the monumental success of George Catlin's images of Native Americans in the 1830s and 1840s, who were dressed in ceremonial garb and made up with traditional face paint, these same audience members who witnessed his performances in New York and other locations would have been familiar with the notion of the colorfully painted Indian.[43] Moreover, these same audience members would also have been familiar with perhaps one of the most famous depictions of an Indian, namely Charles Bird King's 1828 painting of the Cherokee leader Sequoyah (Figure 3.2).

Sequoyah is perhaps best known for his development of a syllabary, or an "alphabet," as it was known, that translated the eighty-five syllables of the Cherokee language into English. The result of this endeavor was that a host of Cherokees learned to write, but, as Steven Conn notes, it also sped

Figure 3.2 "Sequoyah," by J. T. Bowen Lithography Company after Charles Bird King, 1837.
Source: National Portrait Gallery, Smithsonian Institution.

the forced assimilation of the Cherokee nation, making it easier for the white establishment to extend the domain of empire.[44] In King's image of Sequoyah, he stands gesturing to his alphabet, and while not writing directly on the Indian body, this image nevertheless equates the figure of the Indian with the act of writing. By having Sequoyah's hand point to the alphabet, King creates a gestural link between the Indian's body and his writing, and by doing this, he is, in effect, writing on the body of the Indian, inscribing the will to power of the white establishment onto the only other figure in the painting, Sequoyah. Sequoyah becomes objectified in this way, made to stand not as active agent but as an extension and embodiment of the act of decoding and translating white power. King's image, therefore, creates two levels of equation—Sequoyah's Cherokee language becomes equivalent to the English language, and Sequoyah becomes equivalent to his alphabet—and it works by constructing these equations as complete and total. With the alphabet, in short, white imperial power knows everything the Cherokees are saying, writing, or thinking. Likewise, Sequoyah, with his alphabet, is the only kind of Cherokee, the only one the white imperialists need to know: complacent, not rebellious, and cooperative, not resistant.

The image of Ginger Blue as the mummy thus draws on this idea of the Indian in the popular imagination, except that with Ginger Blue, the figurative equivalence of Indian body and writing has become literal. Unlike King's image of Sequoyah that works to decode the other completely and totally, the image of Ginger Blue works against this same idea. Ginger's body is a mismatch of signs and symbols that are not and cannot be decoded; if Ginger is the figurative equivalent of the Cherokee alphabet, he is an alphabet that is totally obscure. Unlike Sequoyah's alphabet, Ginger's bodily inscription refuses to be deciphered; he is at once both an object meant to be read, as Charles and Susan attempt to do, and a subject who actively resists any such easy translation. After all, Galen, the pseudoscientist, who has let Ginger into his laboratory only to divine the secrets of antiquity through his black body, discovers exactly the reverse: A black body who assaults his workers and disrupts the scene of total and penetrating vision. As the Indian was so firmly associated with the frontier in the popular imagination, so Rice recodes the notion of a frontier that is easily translated into space for the imperial endeavor by making Ginger's bodily language illegible.

If Rice creates in Ginger a figure who unsettles the notion of an ideologically "translatable" frontier, then he also deploys this same obscurity to sketch out a new genealogy of racial subjectivity. For, while the image of Ginger Blue evokes the frontier through the figures of the Indian and of writing, it likewise evokes the figure of the black chattel slave through the same image of the inscribed black body. The sensationally scripted body of Ginger Blue was a commonplace for the black chattel slave in the United States during the nineteenth century who was often branded or scarred with letters. It was such an egregious but common act that abolitionists could and did invoke it rhetorically to further their causes. Consider Theodore Weld's highly influential tract, *American Slavery As It Is*, written within a couple of years of Rice's play. In it, he gathers a number of testimonials revealing the way black bodies were scarred on purpose by white slave owners. "Ranaway," one testimonial begins, "a negro woman and two children; a few days before she went off, *I burnt her with a hot iron*, on the left side of her face, *I tried to make the letter M*."[45] In the "Witness and Testimonial" section of the work, Weld enumerates the numerous moments of black bodies being marked—branded on the cheek and forehead with an *A* (78), marked with an *S* or an *E* on the arm (78), or burned on a slave's buttocks "from a piece of hot iron in the shape of a T" (80). The horrors of this kind of bodily inscription are explained by Weld as achieving two purposes: one, effecting a horrific punishment, a tradition linked as much to disciplining sixteenth- and seventeenth-century European criminals as to punishing slaves,[46] and, two, preventing escape by creating for the slave owners a "greater security of their 'property'" (Weld 83).

This kind of literal inscription on the bodies of chattel slaves in antebellum America was not only recorded discursively by activists like Weld but was also recorded visually for similar political projects. One of the most famous of these was the image depicting the hand of Jonathan Walker, a man prosecuted in 1844 for attempting to run slaves from Florida to the Bahamas, where they would have been manumitted. Walker's punishment, and the source of his enormous popularity and celebrity as an abolitionist martyr, was literally written on his flesh, for he was not only fined and pilloried for his crimes, but he was also branded on the hand with the letters SS for "Slave Stealer." "Walker's hand," summarizes Marcus Wood, "became the most infamous hand and the most visible brand in the history of American slavery" (246). The image of his hand, originally captured in a photograph, was duplicated and circulated in periodicals, children's books, and even remembered, poetically, in John Greenleaf Whittier's "The Branded Hand" (1859) (Figure 3.3).

Texts like Walker's image, Weld's tract, and Whittier's poem helped fuse the idea of chattel slavery and bodily inscription in the popular imagination. Black bodies were deformed and scarred by the lash and the whip, and

Figure 3.3   Branded hand of the abolitionist Jonathan Walker.
Source: Courtesy of the Rare Book Division of the Library of Congress.

white sympathizers who risked their lives to free these slaves were punished in a similar method. This idea is figuratively mastered by Frederick Douglass in *My Bondage and My Freedom* (1855), his rewriting and expansion of his original 1845 *Narrative of the Life of Frederick Douglass, an American Slave*. Playing with these ideas and tropes, Douglass deems himself a "graduate from the peculiar institution" of chattel slavery, "*with my diploma written on my back.*"[47] Douglass mockingly aligns the educational stylus that can inscribe names of successful graduates of its institution with slavery's whip that can also inscribe the names of "successful" graduates of its institution. While Weld's branded letters and Douglass's whipping scars are not synonymous, they both betray a desire by the white slaveholding power to discipline the body of slave and slave sympathizers alike through the act of violent inscription. What precipitates from Douglass's discursive confluence is the way black bodies become synonymous with spaces for writing out the horrors of the institution of slavery.

The image of Ginger Blue as the mummy thus evokes both the politicized imagery of a figure like Walker and the figurative architecture of an artist like Douglass. Ginger's body is also a body that is inscribed by the white establishment, and within the play, this inscription functions as a kind of control that Rifle attempts to gain over Ginger, an attempt to own the black body and deploy it as an object for securing Rifle his prize. While not nearly as violent as the cropping or branding of bodies that was employed in the South to mark slaves, Ginger's body nevertheless registers this history tangibly on the stage.

More emphatically, the racial power dynamic is literally transferred to Ginger's body through the image's tonal qualities. These markings are white, or at least light, glyphs that coat Ginger's body, a whiteness that makes the blackness of his body even more striking. This racial polarization functions to accentuate exactly how white power, here emblematically imagined as the white runes and letters, is physically written on the slave body whose blackness helps bring out and clarify the power dynamic of the white slave establishment. Reading these racial markings through Rice's recoding of the frontier allows us to see how Rice is, ironically, using Ginger's obscurely illegible body to rewrite a notion of racial subjectivity that resists the inscription of power, and the power of inscription, at the core of the white establishment. Ginger's illegible body helps to obscure the "visibility politics," as Peggy Phelan calls it, of the dominant power structure, where bodies are meant to be clearly visible and easily read as signs of their own productivity within a capitalist society.[48] If the "terms of... visibility," even for underrepresented groups, "often enervate the putative power of these identities" (Phelan 7), then Ginger's maneuvering of the frontier to obscure racial subjectivity offers one method for sidestepping this kind of enervation.

Through this image, as through our discussion of Rice's play's interactions and exchanges with Paulding's work, we have discovered Rice's "spectacular opacity," to use Daphne Brooks's term, a "cultural phenomenon emerg[ing] at varying times as a product of the performer's will, at other times as a visual obstacle erupting as a result of the hostile spectator's epistemological resistance to reading alternative racial and gender representations. From either standpoint, spectacular opacities contest the 'dominative imposition of transparency' systematically willed on to black figures" (8). Yet what we have also discovered by tracing this minstrel show's genealogy of performance is that the "performer's will" and the "spectator's resistance" did not function in isolation, that it was not simply a matter of individual or audience agency but rather a complex mechanism involving surrogacy, ghosting, and repositioning of the cultural forces of antebellum America. To say that it was just individual willpower or that it was simply audience reaction simultaneously flattens out the performative interplay existing in the antebellum period at such flashpoints as blackface minstrel performances and blinkers us to the way those multilayered performances were in constant dialogue across generic and formal boundaries with a range of performances that did not simply represent black figures. To say that a performer like Rice enjoyed a kind of spectacular opacity without mapping out how that opacity was composed of a number of competing performative modes and genres and was energized through exactly this kind of modal and generic tension is to miss seeing how blackness was no more based simply on representing black figures than the frontier was on representing the West.

By yoking two seemingly distinct historical and performative traditions, blackface minstrelsy offered a different notion of the frontier, one that was unsettled and thus helped unsettle the dominant ideology. Moreover, Rice's continual deployment and redeployment of this fantasy of the frontier in order to obscure racial markings and escape what might be figuratively called border patrolling in antebellum America's most public and visible aesthetic milieu did nothing less than frustrate traditional notions of the theater as a "place of seeing." What precipitated out of this reconfiguring of the frontier on the blackface minstrel stage was a new place of seeing, an aesthetic that actively resisted the racist and imperial ideology of antebellum America—directly through kicking and biting, as Ginger does, or indirectly through the strategic use of opacity, as Rice does. In doing so, Rice's theatrical endeavors helped imagine a more flexible form of subjectivity and, simultaneously, a more socially provocative and aesthetically diverse form of theater. That this minstrel theater was enormously popular speaks to the ways this new aesthetic both responded to a much more variegated and heterogeneous American public than has previously been imagined and, at the same time, helped construct that same public. As a newspaper reported after one of Rice's performances in which he sang and danced as the character of Jim Crow, the next day " 'Jim Crow' was upon nearly everybody's tongues; boys whistled it on the street, ladies sang it in the parlor, while it was heard in the mart of trade and in the workshops."[49] Rice's performative style, in short, reached from the "boys" in the "streets" to the "ladies" in their "parlors," inflecting the lives of the bourgeois men of "trade" as well as the working-class men of the "workshop." These various and wide-ranging constituencies of the American public both responded to Rice and were activated by him; they encouraged him through patronizing his act and were influenced by him as we can witness in their whistling and singing his songs in their private spaces. Thus, while Rice's performance might have troubled the usual dynamic of the theater, this new performative aesthetic helped carve out a new theatrical terrain—funneled through his reframing of the frontier—that could be shared by both the bourgeoisie and the underclass.

Though minstrelsy was incredibly popular and pervasive, I do not want to suggest that Rice's performances changed the course of history. What I do want to suggest is that the minstrel stage's aesthetic pas de deux with the performance of the frontier on the antebellum stage helped frame a new theatrical experience for the American populace. If Rice's performance was "unique," as one reviewer mentioned, then part of its uniqueness was the novel way it helped map a new aesthetic landscape, a landscape whose heartland was not on the plantation nor in the city but rather on the frontier.

CHAPTER FOUR

✧

What Is It?

The Frontier, Melodrama, and
Boucicault's Amalgamated Drama

Dion Boucicault's *The Octoroon; or, Life in Louisiana*, a racial melodrama about a tragic mulatta named Zoe and her doomed interracial relationship with the young white gallant George Peyton opened at the Winter Garden Theatre in New York City on December 6, 1859, four nights after John Brown was hanged and on the same night that a pro-Southern candidate was elected mayor of New York City. Boucicault's drama of tragic, cross-racial love, interracial murder, and sensational catastrophes was therefore exquisitely timed to cause a stir, and if the *New York Times* of December 15, 1859, is to be believed, it did: "Everybody talks about the 'Octoroon,' wonders about the 'Octoroon,' goes to see the 'Octoroon;' and the 'Octoroon' thus becomes, in point of fact, the work of the public mind."[1] Boucicault, in short, knew how to cause a theatrical sensation. Not only had he introduced a play that dealt with the issues of cross-racial "amalgamation,"[2] murder, and slavery, but just a day before the play opened, his wife, Agnes Robertson, an accomplished actress playing the title role, received an anonymous letter stating that if she essayed the part of Zoe, she would be shot. "In all probability," suggests one of Boucicault's biographers, Richard Fawkes, "the letter was written by her husband, but its mere existence enabled Boucicault to gain column inches of free publicity."[3] Like his contemporary, the master showman P. T. Barnum, Dion Boucicault was an apt manipulator of public sentiment, and the play, in no small part because of Boucicault's craftsmanship, became *the* hot topic.

The Octoroon not only aimed to cause a sensation but was also, as Boucicault himself argued, invested in social change. "I believe the drama to be a proper and very effective instrument to use in the dissection of all social matters," Boucicault declared. "It is by such means that the drama can be elevated into the social importance it deserves to enjoy."[4] More specifically, as he expostulated on why the octoroon must die at the end of the play, drinking poison to avoid becoming the forced concubine of the evil overseer, Jacob M'Closky, Boucicault states: "In the death of the Octoroon lies the moral and teaching of the whole work. Had this girl been saved, and the drama brought to a happy end, the horrors of her position, irremediable from the very nature of the institution of slavery, would subside into the condition of a temporary annoyance."[5] The text Boucicault cites as a source for his play ends with the marriage of the octoroon to her suitor,[6] and so, Boucicault clearly saw his play—one that ends not in benign marriage but in the death of the octoroon—as critically engaged in the debate over the institution of slavery.

However, while many American newspapers blasted Boucicault for "misrepresent[ing] and vilify[ing] the South" and for creating in Zoe an amalgamated racial identity that was "preposterous, unnatural, and profane,"[7] many critics saw the play as merely entertaining, taking no real position in the slavery debates—a vision that seems to trouble Boucicault's claims to his drama's social activism. Joseph Jefferson, who played Salem Scudder in the Winter Garden production, recounts in his memoir that "the truth of the matter is, [the play] was non-committal."[8] Likewise, a later review of Boucicault's work on December 15, 1859, in the *New York Times* echoed this sentiment. "[W]e own ourselves still unable to see what possible reason or common sense there can be in regarding [the play] as a formidable political engine," the reviewer states. "It seemed and seems to me to be merely a cleverly-constructed, perfectly impartial, not to say non-committal, picture of life as it is in Louisiana. Its negroes are negroes, and nothing more—with the least imaginable likeness to TOUSSAINT L'OUVERTURE or DOMINICK VESEY." By insisting that the play was "non-committal," these sources index how the death of the octoroon, while gesturing to the potentially explosive issue of slavery, ultimately defused it by eliminating the disruptive figure of the mulatta from the play's racial calculus. Read this way, the death of the mixed-raced figure of Zoe underscored the play's essentialized racial ideology—"its negroes were negroes," as the reviewer noted, "and nothing more."[9]

These critics have suggested that Boucicault's reliance on the tragic mulatta plot helped reinforce a debilitating scheme of racial difference, one that writers like Frederick Douglass, Martin Delany, and William Wells Brown were actively working against in antebellum America.[10] But even when the tragic mulatta plot was replaced in its British version by one that ends in marriage, not death, in an effort to please an audience much less anxious about the specter of slavery, the play's thematic investment in place still muddied its political content. For no matter where *The Octoroon* was put on to entertain audiences, the play always unfolded in Louisiana, or as it is called in text, "the selvage of civilization."[11] For Joseph Roach, the term *selvage*—the interwoven edge of a piece of fabric—is a key to unlocking what is at work in the play, for the selvage "more figuratively suggests a margin, a boundary, or a perimeter that by opposition defines the center—in short, a frontier."[12] While the play, in the main, takes the form of a mortgage melodrama, its interweaving plots also allow it to reference itself as a frontier drama.[13] Understanding this, Roach argues that it ultimately uses this frontier setting to "thematize the 'law' of manifest destiny and the doctrine of monoculturalism that it inscribes" even as it gestures to "the historic opportunity to accept or reject an alternative to the bloody frontier of conquest and forced assimilation" (182).

I posit that it is precisely the way Boucicault maintained the play's thematic development of the frontier setting and mobilized it to inflect the formal shape of the text, no matter where the play was staged in the transatlantic world, that substantiates Boucicault's claims about the play's social and political critique. By reading the way theme engages form, and vice versa, in *The Octoroon*, I will argue that it actually lives up to Boucicault's claims in two ways. First, he pulls the curtain back on the politics of melodrama, linking its black-or-white mode to the suffering of the hero and heroine in the main plot. By reading racial identity construction through melodramatic performance, Boucicault's play dramatizes Saidiya V. Hartman's argument that "the corporeal enactment of blackness [is] a pained one,"[14] that melodrama's logic of suffering in antebellum American theater was often racially coded and depended on that codifying to generate its power. By attending carefully to the formal maneuvers of the main plot, we see how Boucicault draws our attention as audience members to this racial encoding in an effort not only to distance us critically from the melodramatic mechanisms of oppression operating within the main plot but also to italicize its artificial claims to authority. In this sense, while the tragic mulatta plot may be "non-committal," resting on an essentialized, damaging notion of racial subjectivity, Boucicault problematizes this plot by metatheatrically highlighting and puncturing its claims to authority.

Second, if *The Octoroon*'s main plot problematizes the melodramatic enactment of racial violence, then its subplot, involving a frontier character, the Indian Wahnotee, uses an ideologically loose and aesthetically blurry fantasy of the frontier to offer a productive countermand to melodrama's power play. By focusing on the subplot and the way Wahnotee shadows Zoe in terms of identity construction, aesthetic characterization, and dramatic action, we shall see how Boucicault's play—read in its totality—does not buy into a coding of the frontier as an extension of American imperial power, as Roach insists. Rather, through the particular fantasy of the frontier Boucicault generates, it gestures to what I will call an amalgamated drama that does not suffer from the black-or-white modalities of melodrama.

Finally, by placing Wahnotee in context and reading his character through the play's performance at P. T. Barnum's American Museum in 1860, which was also exhibiting the showman's nondescript "What is It?"—a half man, half ape creature from the "Wilds of the Prairie"—I will show how this double bill (re)focuses our attention on the performance of identity. By tracing how both Barnum and Boucicault reenvision the frontier onstage, I will reveal how their two "creatures" helped craft a black-and-white mode that exchanges melodrama's politics of suffering for the liberating effects of what Boucicault called the "pleasure" of "amalgamated" performance. Boucicault complicates the notion that the frontier on the nineteenth-century stage was only an extension of imperial ideology, as critics have suggested.[15] He employs the frontier not as a means of reinforcing the codings of savage versus civilized, black versus white, but rather as a way to advance a new performative practice that found pleasure in black-and-white identity politics and thus also served as a vehicle for reimagining what it meant to perform America that way. "What is It?" is a question, therefore, that could be asked not just of Barnum's creature and of Boucicault's play but of an American nation confronting a host of amalgamated identities on the eve of the Civil War.

I SUFFER, THEREFORE, I AM

George Peyton, one of the protagonists in *The Octoroon*, seems to embody perfectly the melodramatic hero, for when he is courting Zoe, George's language reveals all of the traits of melodramatic virtue. "I shall see this estate pass from me without a sigh," declares George, "for it possesses no charm for me; the wealth I covet is the love of those around me—eyes that are rich in fond looks, lips that breathe endearing words; the only estate I value is the heart of one true woman, and the slaves I'd have are her thoughts" (465). A melodramatic lover's speech par excellence, George's statement of sentiment eschews all qualifications and makes his character, as Robert B. Heilman suggests about melodrama generally, "monopathic."[16] All the hero wants is love, or as George phrases it, "the heart of one true woman." The melodramatic mode that George emblemizes so directly rests on a dynamic of black-or-white systemic formations, on what Peter Brooks has called melodrama's "polarized" mode. In this mode, characters attempt to make the "moral occult" completely visible, either by performing its goodness wholeheartedly, as its heroes and heroines do, or by attempting to subvert it wholeheartedly, as its villains do.[17] In this instance from Boucicault's play, therefore, George is the consummate melodramatic lover; his goodness is, to use Linda Williams's term, a kind of "moral stereotyping,"[18] for its love is unchecked and admits no exceptions.

Boucicault demonstrates the black-or-white nature of George's identity even more emphatically just before the revelation that Zoe is a slave. Torn between his love for the octoroon and his devotion to his family and realizing that a strategic marriage to Dora Sunnyside would save his plantation, George proclaims: "My dear mother—Mr. Scudder—you teach me what I ought to do; if Miss Sunnyside will accept me as I am, Terrebonne shall be saved: I will sell myself, but the slaves shall be protected." George's melodramatic exaggeration here meets with his ever-practical mother's retort: "*Sell* yourself, George! Is not Dora worth any man's—" which Scudder then interrupts, chiding her, "Don't say that, ma'am; don't say that to a man that loves another gal. He's going to do an heroic act; don't spile it" (472–473).

What we see here is a disjuncture of modes that gestures to both the tenuous authority of the melodramatic form and the way that form helps limn the American color line all the more clearly. Take, for instance, Salem Scudder's response to Mrs. Peyton. His admonishment that George is engaging in a heroic act that should not be "spiled" makes plain that what we are witnessing is not so much an act of heroism but rather a melodramatic effect aimed at constructing George as a hero—a fragile act that could be easily derailed by Mrs. Peyton's failure to play along. Moreover, George has recently returned to the Terrebonne Plantation from Paris, the birthplace of Rousseau's *mélodrame* and the home of René Charles Guilbert de Pixérécourt, one of the most influential figures in the American melodramatic theater.[19] George thus comes to embody not only the melodramatic hero but also melodrama itself. Scudder's dramaturgical self-reflexivity, therefore, works to alienate us from the action of the play's melodramatic hero. By critically denaturalizing the melodramatic mode in this way, Boucicault questions the logic involved in characterizing George as the dashing hero of a typical nineteenth-century melodrama.

While it might seem a kind of overreading to suggest that Boucicault was "self-reflexive" in the mid-nineteenth century, in some ways anticipating poststructural infatuations with play within his text, this kind of "mixed consciousness," as Marc Robinson calls it, was prevalent in many antebellum American texts. As he says:

> Any study of mid-nineteenth century American theater must come to terms with this "mixed consciousness"—the experience of being both inside and outside the performance, and the process by which a spectator's surrender to visual pleasure,

a surrender that typically involves self-forgetting, results in self-recognition of the kind James describes…. Such an experience enlarges one's sense of the purpose of theatrical seeing. Instead of being passive and anonymous, spectatorship in the nineteenth century is often a form of intervention, as audiences are invited to become witnesses, analysts, historians, and even reformers, able by the care with which they observe a production to practice the skills of self-scrutiny and social diagnosis necessary outside the theater as well.[20]

Throughout *The Octoroon*, Boucicault continues to disrupt the black-or-white vision of melodrama through creating this kind of "mixed consciousness" in his spectators, a shuttling between what Robinson refers to as "analytic and ecstatic seeing" (43). This double vision occurs again when George speaks of either selling himself or retaining his integrity, either letting the slaves be abused or protecting them. To be heroic thus involves not just personal sacrifice but also the public declaration of how he will suffer because of his choice. The kind of suffering George is invoking was required in melodramatic subjects, for as Linda Williams argues, the melodramatic mode defined itself by "staging virtue through adversity and suffering" (15). As we have already noted, melodrama trades in a kind of "moral stereotyping"—a black-or-white bifurcation of virtue and villainy—but it needs a means by which to make that moral division visible. Suffering provides just such a means, not only separating virtue from villainy but also equating virtue with a highly visible kind of victimhood as a way of marking the hero as heroic. As Boucicault was aware, one of the bedrock principles of melodrama was that heroism emerges from virtue's suffering.

In the nineteenth century, that understanding of heroism and, thus, of identity was codified by the theatrical predecessor of *The Octoroon*—the stage blockbuster *Uncle Tom's Cabin* (1851). "From the moment Simon Legree's whip first lent Uncle Tom a paradoxical visibility and dignity as a suffering, and thus worthy, human being," Linda Williams insists, "the political power of pain and suffering has been a key mechanism of melodrama's rhetorical power" (43).[21] The move from white to black suffering in Uncle Tom effectively recalibrated identity, making that suffering the defining feature of hitherto disenfranchised individuals: "I suffer, therefore, I am," the speaker suggests. When George thus proclaims, "I will sell myself, but the slaves shall be protected" (472), he is embracing this method of identity formation, metaphorically blacking up by representing himself as a piece of chattel like Uncle Tom that can be sold in order to insert himself simultaneously into a tradition of suffering, melodramatic heroes.

The problem with George's performing this melodramatic suffering, however, is that he is no Uncle Tom. George is not a slave; he is not subject to the whip of Simon Legree; he does not suffer from the humiliation of servitude. Uncle Tom's heroic suffering helped construct a fraught version of black subjectivity through melodrama, whereas George's self-inflicted wound, by contrast, is an attempt to construct his heroic self by taking over the suffering, melodramatic identity of the slave. Since George is a privileged member of the white Southern aristocracy, his heroic statement that he will "sell" himself can be read as a kind of performative slumming, a fact underscored in the text by Mrs. Peyton's immediate, instinctive response: "*Sell* yourself, George!" (472). By highlighting the exact term central to George's performance, Mrs. Peyton's comment draws our attention as audience members to the way melodrama is implicated in the repressive structures of racial power. George's appropriation of the role of a suffering, black melodramatic hero can only occur through his expropriation of one of the few modes of identity construction accorded black chattel slaves. George's "blacking up" works, in other words, not to address the inequalities and devastating ironies such a cross-racial performance reveals but rather to use these very inequalities to reveal his character as a melodramatic hero.

If Boucicault wants to make us critically aware of his play as a melodrama and of George as its heavy-handed hero, then he equally wants us to see the title character, the famous octoroon, together with the tragic mulatta plot she inhabits, in a critical light. Like the previous exchange, Zoe's revelation of her true identity to George at the climax of the play creates a slippage in the modal configuration of the play, a slippage that also implicates the melodramatic mode in the enactment of racial power. In this scene, Zoe tells George, "There is a gulf between us, as wide as your love, as deep as my despair." When George then insists that she explain herself, Zoe produces a litany of signs of her own abjection, ending the list by proclaiming: "I am an unclean thing—forbidden by the laws—I'm an Octoroon!" (466–467). At this exact moment when the future of the characters in this play hangs in the balance, George seems unwilling to let Zoe suffer as the tragic mulatta; he is unwilling, in other words, to abide by the rules of melodramatic suffering.[22] In a moment that has escaped critics' attention, George seems willing to toss aside Zoe's definition as an octoroon because of love, declaring, "Zoe, I love you none the less; this knowledge brings no revolt to my heart, and I can overcome the obstacle" (467). George's about-face in terms of characterization—from melodramatic champion to melodramatic challenger—becomes a device used by Boucicault to suggest not only how fluid and nonmonopathic dramatic characters can be but also how artificially conditioned melodramatic characters are. In this instant, after all, the play could end happily, as Reid's narrative does with Edward and Aurore living a "tranquil" life together (367). Yet, this dramatic possibility is quashed by Zoe's next line, "But *I* cannot" (467). George's momentary dismissal of the melodramatic plot for one that might avoid its calamitous conclusion is thus abruptly undercut by Zoe's declaration. Her emphasis on I, moreover, not only highlights that she disagrees with George but figuratively underscores that it is precisely Zoe's mulatta identity for which the play is named that forecloses any possibility of avoiding a tragic end. She *is* the tragic mulatta, she insists, and her reproach to George indicates that he has misread her scripted end. Like the scene between George, Mrs. Peyton, and Scudder, this exchange between melodramatic hero and heroine introduces a critical "mixed consciousness." Just when the audience watching this production would be most heavily invested in the melodramatic nature of the play, Boucicault creates a slippage that allows a critical space to develop for them within the confines of the drama itself.

What we see in this critical moment is that if Zoe will play the tragic mulatta triumphantly, she will necessarily have to suffer as the result of this choice precisely because of her commitment to melodramatic performance and the identity it entails. Nancy Bentley argues that "the idea of the inviolate soul in [mulatta] fiction modulates all too easily into notions of a soul that thrives upon, or even requires, the humiliation of the body. By definition, the tragic Mulatta is granted her most pronounced symbolic power by virtue of her worldly suffering" (505). Russ Castronovo goes further, stating that figures like Zoe can only achieve freedom through suffering a tragic death since death "liberates the subject from social meanings of race."[23] Lauren Berlant has recently argued, however, that melodramatic suffering, like Zoe's, became a means not of erasing identity but of ironically—if not unproblematically— mapping out a new kind of personhood. Starting in the early nineteenth century, when the sentimental mode's stock was on the rise, its appeal to the emotions, Berlant argues, created a new way to conceptualize identity. It worked to bind people to the nation not by deploying a rhetoric of citizenship or of individual rights but rather by creating a rhetoric that depended on "the capacity for suffering and trauma at the citizen's core."[24] To make oneself into a true citizen, as we see Zoe do, involved identification with pain and suffering and, more importantly, the embracing of this identification as identity.

Zoe's desire to suffer as the melodramatic tragic mulatta can be read as a desire for identity, for mixed race women like Zoe were not officially recognized as mixed in the nineteenth century but were instead identified as black and thus considered chattel property.[25] Brooks argues that Zoe is "blackened by the act of suffering" (41), and while Boucicault's play stages this argument, the playwright is likewise keen to draw his audience's attention to how the form of melodrama itself—with its reliance on suffering—is implicated in the scripting of the play's tragic end. Zoe's desire to suffer, in other words, marks her blackness but also seals her fate, for not ten lines after Zoe's melodramatic declaration of intent, George attempts to dissuade her, asking if they must "immolate" their lives to the societal prejudice around them. Zoe can only insist: "Yes, for I'd rather be black than ungrateful! Ah, George, our race has at least one virtue—it knows how to suffer!" (467). By embracing a racial understanding of herself, Zoe thus also embraces the ne plus ultra of melodramatic identity, the capacity for suffering not as a plot device but as a conduit to personhood. As Boucicault reveals, her melodramatic understanding of who she is in a genre that makes everything black or white drives her to freight her blackness, her "suffering race," with the responsibility for her suffering.

Like George's performance of heroism, Zoe's playing the suffering victim shows how implicated the form of melodrama is in the reinforcement of the racism of antebellum America. Ironically, to wrap herself in the mantle of the suffering melodramatic heroine, Zoe must first figuratively black up, just as her paramour, George, did earlier. In Zoe's case, however, such a choice also dismisses the complexity of her paradoxical nature as black –and white, and in doing so, denies that racial identity can be anything other than an enslaved— and enslaving—stereotype. While Zoe's pathologizing of her black blood as the reason for her suffering gives her access to the melodramatic equation of suffering with subjectivity, this same melodramatic indictment simultaneously buttresses the idea that her identity as a hybrid is profane, pathological, and thus unacceptable. Zoe scripts her own tragedy when she makes her black-and-white identity visible in the black-and-white world of melodrama, a world that cannot and will not admit the blending of those or any categories. Through George's repeated theatrical disruptions of the otherwise seamless melodramatic scripting of the play, disruptions that occur at the most crucial moments in the main plot's formal justifications—his willingness, even eagerness, to undercut the melodramatic power play—Boucicault clears a space formally for his audience to entertain alternative forms of theatrical self-definition that might be able to accept an amalgamated identity like Zoe's. Marc Robinson calls this kind of problematized genre "sophisticated melodrama" (9), but as we can see, this self-reflexive melodrama could also do more than simply interrogate the aesthetic limits of a theatrical mode. If Boucicault scripts Zoe's dependence on melodrama's "poetics of pain," as Brooks calls it (37), leading to her ultimate destruction, then his play's main plot repeatedly highlights and questions melodrama's shadowy but nonetheless foundational role in the nefarious logic of racism in America.

THE PLEASURE OF BAD TASTE

The melodramatic mode that Boucicault problematizes was already starting to lose its popular appeal with audiences by the mid-nineteenth century. By 1859, the American theater was in the midst of change, shaking off an older form of melodrama stemming from the French plays of Pixérécourt and latching onto a new, more parochial—and more realistic—form of drama originating with the works of Eugène Scribe.[26] Boucicault himself reflects this shift in an essay written in 1877, where he insists that there are two kinds of drama: The first is what he calls the "*contemporaneous* or *realistic* drama, which is a reflex of the features of the period, where the personages are life-size, the language partakes of their reality, and the incidents are natural," while the second is what he calls the "*transcendental* or *unreal* drama, where the personages are larger than life-size, their ideas and language more exalted than human conversation, and the incidents more important than we meet with in ordinary life."[27] Well before the crystallization of dramatic realism by James Herne's *Margaret Fleming* in 1882, Boucicault defines the competing modes of drama as "realistic" and "transcendental," which, from the way Boucicault describes it, is melodrama.

However, while Boucicault saw the drama of the period developing in two ways, his own play exists at some distance from both of these definitions. *The Octoroon* is a problematic or "sophisticated" melodrama rather than unreal in the way he defines it, and even if we look no farther than Boucicault's own definition of realism, we can see how this play is likewise not realistic. *The Octoroon* was moving in a new direction, and Boucicault attempted to lay the groundwork for this shift by imagining what this new style of drama might contain. In an article for the *North American Review* in 1875, he defines this new dramaturgical style, arguing that the "liberty of imagination should not be sacrificed to arbitrary restrictions and traditions that lead to dullness and formality. Art is not a church; it is the philosophy of pleasure."[28] Here, we see the theoretical basis for Boucicault's reluctance to write dramas that were either "transcendental" or "realistic," in the vein of Pixérécourt or Scribe. Following the playwright's suggestion, we can read *The Octoroon* as not only reproducing while criticizing melodrama but also using the critical space carved out from melodrama to stage what he calls "the philosophy of pleasure."

While Boucicault's statement helps us see his discomfort with the dramaturgical modes available to him, it only gestures to what his new style might look like. To discover what might be "pleasurable" about *The Octoroon*, we need to situate it more fully within its theatrical moment. On September 15, 1859, the *New York Herald* noted that the newly renovated Winter Garden Theatre had eliminated a good portion of the stalls to make room for the parquette, or what we would call "orchestra seating." Just three months before the opening of Boucicault's play, in the same theater where it would be staged, this remapping of space simultaneously remapped the class dynamics of the theater. This new theatrical space, in effect, catered more to the burgeoning bourgeois audience that would have been put off by "the pit" of the older theater. Moreover, the *Herald* suggests that what really defined the new Winter Garden was "the exceeding good taste which has prevailed in all the arrangement, and the liberally lavish way in which everything has been done .... The house is sumptuous, elegant, and tasteful throughout."[29] This emphasis on "taste," twice mentioned, illustrates two distinct trends. First, it indicates the increasing desire among theater managers to offer more "respectable" theatrical fare. Unlike the Bowery theater experience—"no dainty kid-gloved business," Walt Whitman recalled, "but electric force and muscle from perhaps 2000 full-sinew'd men"—the theatrical entertainments of midcentury aimed to be more respectable and, what is equally clear, less working class. By midcentury, in other words, the tasteful applause at the Winter Garden had replaced the "long-kept-up tempests of hand-clapping peculiar to the Bowery."[30] Second, the emphasis on taste indexes the burgeoning middle-class's investment in it as a means of constructing their identity by simultaneously enforcing class lines and racial boundaries. In a mid-nineteenth-century social mix, when social mobility threatened clearly delineated class divisions, one could perform one's "good taste" and thus one's superior class, by seeing and being seen at "tasteful" performances.[31]

In contrast, *The Octoroon* was a play in bad taste. Boucicault's dramaturgy not only demurred from engaging fully in the traditional mode of melodrama but actively went about undermining its legitimacy. However, the play was not a realistic *pièce bien faite* either, as Scribe's drama came to be called. Thus, his play chafed at the "arbitrary restrictions" guiding both melodrama and the well-made play. Yet, because of its bad taste, *The Octoroon* ironically offered its audience something new, a less restricted, more amalgamated idea of what drama—as well as identity—could entail. Nowhere is this more explicit than in the play's relatively unexplored subplot. By examining this plot's interaction with the main plot and the way the characters from this subplot resist having their performances conditioned by the "arbitrary restrictions and traditions" of the melodramatic mode, we see how Boucicault traded the melodramatic aesthetic of "tasteful" suffering for a new aesthetic of black-and-white pleasure, the result of which I am calling Boucicault's amalgamated drama.

BOUCICAULT'S AMALGAMATED DRAMA

Up to this point, the investigation of Boucicault's demystification of the racism and identity in the melodramatic mode has only attended to the main plot, a plot that William Winter, the playwright's contemporary theater critic, was focusing on when he said that Boucicault was "more adroit than original."[32] Yet it must be remembered that intersecting the main plot's north-south axis of shrewd Yankees and plantation overseers is a subplot running east-west and centered on the frontier figure of the Indian, Wahnotee, a part that Boucicault played in the drama's first run. His Indian was unprecedented in mulatta stories, but its real importance lay not so much in its novelty as in the way Boucicault employed a frontier aesthetic to incarnate in Wahnotee—quite literally—his dramaturgy of pleasure.

Boucicault gestures to this aesthetic when he introduces the Indian in the first act. Just as Boucicault reinforces his equation of George with melodrama by noting his association with Paris, the playwright likewise associates Wahnotee with the frontier by having him come from a "nation out West" (457). Wahnotee thus embodies the frontier. While most of the characters from the main plot want to send him back there, Zoe objects.

> Wahnotee is a gentle, honest creature, and remains here because he loves [the slave boy, Paul] with the tenderness of a woman. When Paul was taken down with the swamp fever the Indian sat outside the hut, and neither ate, slept, or spoke for five days, till the child could recognize and call him to his bedside. (457)

What has been overlooked by critics is the fact that *The Octoroon* features a second interracial union that also ends with the death of one of the characters. However, if the tension of the main plot is generated by the inability of the interracial couple to transcend melodrama's prescribed suffering, the subplot highlights an interracial union that sidesteps melodrama entirely and, in doing so, flourishes. While both plots end with the death of one of the partners, it should be noted that Zoe chooses her suicide, while Paul's death comes at the hands of M'Closky. Unlike the relationship between Zoe and George, that between Wahnotee and Paul would have continued if it had not been cut short.

These two plots of the play parallel each other in another way as well, for both Zoe and Wahnotee are hybrids. While Wahnotee later plays the avenging, masculine hero who hunts down and kills the villain of the play, before then he seems comfortable playing the woman, as Zoe observes, by tending to Paul. Unlike Zoe's internal schism between black slave and white heroine, however, Wahnotee seamlessly joins two competing gender performances, playing the masculinized character of the violent savage at the end of the play just as he easily portrays the maternal caregiver to a slave at the beginning. Even Wahnotee's language reflects his hybridity, for while Zoe mouths the pure language of the melodramatic heroine, Paul recounts that Wahnotee "speaks a mash-up of Indian and Mexican" (457). Unlike George and Zoe who suffer from the black-or-white scripting of melodrama, Wahnotee lovingly embraces his black-and-white identity just as he both loves and avenges Paul. Unlike George and Zoe's representation and embodiment of melodrama, therefore, Wahnotee's incarnation of a "mashed-up" frontier stages a provocative alternative to the main plot.

Boucicault fine-tunes Wahnotee as an avatar of an alternative frontier dramaturgy by drawing a sharp contrast between character development in the main plot and in the subplot. We can see this by recalling how fully and uncritically Zoe embraces her role as the tragic mulatta and, as such, how she repeats the mantra, "I suffer, therefore I am," right up to her death. George also seems to manifest fully this same adherence to melodrama's equation of identity and suffering. Thus, in the scene where Zoe has just been sold to the lascivious M'Closky, George leaps at the villain, knife in hand, snarling, "Yelping hound—take that." M'Closky quickly draws his own knife, and for a moment, the hero and villain are poised to fight—the melodramatic agon of the play thrust center stage. Yet, that tense moment is deflated as Scudder darts between them, saying: "Hold on, George Peyton—stand back. This is your own house; we are under your uncle's roof; recollect yourself" (482). The knives are replaced, the conflict is forgotten, and the plot moves forward. Despite what has happened, George will not become an avenger: He must not dispatch the sole impediment to his life with Zoe. Instead, he must heed Scudder's advice—he must "recollect" himself—and learn to suffer more visibly for us if we are to see him as the melodramatic hero.

To recollect oneself can be understood in this context in at least two distinct ways. In one sense, Scudder advises George to *remember* himself. Like Scudder's commentary earlier in the scene between Mrs. Peyton and George, this term allows us to see how Boucicault is drawing attention to the limits of the melodramatic mode: George seems to have forgotten that he is playing the hero, and by heeding Scudder's advice, as an actor would a director's, he will remember that he must suffer in order to be one. Boucicault's use of Scudder in this instance calls attention to the self-hatred at the core of the melodramatic imagination. However, in addition to understanding *recollect* as remember, the term also means to collect oneself again, to re-collect oneself. Reading the term in this way does not so much illustrate the nature of melodramatic identity as show the ways that identity is managed. To be a melodramatic hero means not only embracing one's identity as victim but also relentlessly policing it. Melodrama, in other words, is not so much about revealing one's emotions, as our contemporary understanding of melodrama might suggest it is. It is rather about revealing and displaying the right emotions. As Boucicault's culture insisted, melodrama was about the tasteful display of emotions. Letting go of your emotions, as George was about to do, is tantamount to letting go of your identity in Boucicault's bourgeois America. Only through constantly re-collecting himself as the suffering, stoic hero, keeping a lid on his more fervent passions, will George be able to perform his "tasteful" melodramatic self.

By contrast, Wahnotee feels no such need to recollect and police his own identity. Whereas George understands suffering as something to be embraced, Wahnotee understands it as something to be resisted and overcome. Boucicault dramatizes this difference, moreover, when Wahnotee, like George and Zoe, is made to suffer. At the Peytons's request, Wahnotee and his partner, Paul, go down to the dock to get the letter that, unbeknownst to them, will save Terrebonne Plantation and thwart M'Closky's dastardly plans to buy it, its slaves, and most importantly, Zoe. When Wahnotee and Paul later find a camera that Scudder was using to take pictures of Dora, Paul insists that Wahnotee take his picture. After bribing him with the promise of "fire water," Paul convinces him to do it. As soon as Wahnotee has done his part, he runs off to get his drink. Paul, meanwhile, sits waiting for the picture to develop, and as he does so, M'Closky discovers him, takes up Wahnotee's tomahawk, and kills the young boy in order to get the letter. M'Closky then escapes, assuring himself and the audience that the Indian will take the fall for the death of the boy. When Wahnotee comes back onstage, he sees Paul and mistakenly thinks he is still alive. Believing Paul is "shamming sleep," the Indian "gesticulates and jabbers," gives him a nudge with his foot, and then "kneels down to rouse him." To his "horror," Wahnotee discovers that Paul is dead, and as the stage directions indicate, he "expresses great grief" (469).

Like Zoe and George, Wahnotee suffers here. Rather than simply embracing it, however, he lashes out. Instead of stemming the flow of emotions as George did, he expresses his fury passionately. Seeing the camera, he lets out a "savage growl, seizes [his] tomahawk and smashes [the] camera to pieces" (469). On the one hand, Wahnotee's smashing of the camera seems futile—a far cry, for instance, from what would have been the potentially deadly and plot-altering result of George's tussle with M'Closky. On the other hand, while he does not sink a dagger into the villain's heart, Wahnotee's passionate outburst stands in stark opposition to George's inert rage. When it matters most, when the plot of the play hangs in the balance between a melodramatic ending and one that rejects this aesthetic, George retreats into the melodramatic formula of suffering heroism. Wahnotee, on the other hand, when his actions mean little, when suffering would allow him a modicum of melodramatic heroism—and the identity it provides—explodes in passion. What we see in this contrast are distinctly different aesthetics and modes of self-definition: recollecting the self versus releasing the self; meaningless words versus wordless meaning. By comparing these two suffering figures—as Boucicault intends us to do—we see the glimmer of an aesthetic alternative to melodrama's command that its practitioners script their own destruction. Tending to the subplot, we see a mode of expression that encourages its artists to resist the problematic black-or-white semantics of melodrama's formulation.

As this alternative mode's key figure, Wahnotee avoids the sinister effects of operating within the melodramatic mode in a way that George, and Zoe in particular, do not. While Zoe was incapable of sustaining an amalgamated identity—constructing her identity through the problematic denial of her hybridity in order to perform the tragic mulatta of melodrama—we can see how Wahnotee avoids this self-destructive construction of identity by embracing exactly what Zoe's melodramatic mode did not allow. Boucicault highlights the amalgamated nature of Wahnotee's identity most clearly in his "haunting" of M'Closky after he discovers in the play's trial scene that it was indeed M'Closky who killed Paul. Wahnotee is a "mashed-up" character, and as he begins pursuing M'Closky through the swamp, the Indian's hybridity is what terrorizes the villain. "In some form, human, or wild beast, or ghost," M'Closky enunciates breathlessly, "it has tracked me through the night. I fled; it followed" (491). Boucicault underscores how Wahnotee's identity is hybrid here in two ways. First, in the dialogue, we see how the Indian's identity becomes not only an "it" rather than a "him" but how he also becomes both a "human" and a "wild beast." Second, as David C. Miller has shown, the swamp through which Wahnotee pursues M'Closky was a space of terror in the minds of white antebellum America because its uncontainable geography—simultaneously both fluid and solid, fecund and decaying—symbolically reflected the terrifying uncontainability of the ever-increasing numbers of violent, murderous slave rebels, like Nat Turner, who found the swamp a perfect location from which to organize their attacks.[33] Through both dialogue and setting, Boucicault codes Wahnotee as not only hybrid and unsettled but, because of this hybridity, also terrifying and unsettling to someone like M'Closky. Thus, although Wahnotee and Zoe are both hybrids, Wahnotee's identity remains hybrid, while Zoe restricts hers to the black "taint" of her body. For Zoe, in effect, hybrid identity leads to her own destruction, while for Wahnotee, his hybrid identity effects a kind of moral justice. If Zoe is haunted by the persistent presence of the black blood in her veins, M'Closky is haunted by the almost absent Indian who is nevertheless persistently present in his imagination.

To be sure, Wahnotee is, in many ways, the stereotypical stage Indian, just as Zoe is, in many ways, the stereotypical tragic mulatta, but whereas Zoe suffers because of the melodramatic role she accepts, Wahnotee resists the black-or-white mode of melodrama. Boucicault's Indian is pointedly not the inhuman villain of Manifest Destiny, killing settlers and terrorizing the nation. He is not the monstrous bogeyman, the "ruthless savage" demonized in the American imagination during this period.[34] While George can only helplessly and mutely record the tragedy of Zoe's death, Wahnotee acts, his humanity fully displayed as he responds with passion to the death of Paul. That being said, Wahnotee is not a version of the staged noble savage either, heroically helping imperiled white citizens and then leaving the scene at the end of the play.[35] Wahnotee's violent acts and feelings, his "savagery," are neither condemned nor dismissed in the play but are rather celebrated, for it is the Indian and not George who dispatches the villain and restores moral order. In this way, Boucicault avoids essentializing Wahnotee's identity, allowing him to operate within both the subplot with Paul and, substantially, in the main plot with M'Closky.

In the first run of the play, the fact that Boucicault performed the role of Wahnotee helped underscore the character's easy hybridity, for the playwright was a hybrid: He was an Irishman of French descent writing an "American" play as well as being a white man playing a "red" one, a "civilized" European playing an American "savage." Part of the pleasure the audience experienced in Boucicault's performance must have come from the staging of his "mashed-up" identity, an identity that underscored what Wahnotee stands for in the play. I suggest the playwright's recoding of how the frontier was performed clarifies what he meant when he wrote that drama should entail a "philosophy of pleasure." Distancing his play from melodrama's fetishizing of suffering, Boucicault imagines the frontier embodied in Wahnotee as a pleasurable and nonessentialized shuttling between various overlapping and interweaving performances of the self—an amalgamated drama in which the fluidity of this frontier fantasy stands in stark contrast to the monopathic characters of the main plot. Unlike Zoe's anxious roleplaying that limits her to her blackness and trades on her suffering, Wahnotee's performance stitches together a range of identities that allow him both to feel passionately for Paul and to avenge him. The pleasure involved in this performance springs from all of the ways it avoids melodrama's insistence on re-collecting a character's suffering self as he or she goes down the path to self-destruction. For an antebellum American audience dependent on the melodramatic fetishizing of good taste, Wahnotee offered this audience another flavor of American identity.

THE FRONTIER FREAK

When *The Octoroon* finished its brief initial run at the Winter Garden Theatre in New York City in 1859, and after simultaneous performances at both the Old and the New Bowery Theaters in 1860, it traveled uptown to the stage at P. T. Barnum's American Museum. As theater historian George C. D. Odell suggests, it landed at Barnum's venue "to reap the golden harvest of provincial awe," for it "ran comfortably to mid-March, largely aided by the presence in the hall of freaks of Barnum's What is It? a 'most marvelous living creature found near the source of the River Gambia,' a combination of gorilla body and human intelligence."[36]

As we can see in the figures that follow (Figures 4.1, 4.2), taken from a rare double-sided theatrical broadside, part of the pleasure of going to Barnum's Museum on March 10, 1860, was not only seeing Boucicault's popular work but also encountering Barnum's equally popular freak. They were two sides, as it were, of the same aesthetic experience. As we can see from

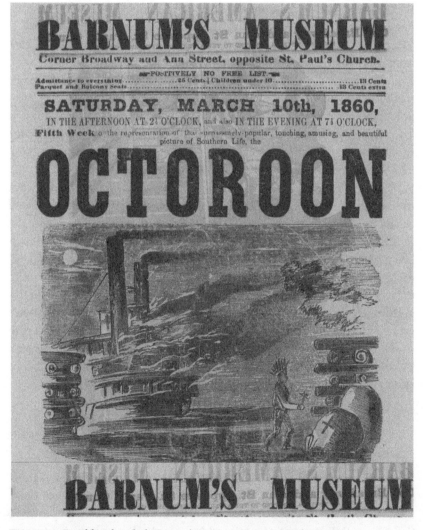

Figure 4.1   Detail from broadside, Barnum's American Museum, March 10, 1860.
Source: Harvard Theatre Collection, Houghton Library, Harvard University.

Figure 4.2   Detail from broadside, Barnum's American Museum, March 10, 1860.
Source: Harvard Theatre Collection, Houghton Library, Harvard University.

these images, what attracted audience members to the play was not only the drama's sensational steamboat fires and the relentless hunting of the villain by a tomahawk-wielding Indian, such as we see in Figure 4.1, but also the strange and perplexing creature we see in Figure 4.2. For, as the broadside relates, this creature, presented as the Missing Link in human evolution, would be displayed in between the acts of the melodrama about cross-racial love on the Southern frontier. What you got as an audience member was a two-for-one deal: two "freaks" for the price of one.

Half man, half ape, Barnum's What is It? drew a crowd because it was an amalgamation, and Boucicault's play is perfectly paired with it because the play is also an amalgamation. There are the amalgamations that are Zoe and Wahnotee, but the play itself, with its two different plots, was a generic hybrid, an amalgamation as well. The main plot was a melodrama, though a self-conscious one, scripting character and action as natural and essential-ized and deploying standard character types and set pieces. The subplot, by contrast, was a new mode of drama, trafficking in a more performative conceptualization of identity in the context of the frontier, recalibrating the meaning such stereotypical figures as the Indian could have on and for the ideology of the play. In short, like the nature of its melodramatic heroine, *The Octoroon* was both black-and-white.

Turning our attention to the broadside again and focusing on the section of it directly below Figure 4.1, we can see how the presence of Barnum's freak has permeated, quite literally Boucicault's play (Figure 4.3). In this space, where *The Octoroon*'s cast is enumerated, we see an inverted image of What is It? that has bled through the paper and becomes, as Wahnotee did to M'Closky, a ghostly presence haunting the characters of Boucicault's play. While this is, of course, inadvertent (likely due to the printer's failure to have used sufficiently thick paper stock or to have put too much ink on the press), we cannot also help but read this tantalizing mistake symbolically: Hybridity defines not just What is It?, Zoe, and Wahnotee but all of the characters in this play and, by extension, all of the people seeing this performance. "What is It?" was the question Barnum insisted his audience ask of his creature, but it was also the question that both Barnum's and Boucicault's shows made their audience ask of themselves.

What is also evident about both performances is that the drive to question one's own identity was at least partially generated by redefining what the frontier might mean in antebellum America. For, in addition to being sold as a freakish creature who refused categorization, Barnum's "amalgamation" was also sold, in several instances, as "The Wild Man of the Prairies," a creature discovered in "the wilds of California," where "for the last 10 months it has been living with a tribe of Indians."[37] The broadside gestures to this same idea, for at the bottom of Figure 4.3, we can see how it is being

Figure 4.3 Detail from broadside, Barnum's American Museum, March 10, 1860.
Source: Harvard Theatre Collection, Houghton Library, Harvard University.

paired with a "Black Sea Lion" and a "Grizzly Bear," both "[j]ust arrived from California." All of these attractions, Barnum suggests, are frontier creatures, even if What is It? is the most important in that it fixates directly on the notion of human identity. Barnum often changed the supposed origin of What is It? to capitalize on the interests of different audiences, but what is important here is the parallel between Barnum's frontier amalgamation and Boucicault's Wahnotee, who was one as well. Showcasing What is It? between the acts of *The Octoroon* thus made sense aesthetically. Just as Wahnotee's performance resisted the melodramatic ideology of the frontier—noble savage versus ruthless killer—What is It? pushed against the same ideology that insisted on a clear black-or-white line dividing savagery from civilization.

What is It?, however, also achieved something as an entr'acte spectacle that Wahnotee never could. Barnum's freak radically altered the stage machinery that insulated its audience members from the presence of this performative identity, bringing them face to face with a kind of radically "nondescript" performance of the self. In this Currier and Ives's print of What is It? at Barnum's American Museum (Figure 4.4), we encounter a performance with none of *The Octoroon*'s formal mechanics to work through, no plot twists to account for, no character development to follow. As James W. Cook has shown, What is It? was a black man from New York City; unlike other Barnum freaks—the Siamese twins, Chang and Eng, or the dwarf, Tom Thumb, for instance—the various actors who played What is It? throughout its tenure at the American Museum were, as a contemporary writer noted of one of them, "unexceptional" (128). The identity of What is It? as a freak was entirely a matter of performance, and thus when he thrilled audience members, he was simultaneously highlighting how performative identity really was. As Boucicault's dramaturgical innovation involved the aesthetic encounter between the main plot and subplot, What is It? energized audiences by confronting them directly and tangibly with the question of identity—an identity, as the lithograph illustrates, that could be observed, experienced, and even touched by an entire middle-class family. Moreover, Barnum's refusal to pin down What is It?—it was both man and ape, African and Western, black and white—helped accentuate not the terror of social blurriness but rather the pleasure of performative identity, for as the lithograph's caption states of Barnum's creature: "He is playful *as a Kitten and in every way pleasing, interesting, and* amusing." This language may have been used to alleviate middle-class fears of miscegenation: The caption obliquely reassures us that What is It? is not the savage black rapist of the white American imagination. Instead, it is presented as being as playful as a kitten but a creature nevertheless "*pleasing, interesting, and* amusing" for all of the ways it flirted with identity itself as an amalgamation. Like

Figure 4.4   Circus poster: "What Is It?" or "Man Monkey," circa 1860.
Source: Currier and Ives, The New-York Historical Society, negative no. 67612.

Barnum's exhibit, Boucicault's self-conscious melodrama was pleasurable precisely because it offered to its audience in its vibrant subplot what this same group of citizens had been told would not be tolerated in the main plot: identity as an amalgamated, black-and-white performance.

Boucicault's play, like the spectacle of What is It?, used its critical distance from the melodrama, with its black-or-white ideology, to develop a new kind of performative practice, one epitomized in a scene that occurs at the end of the play in which Salem Scudder condemns a group of white settlers who are bent on lynching Wahnotee for the murder of Paul.

Here's a pictur' for a civilized community to afford: yonder, a poor, ignorant savage, and round him a circle of hearts, white with revenge and hate, thirsting for his blood: you call

yourselves judges—you ain't—you're a jury of executioners. It is such scenes as these
that bring disgrace upon our Western life. (485)

Here, Boucicault again complicates the "moral stereotyping" of melodrama,
for it is the settlers, not the Indian, who are the "savages" in their "thirsting
for ... blood." With this kind of role swapping and racial remarking, the scene
undercuts the melodramatic ideology of the frontier even as it gestures to
a new kind of performative practice that understood subjectivity itself as
something black –and white.

Moreover, by dubbing this moment both a "pictur'" and a "scene"—a
kind of theatrical spectacle—Boucicault also highlights the self-consciously
theatrical nature of the "Western life" Scudder outlines: The frontier is not
so much a historical or geographical boundary as a set of performative practices inflected by history and geography. By presenting the frontier as something always and already a "scene," *The Octoroon* usefully illustrates one
configuration of these performative practices, a configuration that offers
both an alternative to the melodramatic mode and evidence of exactly how
fungible the concept of the frontier really was. In linking frontier performance to hybrid identity, What is It? also coded the frontier as a performative practice. To see What is It? was to see the frontier enacted. More
important, Barnum's refusal to categorize the creature by referring to it as
a "nondescript" effectively avoided the scripting of the frontier as the ideological extension of Manifest Destiny and American imperial power.

In essence, Boucicault's play did three things simultaneously. First, it
destabilized the melodramatic mode by alienating the audience from the
main plot's melodramatic investments and pointed to the way melodrama's black-and-white mode, which could not tolerate figures who were
black and white, had become the common language for the articulation
of racial power in America. Second, the pleasure involved in undermining
the melodramatic mode laid the groundwork for the way Boucicault then
recoded the frontier through Wahnotee as an alternative to the melodramatic modes of identity. Finally, by focusing on the fact that the play was
put on in the same venue where Barnum presented What is It?, we see how
Boucicault's version of the frontier generated a new kind of performative
practice that opened up the meaning of the frontier even as it substantively
framed identity differently. If "[e]verybody talk[ed] about the 'Octoroon,'
wonder[ed] about the 'Octoroon,' [and went] to see the 'Octoroon,'" as
the reviewer for the *New York Times* stated, then this drama played a vital
role in revealing antebellum America to itself. Punctuated by the entr'acte
spectacle of What is It?, Boucicault's play showed its audience how a stage
performance could rescript what it meant to perform or "act" as an American offstage as well.

If we study the *carte de visite* below from Barnum's American Museum (Figure 4.5), then we see both the kind of amalgamated identity being performed and the tenor of its performance. On the right we see What is It?, kitted out in boxing gloves and his "wild man" suit, and to the left we see Barnum's Leopard Boy, a young black boy whose body was covered with white splotches, generated by a rare form of albinism, also sporting boxing gloves. Taken as a whole, this image is a blur of racial categorization: The white boxing gloves on the otherwise dark figure of What is It? highlight his racial mixing by figuring him, literally, as both black-and-white. To an

Figure 4.5   What Is It? and Leopard Boy.
Source: Cabinet photographs, Harvard Theatre Collection, Houghton Library, Harvard University.

even greater degree, Leopard Boy reinforces this racial amalgamation by again literally figuring in his body the racial mixing going on—he is, as was abundantly clear to Barnum's audience, both black-and-white. Yet it is the arrangement and narrative of the scene that most dramatically punctuates the effect of both Barnum's freaks and Boucicault's "freak." As with *The Octoroon*, the scenery is natural and wild, not Africanized or exotic, a cognate for the frontier in the antebellum American imagination, thus helping to code both of Barnum's freaks as frontier figures. What is even more startling about this image, however, is the narrative the two people perform. While it is clearly meant to evoke a boxing match, it is also clearly not about their sparring with each other or, for that matter, their involvement with each other. If it is a boxing match, in other words, it is evidently not about the contest between the two figures. With their three-quarter profiles and the directness, even aggressiveness, of their body language—particularly Leopard Boy's crossed arms—the image suggests a kind of combativeness with the viewer, a steady and unflinching return of the viewer's gaze. What this image captures is far different from the Currier and Ives's depiction of What is It? as safe and "playful as a kitten" (Figure 4.4); rather, it frames these figures as dangerous, aggressive, and self-aware, aware of their own socially problematic identity as black-and-white and, through the performance involved in this image, committed to pushing that identity right up in the face of the viewer. Like Wahnotee's smashing of the camera, these figures do not play by the rules of melodramatic identity—they are not content to espouse the black or white dictums of melodrama. Rather, if we look at the pendant hanging from the chest of What is It? depicting both the profile and name of Washington, perhaps the most celebrated of Americans, we see how these figures are making a claim to Americanness, aggressively performing another idea of what it means to "act" American, this time in black-and-white. If the performance of figures like Wahnotee, Leopard Boy, and What is It? were "pleasurable," these performances were also provocative and political. Unlike the doomed octoroon who perishes at the end of Boucicault's play, these two aggressive figures subversively refused to disappear from an American social scene that was always already amalgamated.

CHAPTER FIVE

৵৹

The Great Divide

Pioneer Performances after the Civil War

Where memory is, theater is.

—Herbert Blau, *The Audience*

[T]he most persistent mode of forgetting is memory imperfectly deferred.

—Joseph Roach, *Cities of the Dead*

With the fall of Fort Sumter to Confederate forces in April 1861, interest in the frontier was replaced by the nation's fixation on the Civil War and the key role it would play in defining the future of the American nation. "The epic clash of North and South at Shiloh, Gettysburg, and the Wilderness," recounts Louis S. Warren, "absorbed the energies of almost every American historian for the next three decades. Few attempted unpacking the West until after the 1880s."[1] Yet when theaters attempted to "unpack" the frontier after 1865, they did so with a frenzied intensity. The frontier became a palliative for a nation reeling from the catastrophe of the war—settling the frontier became a way of stabilizing an unsettled nation, a nation shaken by a violent, long-lasting, and deadly conflict. It should come as no surprise, then, that by the late nineteenth century, approximately 5 to 10 percent of all theatrical touring productions in the United States, from the urban Northeast to the agricultural South to the rural West, were plays about the frontier.[2]

As it acquired more and more layers of meaning, the frontier became, in Pierre Nora's term, a *lieu de mémoire*, a "site of memory" with "no referent in reality, ... a pure, exclusively self-referential sign."[3] The frontier, in other words, began to slip away from its geographic specificity and to become a self-sustaining imaginary space. The memory of the frontier was a "moment of history torn away from the movement of history," suggests Nora of similar *lieux de mémoire*, "like [a] shell on the shore when the sea of living memory has receded" (12). As with other sites of memory, like museums, festivals, monuments, and fraternal orders, the post–Civil War frontier existed in a tension between the reality of history and the fantasy of memory, and the stage became a way for negotiating this tension productively.

While modern critics like Roger Hall have suggested how this *lieu de mémoire* helped to codify and propagate the ideology of American empire (3, 228), we have already seen how the theater can be remembered differently. By treating the frontier theater as a "rhizomorphic structure," to use Paul Gilroy's term,[4] we can see that the memory of the frontier onstage always nurtured other kinds of political and ideological growth, even as their competing ideological roots blossomed into more distinct, and divergent, aesthetic formations after the Civil War. This growth along two distinct ideological axes, already evident in Boucicault's doubly emplotted frontier play, can be traced in two competing and celebrated post–Civil War pioneer performances: Augustin Daly's *Horizon*, which opened at the Olympic Theatre in New York City in March 1871, and Joaquin Miller's *The Danites in the Sierras*, which opened at the Broadway Theatre in New York City in August 1877.[5] While these plays share a degree of importance in the history of staging the frontier, their politics stand diametrically opposed to each other, as did the playwrights who wrote them. Their stage histories, too, progress along different lines, for while Miller's play was a much more pronounced success than Daly's in the nineteenth century, Daly is known to us now, ironically, as one of the most important figures in American theater history while Miller has been marginalized. For all of their differences, we also understand that their plays were each generated in the same cultural moment and respectively hailed as authentic representations of the frontier. Moreover, while at first glance these plays may seem to have little in common, we can see how these playwrights stage similar tropes and themes, so that by investigating these wildly divergent plays' echoing of each other, we can chart the complexity of the transmission and reception of the cultural memory of the frontier in the postbellum era. By exploring the way the two plays' developments of similar frontier themes—gender and sexuality, community and commodity, and melodrama and theatricality—I will show how they are actually remembering the frontier differently. Furthermore, by focusing on the different deployment of similar themes, I will show how the plays complicate the memory of the frontier as what New Western Historians like Patricia Nelson Limerick call simply a "legacy of conquest" by bringing to mind a particularly neglected "residue of cultural memory" that exists on the other side of the great divide of American history. Finally, by looking at these two works side by side, I mean to suggest not only how they bear witness to the ideological tensions structuring the previous performances in this study but also how they tear them apart. It is this bifurcation of aesthetic and ideological lineages that sets the stage for the aesthetic development of two distinct types of the performed frontier in the twentieth and twenty-first centuries.

GENDER AND SEXUALITY

When producer Augustin Daly turned to the frontier in his drama *Horizon*, he had already earned the reputation of being a strict, ruthless theater personality. Even his brother, Joseph Francis Daly, his most ardent supporter, admitted in his biography of Augustin that from "the beginning he got the reputation as an unyielding disciplinarian."[6] Augustin Daly embraced this role and thrilled to the power it conferred on him. "I went upon the stage," he confided to his brother, "and felt as one who treads the deck of a ship as its master" (qtd. J. Daly 88). Daly would be a production's "master," but if he was strict, even draconian, he was also deeply invested in using this same discipline to change the methods of the American theater. "This manager is a general," starts off one of his reviewers, continuing the usual assessment of Daly's character, but then qualifies this line of argument by saying, "his ability is nothing less than that of a great commander, when you reflect that he is managing and directing every day some two hundred people on his actual list."[7] If the general, as he was called, was prickly and stringent, offering no quarter for mistakes and miscues, then his overall project, as this reviewer suggests, was to make the theater efficient and productive by regulating how the production was put together. Like the bourgeois businessmen Daly hoped to attract, he saw that the way to make the theater better was to control every aspect of production, to regulate and police what the audience saw when they entered an auditorium. As George Parson Lathrop noted, Daly "plans, notices, and controls every smallest detail of scenery, furniture, bric-à-brac, in the setting, down to an inch or an angle" (270). Daly would control the theatrical product, even if it meant that he had to adjust, shift, and nudge it himself.

Daly was not only interested in making the American theater more efficient and productive, he was also deeply involved in purifying and policing the theatrical enterprise in general. Daly wanted to see the sullied image of the theater as a den of vice and sin purged and the American stage brought to respectability. One way he effected this in the theater was by closely regulating the space of the theater itself. In the theater he operated in 1869, for instance, he eliminated all of the lower-priced seats on the ground floor, thus regulating the class of patrons that would be coming to his shows. In addition, as Bruce McConachie details, Daly plated the walls of this small, 900-seat theater with mirrors, "partly to give the illusion of a larger space, but also to allow his audience to watch themselves and others playing their social roles."[8] One might add that these mirrors also encouraged the audience to regulate and to modify these same social performances. Daly's mirrors reflected back to the audience not only an image of what they were doing but also an image of what they *should* be doing.

In addition to monitoring his audience and having them monitor themselves, Daly policed his actors by imposing a set of fines for behavior that he saw as detracting from the play's production or his theater's bourgeois sensibility. In an April 3, 1889, notice to his actors, he stated: "I must positively protest against the spirit of carelessness and disposition to alter the business of lines in this play which is creeping upon the principals in the cast. I want my lines spoken, and I want the business I gave at rehearsals followed. Anything else is contrary to my directions and will be punished by an exemplary fine."[9] Making his fines exemplary, for Daly, also meant making them steep. "There were fines for being late, for making the stage wait, for lack of courtesy. For addressing the manager on business outside of his office there was a fine of $1 for the first offence; considering that salaries started as low as $7 a week and averaged about $35, this fine was actually quite stiff" (Felheim 33). Daly thus controlled his actors' behavior and their acting by making them accountable, financially, for their each and every deed.

It was this policing of audience and actor alike in his theater that contributed to ushering in a new era of American drama that made it more attractive to the growing business class of patrons that the industrialization of the urban Northeast made possible. His careful attention to every aspect of the production allowed Daly later to reflect that the

> best portion of the community has taken possession of the theater, as it ought to take possession of all public amusements, and has made it its own. The purification of the temple of the drama has been so thoroughly effected that the worthiest people find it worthy of their affectionate regard. The "third tier" and the pit of thirty years ago, with their bars and their lounges, have disappeared. There is no attraction for the vicious. The constant patrons of the drama belong to the class of people who are strictest in the performance of every duty, moral and social.[10]

The theater, according to Daly, had been thoroughly "purified," and for this impresario, purification was a measure of success. Moreover, as he relates in another piece, "Not only is the drama pure and the theatre respectable, but the morale of actors in this country is unsurpassed by that of any other country or age."[11] If Daly's reflections are to be believed, then he succeeded in elevating the status of audience and actor by meticulously policing how people both before and behind the footlights "acted."

Yet, the "general's" campaign to make the theater more bourgeois did not succeed without several skirmishes. In particular, Daly's efforts to gentrify the theater met determined resistance in the form of his leading ladies, actresses like Clara Morris, Agnes Ethel, Catherine Lewis, Fanny Davenport, Sara Jewett, Edith Kingdom, and, most importantly, Ada Rehan. He made all of them stars, but, as Kim Marra has argued, this involved the "'taming' of purportedly savage actresses" like Rehan, who did not bend easily to Daly's will.[12] I want to suggest that Daly's desire to conquer these women and "the nature and savagery with which [they] were conflated" (Marra 56) became a metaphoric means of acting out the pageant of empire. In monitoring his actresses, Daly was actually mastering the wildness of the frontier and discursively equating his actions as director, playwright, and producer with the larger actions of the United States as civilizer, imperialist, and colonizer.

Nowhere can we see Daly's investment in the taming of female sexuality acted out more clearly than in the way he characterizes Agnes Ethel's role, Med, in his frontier drama, *Horizon*. The play begins in New York City as Mrs. Van Dorp's adopted son, Alleyn, having recently graduated from West Point, is getting ready to make his departure for the "Far West." We learn that Mrs. Van Dorp's real child, Margaret, was kidnapped by her feckless husband and taken west long ago. Vowing to help his mother find her real daughter, Alleyn ventures westward with three companions: the crooked politician, Sundown Rowse; Rowse's naïve daughter, Columbia; and an overly romantic Englishman, Mr. Smith. When they get to the town of Rogue's Rest in the Far West, they encounter a cadre of western stereotypes, including the loner frontiersman, Panther Loder, and the settler, Wolf, with his daughter, Med. Alleyn falls in love with Med, who is already Loder's object of affection, but this rivalry gets short-circuited when the nefarious Indian, Wannemucka, who has been living in Rogue's Rest, tries to kidnap Med in order to make her his "white princess." While Loder prevents this kidnapping, it is attempted once again in one of the most famous scenes of the play—the attack of the riverboat—when the Indians surprise Med and a helpless crew, only to be foiled yet again by Loder. In the last repetition of the scene, the women, sheltered in a fort and left alone by the men of the group, are accosted by the Indians again. Pretending to be repentant,

Wannemucka ingratiates himself with Med only to betray her trust, finally escaping with her to his camp. In the Indian camp, Med and the women of the party await violation and death when Loder, disguised as an Indian, arrives and, with the help of Alleyn and his troops, overthrows the Indians, rescues Med, and helps insure the march of progress across the continent.

Although Daly never states clearly that Med is, in fact, Mrs. Van Dorp's long-lost daughter, the action suggests that she is, and that Wolf is Mrs. Van Dorp's ne'er-do-well husband. While these details are important to the story, what is equally important is the way that Med, separated from the bourgeois life at Waverly Place in New York City and situated on the frontier for most of her life, has become partly savage and has thus abandoned the moral rigidity of her mother and her Knickerbocker family. Near the beginning of the play, as Alleyn and Med are first flirting with each other, Med reveals that everyone has courted her. Shocked, Alleyn retorts: "Why you are only a little girl!" to which Med replies, "Ain't I big enough to love?" Alleyn admits, "Yes, now," and then Med asks, "And I suppose yesterday I wasn't? Oh, that's not true. I've had so many. Everywhere we went, father and I, somebody was sure to say: 'I love you.'" Alleyn responds quite hysterically: "What did you say when they told you they loved you?" "I said—," replies Med, pausing, "I said: 'I love you, too.'"[13] Med's moral looseness is thus highlighted by Daly in this pause, for Med could have easily fit her response into a script of bourgeois sensibility, but this early indication of her moral laxity, like that of Daly's actresses, stands as a "savage" rejection of Daly's imperial desires.

If Med's wildness must be tamed, then the heroic Alleyn is the man for the job, for as a captain in the U.S. Army, he is an imperial agent, literally and figuratively, especially in his relationship with Med. His continued efforts to woo Med, therefore, can be read as efforts to civilize or tame her, making bourgeois love just another mode of empire. Daly makes this link quite explicit when Mr. Smith, the Englishman, and Columbia, Rowse's naive daughter, encounter Alleyn wooing Med. Tittering at the scandal, Columbia says: "Oh, Captain! Caught you in the very act," to which Mr. Smith, taking up the jest, says, "Yes! Very act of besieging the fortress of Beauty." Columbia then makes the comparison plain when she echoes Mr. Smith, saying, "Yes! The very act of throwing the lines of circumvallation around her waist" (122). Daly wants us to see how Alleyn is metaphorically conquering the wild Med, "besieging" her and constructing her as an outpost of empire through the "lines of circumvallation around her." In addition, Daly wants us to see how it is his brand of theater that helps drive this imperial mechanism, for the theater, unlike the novel, allows the audience to see the physical incarnation of Daly's metaphor as Alleyn puts his arm around Med's waist, thus witnessing a visual reinforcement

of Daly's taming of Med. Moreover, by choosing to use the word *lines*—
meaning both lines of defense around a frontier fort and lines of dialogue in
a piece of theater—Daly highlights how Med's loose and unsettled nature,
like the frontier, is being modified and settled through this performance of
a frontier drama.

If Daly was a strict martinet, marshalling his forces to gentrify the theater and write the history of the frontier as a history of imperial conquest,
then Joaquin Miller was a blithe spirit who used his personal knowledge
of the frontier to undercut the juggernaut of imperialism. Unlike Daly,
Miller had lived on the California frontier and traveled far into Mexico
and Central America. During his life, he was, at times, a schoolteacher,
Pony Express rider, newspaper editor, lawyer, judge, and Indian fighter.
He visited Europe several times, joined the gold rush in the Klondike
in 1897, and two years later, went to China during the Boxer Rebellion.
More importantly, he not only experienced the frontier but also identified
with it. "My cradle," he was fond of saying, "was a covered wagon, pointed
west."[14] He understood the frontier as a zone of license that allowed him
a kind of freedom that Daly could not tolerate. Consider this description
of Miller:

> His white beard fell to his waist, and his mustaches were curled up savagely after the
> manner of Emperor Williams, while his wide sombrero was cocked carelessly to the
> northwest. His long, yellow hair fell to his shoulders. The suit he wore was of yellow
> corduroy that matched his hair, and his russet-top boots, fringed at the side, matched
> the corduroys. The buttons on his coat were made of nuggets of Klondike gold; his belt
> was of buckskin with a big silver buckle, and between the bottom of his vest and the top
> of his trousers was a six-inch interregnum of blue flannel shirt. A bright red necktie blew
> out from under the white beard; the trousers were caught over the ears of the dainty
> boots; one hand wore a gauntlet and its mate was carried in a small, white hand, upon
> the middle finger of which was an immense diamond.[15]

A dandy of the West, Miller was a flamboyant self-creation, "the most charm-
ing poseur on this terrestial [sic] ball, but he has posed so long and so well
that his poses have become natural, so he is no longer a poseur" (Hubbard
9). Miller's friend, the western writer Ambrose Bierce, echoes this when
he remembers, "Even now in his age, when from a failing memory of his
famous arrow wound he sometimes limps with the wrong leg, he is obviously reluctant to surrender his lifelong claim to the laurels of the bandit
Joaquin Murrieta" (qtd. in Wagner 213). With this, we see how Miller was
a masterful poseur—an eccentric and theatrical version of himself—who
only in old age, at the limit of his memory, unintentionally let his audience
glimpse the man behind the act.

More importantly, as Bierce references in Miller's claim to be "the bandit Joaquin Murrieta," Miller was a man who used his experience of the frontier to eschew essentialism, rigidity, and everything else that Daly's bourgeois predilections were founded on. Miller, after all, changed his first name as he began his career as an artist, trading Cincinnatus for Joaquin, in order to draw on the notoriety of the nineteenth-century Mexican frontier bandit, Joaquin Murrieta. Yet, when Miller adopted the name of Joaquin, he was doing more than simply paying homage to this legendary bandit; he was, in a sense, appropriating the man's personality, identity, and subjectivity. Miller's adoption of Joaquin was, therefore, also a form of identity construction that drew on a fantasy of the frontier to throw notions of originality, authenticity, and truth into doubt. Consider what Miller said on the issue of his naming himself Joaquin.

> And is it not possible that I am even now the original and only real Joaquin Murrieta? For more than once in the old days I was told (and how pleased I was to hear it said) that no other than Joaquin Murrieta could ever ride as I rode. But here again is confusion.... For his hair was as black as a whole midnight, while mine was the hue of hammered gold. And, after all, was it not my vanity and willingness to be thought Joaquin, rather than pity for the brave boy outlaw ... that made me write of him and usurp his bloody name?[16]

The questions here, mixing with declarations, lead to the "confusion" that Miller highlights. We know this is a hoax, that Miller is wryly grinning at his own statements and provocations, but what remains constant throughout his ironic tone is that what is really funny for Miller—what is really absurd, in fact—is looking for the single truth that cannot exist in a world consistently characterized by confusion. As the modern critic Nathaniel Lewis relates, Miller's "insight (or instinct) was to blur and even negate the possibility of authenticity, even (or inevitably) while claiming to be the real thing. As a work of art himself, he refused to be limited to a single authentic or true self, but labored subversively towards a kind of permanent and infinite reproducibility."[17] Joaquin Miller was a poseur, an actor who never stopped acting, but rather than dismiss him as being merely entertaining, we can see how, in his shameless self-fashioning, this playwright and poet of the Sierras was subverting the same kind of rigid moral order that Daly championed in his own life and writing.

Furthermore, just as Daly used his play's plot of sexual wildness and conquest to solidify the imperial memory of the frontier, Miller used his play's gender trouble to subvert the imperial ideology that Daly subscribed to by remapping the figurative space of the frontier. Unlike Daly's play, all of The Danites in the Sierras takes place in a mining camp in the Sierras, a camp troubled by secretive, dangerous Mormon villains—the Danites of the title—who take their name and their mission from the book of Daniel. These Danites are looking for Nancy Williams, the last member of a group of settlers who killed their leader, Joseph Smith. The miners fear that one in their midst might be a Danite, including the effeminate boy, Billy Piper. Billy nearly meets his death because of the paranoia of the miners but is saved by a missionary woman, called simply the Widow, who arrives to help the camp straighten up morally. As with Daly's play, there is a love triangle between two miners, the lovelorn Sandy, who still pines for Nancy Williams, the Parson, and the newly arrived Widow, who ultimately falls in love with Sandy and marries him while promising to take care of the young and helpless Billy.

As the play progresses, we eventually come to understand, through Billy's confession to the Widow, that he is, in fact, the cross-dressed Nancy Williams, whom the Danites are hunting. Meanwhile, the Widow has a salutary effect on the miners, including rescuing two women, Captain Tommy and Bunkerhill, from ignominy. These women eventually marry two miners, the Judge and Tim, and the play seems to be progressing toward a happy ending. At this point, however, the Danites discover that Billy Piper is Nancy Williams, sneak into the Widow's house to kill her, find the Widow and the child she had with Sandy instead, and kill both of them. With no protector, Nancy's life is in jeopardy, but Sandy, sworn to protect Billy, stands by him. The Parson, who had left the camp after the Widow and Sandy married, returns and discovers the Danites to be the murderers of the Widow and the baby. They are hanged and, in a *coup de théâtre*, Billy is revealed to be Nancy, the long-lost love of Sandy, who promises to marry her.

While the play seems to have a conventional happy ending, there is much in it that does not fit such a conclusion, most notably the character of Billy Piper and the figures of Captain Tommy and Bunkerhill. Having women play men's parts in the theater was nothing new, especially when the woman in a "breeches part" eventually revealed herself to be her "right" gender. Yet, by compulsively staging and manipulating the performance of gender on the frontier in the way he does, Miller was drawing on a subordinated memory of the frontier that had been forgotten in Daly's drama. Miller was staging for his eastern audience not the bourgeois world of the Northeast transplanted to the frontier but another memory of the frontier that he possessed, a memory of the region as an area of "absolute liberty" where "[a]ll great extremes run together."[18] This fluid frontier was perfectly encapsulated by Edmund Booth, a New England miner in Miller's same California frontier, when he wrote to his wife in 1850: "Cal. is a world upside down."[19] "It was confusing," historian Susan Lee Johnson suggests about the southern California mining camps in which Booth was living and to which Miller traveled, "the way that gender relations, race relations, and labor relations coursed into and out of customary channels in California, here carving gullies out of hard ground, there flowing in familiar waterways."[20] To be sure, the experience in the Southern Mines was not ubiquitous—many miners, particularly in northern California, saw a much more hierarchical frontier regulated with increasing force by figures like the Pinkertons. Yet what Miller was representing for his New York audience was not this eastern social structure redacted in California but rather the "confusing" world of the frontier—the same confusing world that he was referencing in his own self-fashioning—a world that possessed a memory of sexual flexibility that vied with Daly's memory of sexual conquest on the frontier.

Miller's cross-dressing heroine, Billy Piper, becomes the mouthpiece for this "world upside down" that Miller encountered in California. Nancy chooses to dress as a man to escape the Danites, and her gamely acceptance of this ambiguous identity in the camp speaks to Miller's own representation of the frontier. "[I]t seems to me," she ruminates, "the highest, the holiest religion that we can have, is to love this world and the beauty, the mystery, the majesty that environ us."[21] Billy could have been terrified about the uncertainty of her gender performance in the camp, terrified that it would not seem authentic enough to save her from the Danites or, conversely, terrified that it would be too authentic to signal to Sandy who she really was. Yet Billy, like Miller himself, eschews authenticity and finds contentment and solace through embracing the "mysterious" world of the frontier mining camp. In this way, the frontier goes from being an environment that is there to be marked with the stamp of empire to being one that helps convey and confer new sensibilities at odds with imperial conquest. The remapping of the frontier of memory to reveal its "mysterious" and "confusing" nature becomes a means of articulating Billy's own subversive performance of sexuality.

Billy's performance of sexuality on the frontier of memory recalls other slippery performances of sexuality that Joaquin Miller encountered in his time in California in the 1840s and 1850s. By reading the echoes of these performances in the presentation of Billy, we will see how this cross-dressing performance not only insists that the frontier be remembered differently but also transforms this difference into a living memory whose every breath stands as a riposte to Daly's standard sexualized conquest of the "wild" frontier. Consider the following popular image of a California miner, a daguerreotype that circulated widely in the boom days of the California gold rush (Figure 5.1). This image was exceedingly popular with male viewers, who saw the figure as a "girl." Even though the girl was dressed as a man—like Billy Piper is in Miller's play—frontiersmen found this image of a masculinized girl with a suggestively placed handle emerging phallically from

Figure 5.1   John B. Colton.
Source: Courtesy of The Huntington Library, San Marino, California

her trousers both attractive and arousing. Recently, however, as Jennifer A. Watts of the Huntington Library has discovered, this female miner was actually a young man named John B. Colton. Far from being aberrant, this image's slipperiness as a text—the way it continues to confuse the binary of maleness and femaleness—attests to the gender trouble in the California gold mines in the 1840s and 1850s that Miller bore witness to, the way the frontier, as Johnson argues about the same image, "marked a time and place of tremendous contest about maleness and femaleness, about color and culture, and about wealth and power" (Johnson 51).

When the actress Kitty Blanchard played Billy Piper in Miller's *The Danites* in New York City in August 1877, there was little doubt for the audience that she was a woman playing a man. Consider this image of Blanchard as Billy Piper from the production (Figure 5.2). Nevertheless, while this is more evidently a woman, the same sexual dynamics of attraction exist here as they did with the image of Colton, for male audience members were enticed by this cross-dressing performer who had an even more pronounced and suggestively phallic "handle." Both images point up the instability of the gender performance occurring, the way it falls between maleness and femaleness. While Miller may not have been recalling Colton's image per se,

Figure 5.2   Kitty Blanchard in "The Danites in the Sierras."
Source: Billy Rose Theatre Division, The New York Public Library for the Performing Arts, Astor, Lenox, and Tilden Foundations.

his smudging of the line between maleness and femaleness with Blanchard evokes the memory of the frontier that Colton's image captured. Reading Blanchard's subversive performance through Colton's image, moreover, helps establish how the representation of Billy Piper's embracing of the frontier's "mystery" caused an urban Northeast audience the same sexual titillation that characterized a memory of the frontier at odds with what Daly had produced in his drama. What the audience members experienced every time they hooted and hollered for Billy Piper, in short, was the exhilaration of a frontier memory that undercut Daly's taming of the wild frontier.

If this exhilaration always came to a close with the end of the play, where Billy Piper again donned the restrictive petticoats of Nancy Williams's bourgeois sexuality, other forms of subversive pleasure accompanying the remapping of frontier memory were continuously available to audience members, forms whose lack of closure stand as the most blatant displacement of Daly's memories of conquest. If Billy finally became Nancy, in other words, then Captain Tommy and Bunkerhill, the obstreperous fallen women of Miller's play, always remained Captain Tommy and Bunkerhill. From the first reviews of *The Danites*, Captain Tommy's and Bunkerhill's positions in the sexual calculus of the play were always in question. In his reading of reviews of the play, George Odell wrote in his *Annals of the New York Stage* that Ida Jeffreys played Captain Tommy and Ada Gilman played

Bunkerhill, "two mining camp 'ladies.'"[22] While Odell's quotation marks around "ladies" indicate, in a certain way, that these two fallen women would never be proper ladies, they also identify them as women whose sexual performances fall outside standard definitions of femaleness.

As we have seen, the rules of sexual performance on the frontier were more confused and abstract. Women on the frontier discovered, in other words, a degree of freedom and license unavailable in the East. One such eastern-born woman who found freedom on the California frontier, for example, was Mary Jane Megquier. "I have seen so much of things a little more exciting," she admitted in an April 8, 1850, letter to her family in New England, that "I fear I shall never feel perfectly satisfied with [her family's] quiet ways again. Here you step out of your house and see the whole world spread out before you in every shape and form."[23] For Megquier, the frontier represented freedom—a zone of boundlessness where you encounter life in "every shape and form"—that made a return to New England seem perfectly awful. Another woman, Louise Amelia Knapp Smith, called Dame Shirley in the mines, echoed this sentiment more bluntly. "I *like* this wild and barbarous life," she stated boldly. "I leave it with regret."[24]

If figures like Dame Shirley eventually left the diggings to return to the East, then characters like Captain Tommy and Bunkerhill from Miller's play pointedly never returned to the East, literally or ideologically. The first entrance of the "ladies" shows how much distance they have from notions of northeastern gentility and how much they have embraced the fluidity of gender on the frontier. The Judge and Tim are about to get into a fight with Billy Piper because they fear he is a Danite. Before the first punch is thrown, though, Captain Tommy enters and, with a fist in the face of the Judge, threatens him: "Touch that boy and I'll knock the corn juice out of you. Yes, I will, and you, too.... You bald-headed, gum suckin' old idiot.... Come on, both of you, I'm your match." Standing by her side, Bunkerhill echoes the same sentiment: "Take both of 'em to make one man" (390). What we see here is not only that "ladies" should be placed in quotation marks, but that "men" should be as well. This performance of frontier sexuality is, as Edmund Booth said earlier of California, "upside down." The Judge and Tim are emasculated, unable to measure up to Captain Tommy, who, in offering a "match" between herself and the Judge, calls into question the notion of "normal" sexual performance. When Bunkerhill further diminishes the power inherent in eastern notions of masculinity, we can see how much at odds Miller's staging of frontier sexuality is with Daly's.

Yet, when Captain Tommy and Bunkerhill are "redeemed" by the Widow, as they are in the middle of the play, the fluidity of their frontier performances seems to dry up. In a sentimental scene between the Widow and the "ladies," Captain Tommy admits that there is a "wide river" that divides her and Bunkerhill from the eastern-bred Widow. Miller seems to be actually mapping their different sexual performances in terms of geography: the Widow and the "ladies" represent the two, opposed regions of the country—the urban Northeast and the wild West—regions divided by the "wide river" of the Mississippi. Much like Daly's taming of the wild female sexuality in *Horizon*, the Widow's act of redemption becomes coded as an act of imperial conquest. Reaching out her hand to Captain Tommy and Bunkerhill, the Widow says: "The river is not so wide that my hands will not reach across it. If my feet are on the solid bank, take my hand, hold strong and come up and stand by my side." The ladies "hesitate" but then "grasp her hands and kiss them" (390–391). The scene's movement from West to East, from low to high, from the fluidity of the frontier to the "solid bank" of the urban Northeast, thematically maps the progress of imperialism. The religious reinforcement of the scene's shift in power when the two women kiss the Widow's hand—as a sinner would a saint's—helps assure that this imperial expansion is doubly marked as being, in fact, Manifest Destiny.

This taming of the "ladies" seems to be in full effect by the next act when we see them sewing—a particularly feminine cultural performance—and urging that "[s]ociety must be respected," a particularly bourgeois articulation. At this point, Miller's play seems to be paralleling Daly's imperial attitude toward sexuality. Yet it is precisely the closeness of this dramatic patterning that makes Miller's subsequent reversal of it all the more explosive. While Med is neatly and cleanly tamed by Captain Alleyn's affectionate siege, Captain Tommy and Bunkerhill escape the "lines of circumvallation" that seem so solidly erected around them. Consider the scene when the miners are again going to kill Billy Piper because they fear he is a Danite. While we have already seen how gentrified Bunkerhill and Captain Tommy seem to have become, and thus how well they have been tamed, both women nonetheless come to the rescue of Billy Piper again.

> CAPT. TOMMY: Too many on one, Bunker. I'm goin' in for the bottom dog, and society can just go to the devil [*Throws off bonnet and rolls up sleeves.*]
>
> JUDGE: Now, my Capt. Tommy, just think of what society—
>
> CAPT. TOMMY: Shut up! You bald-headed old jackass! I'm just goin' in on this fight, bet your life.
>
> BUNKERHILL: Yes; we're all gettin' too dern'd respectable, anyhow
>
> [*Throws hat*]. (397)

When Captain Tommy and Bunkerhill throw off their bonnets, they are symbolically throwing off the vestments of eastern gentility, figuratively removing the masculine control symbolized by eastern society and embracing, as did Billy Piper earlier, the fluidity of the frontier and the power it provides.

When Captain Tommy interrupts the Judge's attempt to articulate social control, she is also interrupting the seamless flow of the history of frontier conquest that Daly trumpeted in his play. Captain Tommy's response to the Judge's rhetoric of social control can be read as Miller's dramatic response to Daly's memory of the frontier. These ladies' refusal to be tamed—or brought onto the eastern side of the "wide river"—not only subverts Daly's plot of sexual conquest but also helps spotlight a more fluid fantasy of the frontier that existed just on the other side of the Civil War.

COMMUNITY AND COMMODITY

If exploring how both plays' staging of sexual performance on the frontier discloses the differential circulation of pre–Civil War memory on the post–Civil War stage, then investigating how *Horizon* and *The Danites in the Sierras* imagine community also reveals the way these memories are mapped, sending them in new, divergent directions. Investigating both plays' sexual performances revealed one fault line in the memory of the frontier; investigating how the plays imagine community will put more pressure on that fault line, helping to reveal the contested nature of national memory in the postbellum period.

To begin unpacking Daly's version of community, we should first focus on who is excluded from it and how the playwright negotiates this exclusion. Writing in 1871 on the heels of the Indian Wars, Daly constructs the Indian as his villain, for it would have been easy for Daly's white, bourgeois audience to see the Indian in this way. In his play, as Marvin Felheim relates, Daly "leaned heavily upon the current events of the Indian wars for many details of his plot" (70), events like the Sand Creek, the Fetterman, and the Washita Massacres— all violent and bloody schisms between white soldiers, like those described in *Horizon*, and native populations. Only a year before Daly's play was produced, Major Edward M. Baker and a detachment of cavalry had charged into a Piegen village on Montana's Marias River and slaughtered 173 Indians, mostly women and children, many already incapacitated by smallpox. While the federal government, disgusted by such wanton cruelty, subsequently banned army officers from holding any civil post, the violent white expansion into Indian territories during the period of Grant's ironically named Peace Policy continued unabated. "The Peace Policy," argues historian Robert M. Utley,

> aimed at placing all Indians on reservations, where they could be kept away from the settlements and travel routes and where ultimately they could be civilized. The Indians often had other ideas—if not at first, then after they had sampled the reality of life on the reservation. Virtually every major war of the two decades after Appomattox was fought

to force Indians onto newly created reservations or to make them go back to the reservations from which they had fled. From such perspective, it is not surprising that warfare
characterized the Peace Policy.[25]

As we have already seen with the taming of Med's wild sexuality, Daly was
invested in civilizing and sanitizing the frontier, and thus, it should not
come as a surprise that the real figure of frontier savagery in his play—and
the most obvious object of Daly's imperial aggression—is not the white
woman but the Indian.

Daly describes two such Indians in his play: Wannemucka, the "civilized Indian and 'Untutored Savage' who dwells with the white settlers
in their villages" (103), and Wahcotah, the "friendly Indian who stops
among the white soldiers at their Fort" (104). Both of these figures also
reveal their savage malevolence by the end of the play, and both are erased
from the play's final resolution. However, another Indian exists in Daly's
play who, precisely because she falls under the shadow of Wannemucka
and Wahcotah, complicates this rather clear-cut imperial racism. In act
3, Sundown Rouse, a crooked though comic politician, returns to the
camp after having gone scouting and, to the camp's surprise, is carrying
an Indian child. Showing the baby clinging to him, Rowse recounts how
"I took hold of the little devil when her mother ran away, just to look at
her, when she caught hold of my coat-tail, and hasn't let me go since"
(131). This papoose appears to be far more innocent than the treacherous and dissembling Wannemucka or Wahcotah. The Indian child, symbolically holding on to the coat-tail of white authority, can be read as the
ur-text of white imperialism: Rowse is the symbolic "white father," Daly
seems to insist, who must embrace and tend to his "red children."[26] At this
moment, Daly's notion of community and family could be extended even
to include the Indian, thus productively distinguishing between villainous and victimized Native Americans and complicating the notoriously
clear-cut rhetoric of empire.

Yet Daly merely reinforces this rhetoric by flattening out all difference,
for, as Wahcotah says, "Injun papoose cunning. You capture papoose. Big
chief father come after you" (131). Acting as a beacon for Indian violence,
the child, like all Indians, Daly insists, is treacherous and dangerous. Rowse
underscores this when he snorts: "Then she's hanging on to my coat-tail
as to identify me as the right man for the big chief to kill.... Here you, get
off! Thunder and lightning, what a prospect!...I might as well have a death-
warrant pinned to my back at once. I shall have to dye my hair and black my
eyes—I mean my face—to avoid recognition" (131). Interestingly, Rowse's
response to this threat, like his image of the white father earlier, seems to
call into question its own imperial scripting. To escape almost certain death

at the hands of the vicious Wannemucka, Rowse will have to "go native," dying his hair and blacking his face. Thus, at this point in the play, Daly seems to be offering an incisive though ironic comment on Indian policy: It is Rowse, the white patriarchal imperialist, and not the Indian, who must assimilate in order to survive. Daly seems to be opening a space within his drama to reimagine the parameters of identity and community, for, if we are to believe Rowse, then this Indian child will act as a catalyst for "dyeing" the whiteness of empire redder, thus demanding a commingling of previously distinct and jealously guarded racial communities.

As with Daly's earlier flattening out of difference, however, Daly's flirtation with a less color-coded community only serves to solidify the rhetoric of expansion all the more firmly. In the next scene, Rowse remains white and holds the papoose tighter, cooing to the settlers, "I've got this young papoose in safe-keeping. She's a policy of insurance on all of our lives" (134). Rowse's simultaneous embracing and objectifying of the Indian child ironically comments on the notion of an extended community. Rowse is much more willing to clasp the child to his bosom and keep her in his "safe-keeping," we understand, if he also constructs her not as an Indian child, or even as a person, but rather as an object—a "policy of insurance." This reversal of his previous position, therefore, transforms the child from native subject to capitalist object, from a potential catalyst for extending the notion of community to a chit for extending the imperial marketplace into the frontier. In this way, Rowse's "solution" to the perplexing and potentially deadly problem of the Indian child yokes together the discourse of the market and that of imperial expansion by ironically undercutting the idea that community could be anything other than racially, socially, and culturally pure. For Daly, extending the definitions of community can only occur if the members of that community broker their own sense of who they are through the consumption of all others, thus homogenizing the burgeoning imperialist society. Finally, and perhaps most importantly, by coupling capitalism and imperialism, Daly's continuous negotiations of the imagined community of the frontier reveal the mechanisms by which memory becomes history, for his characters' reversals of previous predicaments erase these memories through acts of dramatic consumption, smoothing over the history of frontier expansion by refusing to remember what a more inclusive sense of community might entail.

While Daly smooths over the history of the frontier through the elimination of memories of alternative communities, Miller works against the grain, finding in the fragments of history visions of extended communities whose memory is at odds with Daly's construction of a monolithic history of the frontier. Ironically, while Daly and Miller differ so widely in the way they imagine community, they fetishize similar objects as the means of imagining these communities, namely children. By probing how Miller echoes Daly's development of the child in his drama, the way Miller seems to ghost Daly on this score, we can see a cross-section of the frontier memory more clearly and, thus, some record of the way the frontier was remembered and forgotten.

Consider Sandy's elegiac monologue about the discovery and loss of Nancy Williams, for instance. He recounts to the miners:

> "Why, poor little bird," I said, and I put my arms about her and took her up when she fell at our feet, boys, and laid her away to rest under the tree, by the bank, Judge, you know, and watched over her, we two did, Judge, as if she'd been our own kid. And then, Judge, when she waked up, you remember, and we fed her, and she talked and told us all. And how we promised and swore to save her, Judge. And then, just as we got all packed up and ready to come back, the Danites came burstin' in upon us, leadin' the Ingins, and all of' em a shootin' at that poor, helpless baby, that never did anybody any harm. (384)

As in Daly's play, the white settlers find a baby, and while not nearly as problematic as the papoose, the infant Nancy Williams has a similar function in the plot. While the babies differ in race, in other words, they similarly act as catalysts of danger and death: The papoose potentially puts Rowse's life in danger from savage Indians as long as he possesses her, while the white baby puts Sandy's and the Judge's lives in danger from savage Danites as long as they protect her. While the baby and the Danites are white in Miller's play, they play roles similar to the Indian baby and Indian warriors in Daly's play. Moreover, the cultural panic about Mormonism in the late nineteenth century would have mitigated this racial difference. As the young boy witnessing Mormons after the Mountain Meadows Massacre in Jack London's *Star Rover* declares: "They ain't white .... They're Mormons."[27] While Mormons were white, they were often racialized as others, most often as "oriental" (Givens 125–132), and as Will Bagley demonstrates, after the Mountain Meadow Massacre of 1857, Mormons were often elided with the "savages" with whom they had committed the atrocious murders.[28]

Yet, even given this historical racializing of Mormons in the late nineteenth century, Miller's representation of this child does not become a "policy of insurance" for Sandy and the Judge, a piece of capital circulated for personal gain. Instead, Sandy and the Judge "battle" (384) for her against the Danites because, as Sandy indicates, they see her as a surrogate child, worth fighting for "as if she'd been our own kid." This phrase highlights how Sandy and the Judge perform the role of parent and protector of this child regardless of the fact that this child is not theirs and that they are merely mining camp partners, not mining camp parents. The stark difference between their treatment of this child and the treatment of the child in Daly's play only serves to index how differently these playwrights understand the notion of community: To survive on the frontier, Daly insists, communities must be defined by their differences and based on a policy of exclusion; to survive on the frontier, Miller retorts, communities must be defined by their inclusions and based on the linking of differences.

Moreover, as Sandy's relentless repeating of the Judge's name makes clear, the responsibility for the child's welfare and for the health of the community lies with each and every member of the mining camp. Rather than shirk this responsibility by transforming the child into an insurance policy, the community in Miller's play embraces the child and thus helps to extend the notion of community as well. The Judge demonstrates this acutely in his speech to the miners when the Widow gives birth to her and Sandy's child. Having never seen a child in the camp before, the miners gather around, and the Judge, puffing himself up for the occasion, orates:

> Gentlemen of—of the committee! Fellow citizens, this, what you now behold is—is—
> [*Stops and* WIDOW *whispers in ear.*] This which you now behold before you is—is an
> —infant. The first white born baby citizen ever born in these Sierras…. Feller citizens,
> this little infant sleeping here in its mother's arms, with the mighty snow-peaks of the
> Sierras about us; this innocent little sleepin' infant, which has been born to us here,
> gentlemen, shows us that—well, in fact, shows us—shows us what can be done in this
> glorious climate of California. (398)

As the Judge makes clear, this infant is not solely the property of Sandy and the Widow, even if the Widow is the one who has to help the Judge name the child. While the scene clearly draws on Bret Harte's short story "The Luck of Roaring Camp" (1868), it also recasts the scene of the baby becoming a commodity in Daly's play: This scene shows how the child makes single ownership—and thus capitalism—obsolete. This is a child "born to *us*," the Judge relates, and thus, if it is a commodity, then it is one that refuses to be circulated in an economy of possession and exclusion, profit and debit.

By relentlessly repeating that the child "shows us" something, moreover, Miller wants to draw attention to the different levels of performance going on. At the level of mimesis—what the child shows the characters onstage—the Judge insists that the child acts as an emblem to the miners. At the level of diegesis—what the child tells the audience members watching the characters onstage—the Judge is telling us that this new construction of the family and of community stems from the frontier, from the "glorious climate of California."[29] This mutually shared infant, in other words, is an emblem of the kind of frontier community that Daly could not abide, a commingling, interdependent, fluid familial unit that undercuts Daly's claim of presenting the one and only history of the frontier. This infant, therefore, rather than helping smooth over the history of frontier conquest, as it does in Daly's drama, stands as a visual cue for showing us—both onstage and in the audience—a submerged memory of the frontier at odds with the history of frontier conquest.

MELODRAMA AND THEATRICALITY

If the theater is a useful site for developing diverse national memories, then the theater's dramatic elements are the tools that allow playwrights to fashion those memories. By exploring how both Daly and Miller develop the same tool—the melodramatic secret—in completely divergent ways, not only will we clearly see the different ways the circulation of memory operates in their plays, we will also see, through the plays' definition and deployment of the secret, the important role played by the theater in the performance of national memory. Ironically, Daly's theatrical failure insured the success of the memory of frontier conquest, and Miller's theatrical success insured that his very different frontier memory would fail to have the same historical visibility.

"Most often melodrama makes dynamic use of a *secret*," posits theater critic Daniel Gerould in his study of melodrama's theatrical elements. "The secret is the most powerful factor in the play's dynamic, permitting the melodramatist to hold the spectator's interest uninterruptedly throughout the performance."[30] Moreover, as Gerould argues, this secret may come in different forms, such as the total secret. The total secret is

> contained in the exposition to the play, and unknown to both the characters and to the spectator. The spectator can only guess as to the nature of the secret (on the basis of scattered "hints"), to which no character has the key. The gradual revelation of the secret, while the spectator attempts to guess it, gives the melodrama its compositional tension. (158)

We encounter just such a total secret in Augustin's Daly melodramatic *Horizon*, for in the exposition we learn that Mrs. Van Dorp's husband kidnapped Margaret, "cruelly taking with him their infant daughter" (106). In the same moment, we also learn that Alleyn was adopted two years after Margaret disappeared, which makes Margaret and Alleyn not related by blood and therefore free to marry. Unknown to both the characters and the audience, though hinted at here, Daly's melodramatic secret helps structure the subsequent action of the piece. After Wolf Van Dorp, Mrs. Van Dorp's husband, dies at the hands of Wannemucka, his daughter, Med,

Mrs. Van Dorp's long-lost daughter Margaret, is entrusted to Loder, the kindhearted frontier loner, for protection. When Alleyn falls in love with Med after taming her wild frontier sexuality, Loder must vet Alleyn. In a telling scene between Loder and Alleyn, we see the way the melodramatic secret structures the play's tension. Exasperated at Alleyn's defensiveness, Loder opines, "If you will only say to me that you love her! I have one duty to perform, and then you will see me no more. A secret—." Alleyn interrupts: "A secret! About Med?" to which Loder cryptically retorts, "To the man who really loves her, a secret worth the world full of gold. For it tells him she is worthy to be his wife.... Remember, it is to be told to one only—the man who is to be her husband." Faced with such a choice, Alleyn grandly states, "Whatever your secret is, it is safe with me," to which Loder, much relieved, warmly responds, taking out a packet of letters and documents: "Come, then; on the road ask me what you will, and every information which this packet does contain you shall have" (141). Daly, thus, uses the melodramatic secret of Med's birth to structure this scene, giving it tension, helping it develop, and insuring its resolution.

Yet if this melodramatic secret "gives the melodrama its compositional tension," as Gerould suggests it does, leading to a "gradual revelation" and the relaxation of this tension, then Daly's play fails to live up to the melodramatic ideal. For when Loder and Alleyn walk offstage, Daly supplies no resolution; he does not reveal what the secret is, nor does he signal to us through his characters, when they return to the stage, what the secret means. We never learn for sure what is contained in that packet of letters and documents even though it is set up so adroitly by Daly in the scene between Loder and Alleyn. While we are entitled to guess, and Daly's melodramatic development certainly suggests to the canny spectator that Med is actually Margaret, Daly never resolves this tension but continues to postpone the plot's resolution.

Even at the ending, when the characters freeze in tableau, Daly still fails to reveal adequately and completely the nature of the secret. Med and the women of the camp have been taken captive by the nefarious Indians, Wannemucka and Wahcotah. Loder, having dispatched Wahcotah, disguises himself as the slain Indian to infiltrate the camp. Just as Wannemucka is about to take Med off to another camp and surely escape for good, Loder casts off his disguise, bellowing, "Indian! Stand back!" Recognizing Loder as his nemesis, Wannemucka springs at him, knife in hand, as the rest of the Indians fall on their captives. As the stage directions then tell us,

Loder seizes Med and fires his rifle at Wannemucka, who falls. In an instant the ravine is filled with soldiers. Alleyn darts forward and passes Med to him just in time to ward her from a blow aimed by Onata [Wannemucka's wife] who darts out of the tent. Rowse and Mr. Smith floor their guards. Columbia runs to Mr. Smith, and, on this picture of triumph, the CURTAIN. (151)[31]

As Martin Meisel argues, a tableau like the one Daly is using demands that actors "strike an expressive stance in a legible symbolic configuration" in order to "crystallize a stage of the narrative as a situation" or to "summarize and punctuate it."[32] The melodramatic tableau was used most often to plot the moral coordinates of the melodrama more firmly, to make plain what might have been confusing, obscure, or merely understated.

Yet this tableau creates more questions than it answers, especially relating to agency and the melodramatic secret. Consider Daly's ambiguous use of the pronoun *him*. We know that Loder is holding Med from the first line of the stage directions. Like a modern-day action hero, Loder grasps the girl with one hand while he blasts the villain with the rifle he holds in his other hand. Med's beau, the valiant, heroic Alleyn, then shows up on the scene, "darts forward," as the stage directions relate, "and passes Med to him just in time to ward her from a blow." Yet if Loder was the one who, like an action hero, was holding the girl and the gun, then who is passing Med to whom? Is Loder the one who darts forward, blocks the deadly blow, and then passes Med to Alleyn? While that would make sense in the moral calculus of the play—partnering Alleyn and Med as Columbia is with Mr. Smith—it does not then make sense that Alleyn is the one passing Med to anyone else. Who, then, is the antecedent to the pronoun *him*?

What I want to suggest about the ambiguity of this pronoun, regardless of who it actually is, is that it points to the bigger ambiguity that remains about Daly's melodramatic secret. While the staging might take care of specifying who the "him" is, this last bit of stage direction fails to bring satisfactory closure to the problem of the secret, no matter how much Daly wants his audience to read this tableau as a "picture of triumph." We do not return to Waverly Place in New York City; we do not inform Mrs. Van Dorp that her daughter has been found; we do not have Alleyn, Loder, or Med even acknowledge that Med is Margaret, failing to reveal—and thus to resolve—the melodramatic secret as Gerould insists all successful melodramas must do. Without this resolution, in other words, the play fails as a melodrama.

The play's flawed construction as a melodrama helps explain why *Horizon*, while not a total flop, met with only lukewarm success in its author's lifetime.[33] As George Bernard Shaw remembers, it was Daly's old-fashioned warmed-over dramaturgy, full of pedestrian stage tricks, stuffy dialogue, and lame resolutions, that demonstrated a "stale pleasantry of a kind for which we are not just now in the humor."[34] Yet even while subjecting Daly's drama to the full force of Shavian wit, Shaw had to confess that Daly was also "an advanced

man relatively to his own time and place, and was a real manager, with definite artistic aims which he trained his company to accomplish" (3:208). If
the play was flawed, then its failures speak to a larger, more complex dramaturgical project—to the "definite artistic aims" that Shaw mentions. As
Don Wilmeth and Rosemary Cullen relate in their introduction to *Horizon*,
Daly's play, "despite its romantic and moral touches, was a major departure
from the then popular and sentimental glorification of the West. Daly chose
instead to portray a more realistic picture" (33). Daly's play was on the cusp
of realism in the theater, and thus its failures to live up to the melodramatic
standards of its time may have sprung from the play's mixed feelings about
the genre. As Brenda Murphy trenchantly notes, the "American theater was
far from realistic in 1880. Its drama was primarily formulaic melodrama or
comedy; its acting was stagy and self-conscious; its stagecraft was sentimental. It should also be evident however, that there were hints of a nascent realism in all three areas. ... The American theater of the eighties ha[d] the raw
materials for realism" (23). Far from suggesting that Daly chose to have his
play fail to show the limits of melodrama, I am instead arguing that the playwright's undercutting of the set piece of the melodramatic secret in his play
may stand as a theatrical record of the eclipse of melodrama by realism in the
last quarter of the nineteenth century.

Moreover, if Daly's dramaturgical aims were to make his productions and
his actors less melodramatic and more realistic, then we see can see how
this play amounts to an imperial scripting of theatricality. After all, Daly's
taming of his wild actresses and his policing of his actors and audiences
more generally were also efforts to make his theater more realistic and less
melodramatic. He "strove to control actresses' embodiments of naturalized
passion," as Kim Marra notes, "to ensure that they fulfilled his own agenda
for heroic conquest and upward mobility. These aims were discernible in
the organizational structure, rules of conduct, and directorial methods
Daly implemented throughout his thirty-year managerial career" (*Strange*
32). Actors under Daly's tutelage "lost their stilted habits because they were
taught not to mouthe their lines, rant, or pose or exaggerate. Inappropriate
ad-libbing and talking between scenes were forbidden. The actors were
instructed never to notice anyone on the other side of the footlights, for the
audience had to be to them as if they did not exist."[35] Read in terms of realism's "rejection of any aspect of the dramatic medium that is reflexive," as
Murphy outlines, "that shatters the fourth-wall illusion by calling attention
to itself as art, such as rhetorical flourishes in dialogue, declamatory style
in acting, of manipulating coincidences in action" (29), it seems clear that
Daly's dramaturgy was invested in doing away with all of the standard melodramatic tropes—exaggerated action, the hitting of "points," the playing to
the audience—in an effort to make his plays more realistic or natural. Yet, if

we remember how Daly also "conquered" his actresses' wildness, demanding that they move the way he wanted, say what he wanted, and behave how
he wanted, then we can see that there is an ideological significance in Daly's
conquest of melodrama through realism.[36] In charging his actors to perform
in a more natural style, Daly was also, in effect, naturalizing empire, making
social meaning out of the way actors performed, the way audiences reacted,
and the way theater would be staged.

Daly's failed frontier drama comes to stand, then, as an unparalleled success, insofar as Daly's realistic predilections played a vital role in helping
to ensure the ascendancy of both theatrical realism and American empire.
Looking back over 200 years of American theatrical history, Arthur Hobson
Quinn declared: "Modern American drama begins with Augustin Daly.... .
Daly was a constructive artist and through the transition decades of the six-
ties and seventies he laid the foundations of the days to come."[37] What we
see from looking at Daly's double project of theatrical and imperial conquest, however, is that Quinn was more right than he might have thought:
Daly laid the foundations of the days to come by helping to craft the modern American realist drama, but he also helped make theatricality itself—
through this crafting—anything but socially neutral. With this in mind, we
can see how correct critic Marvin Felheim was when he shrewdly suggested
of Daly's frontier drama, *Horizon*, that it was itself "a pioneer in a pioneer
field" (68), but a pioneer imbued with the colorings of Manifest Destiny.

If *Horizon*'s failure onstage ironically points up its success in helping to
generate a new kind of socially invested dramaturgy, then the startling success of *The Danites in the Sierras* onstage ironically points up its failure in
helping to sustain a dissenting view of the frontier thereafter. While Daly's
play had only moderate success, Miller's play "emerged as one of the most
famous of all the frontier dramas" (Hall 32). Playbills for *The Danites* often
underscored its popularity as a selling point. A playbill for the McCauley
Theatre proclaimed:

> The "DANITES" has attracted more attention than any other American play ever per-
> formed, having been played to overflowing houses composed of the elite of the country
> in the following cities: 120 nights at the Grand Opera House, New York; 30 nights at
> the Boston Theatre, Boston; 21 nights at the Arch Street Theatre, Philadelphia, and 60
> nights at Haverly's Theatre, Chicago. In many instances thousands of people have been
> turned away, unable to gain even standing room.[38]

To be sure, *The Danites* was far from the best American play ever performed,
as this playbill implies, but the large number of performances in theaters
throughout the United States attests to its immense popularity. The playbill for the 1881 production of Miller's play at the Grand Opera House in

New York City went even further, noting that the play was "the GREAT SUCCESS OF THE LONDON STAGE ... performed at no less than three prominent Metropolitan Theatres, SADLER'S WELLS, THE GLOBE, AND ROYAL STANDARD, to crowded and delighted audiences, composed of all classes of the community."[39] The play was an international success and, equally important, was received well by all theatergoers, which attested to its populist as well as popular success. Unlike *Horizon*, which failed to impress any of the critics on opening night, *The Danites* met with considerable success when it first appeared. As the September 1, 1877, *Spirit of the Times* noted, "It was not surprising that the New Broadway was crowded to excess, not withstanding the heat, on Wednesday week last. The opening of a new theatre and the production of a new play by a well-known writer, were, unquestionably, sufficient attractions to excuse curiosity, although the thermometer stood close on a hundred" (113). So, even though the Broadway Theatre was blisteringly hot in late August, New Yorkers still flocked there to experience Miller's fantasy of the frontier with a fervor they never brought to Daly's play and its frontier fantasy.

This was not to say that Miller's play was without fault, for even the *Spirit of the Times*, while giving the play a favorable review overall, suggested that there were a few drawbacks. Chief among the faults noted was *The Danites'* lack of believability. "The chief defect of this play," quips the reviewer for the *Spirit of the Times*, "is its utter improbability, and, unfortunately, Mr. Joaquin Miller has not M. Victor Hugo's talent of disguising improbabilities and making them appear possible. On the contrary, he renders them more glaring than is quite necessary" (113). This lack of probability was, however, a deliberate choice on Miller's part. In a decided gesture of resistance, Miller played up his drama's lack of realism, creating a theatricality of excess that, like Daly's realism, constituted an ideological gesture and a social critique.

Nowhere does this critique surface more forcefully than in Miller's theatrical ghosting of Daly's use of the melodramatic secret. Unlike Daly's lackluster use of this device, Miller's use of it takes the form not of the total secret but what is called the secret for the characters, and attains—one might even say supercedes—the goals that the device was meant to accomplish. As Daniel Gerould suggests about melodramas containing a secret for the characters,

> in this case the play's compositional dynamics are based on the unfolding of situations which block an "easy" solution to the enigma of concealed relationships. The characters approach the solution, then move away again. ... The spectator, as though a participant in the events unfolding on stage, has a strong "will" to have the secret disclosed, but his desire must remain tense and unresolved until the denouement. (158)

The audience knows quite early in Miller's play that Billy Piper is Nancy Williams—the major secret of the plot—and as the play progresses and the potential moments of unveiling are compounded, the audience's desire for revelation grows. Miller even has Billy Piper confide to the Widow, "[A]lone I must bear my secret, my sufferings and my cross." "O," she continues, tweaking the audience's growing anticipation, "you cannot guess. You will never know the dark and dreadful truth, the mystery, the awful crimes—"(393). Peppering the play with exchanges like this, in effect, helps develop the piece's tension and contributes to the play's overall success as a melodrama.

While Daly's melodramatic secret never gets firmly decoded, Miller's is crisply resolved. One might even argue that while Daly's play operates with a melodramatic deficiency, Miller's play operates not with a melodramatic sufficiency but rather with a melodramatic superfluity. Rather than stall and sputter, as the secret does in Daly's play, in *The Danites* it thrives and flourishes, accruing more and more weighty meanings as it develops. "You hold the secret of my life," Billy tells the Widow, taking her into his confidence. "You hold my *life* itself" (393). This is not merely some trifle, this melodramatic secret, but rather "life itself." Miller wants his audience to see in the melodramatic secret not just a trite resolution to a by-the-numbers melodrama but rather a key for reading life, albeit life construed in a special way.

At the end of the play, in the same spot where Daly's drama fell short, Miller's play offers a striking contrast. Billy Piper disappears into his cabin as the rest of the miners grow restless. Trying to enter the cabin, they are stopped by Captain Tommy, who says, "Stop! Only women must enter that cabin now. For it is a woman who has lived there all these years. Billy Piper is no more." All of the miners cry out together, "What, dead?" to which Bunkerhill, "leading out Billy in woman's dress," responds, "Yes, Billy Piper is dead. But Nancy Williams lives!" Amazed, all of the miners, in unison, respond: "Nancy Williams!" (405). As with Daly's confusion of the pronoun *him* at the end of *Horizon*, Miller's play gestures to a confusion in names at the end of the play as well, for surely, it should be Nancy who is led out "in woman's dress," not Billy.

As with Daly's ambiguous pronouns, the ambiguity in Miller's play would also be resolved in the play's actual staging, but unlike Daly, Miller does not weakly end his drama on this note of ambiguity, using it instead for dramatic effect. He takes the melodramatic secret from a stale set piece for generating interest in the play and transforms it into one of the play's crucial themes and most heavily laden symbolic elements, thus underscoring melodrama's mode of excess. The resolution of the secret in this instance is not merely a confirmation of identity—we do not simply learn that Billy

Piper is Nancy Williams—but rather a ritualistic and symbolic rebirth performed by the community. The ambiguity of naming therefore makes sense in this communal ritual of rebirth, for Billy Piper is still Billy Piper until Bunkerhill names and thus transforms her into Nancy Williams. As a figure invested with religious power, Bunkerhill performs an act of transubstantiation, and the mining community, as a congregation, helps authenticate this "miracle" by responding—all in unison—"Nancy Williams!" This ritual act of renaming and rebirth recalls theater's beginnings in communal acts of ritual that helped confirm the values of that community. The melodramatic secret thus exceeds its usual plot function, taking on a deeper significance. For Miller, the secret that is revealed at the end of his play is not just about identity but is also about the power of community to transform and revive humanity: Billy's secret is thus really "life itself."

This transformation of the melodramatic secret—this heaping of meaning on what had been merely a device used by melodramatists—helps to elevate the moral plotting of the end of the play even as it clarifies why this play ultimately failed to gain cultural currency. Rather than turn to realism, with its imperial leanings, as Daly did, Miller attempted to revitalize melodrama, to resuscitate its impact on society by amplifying its preferred mode of excess. His blatant refusal, as the newspaper reviewer noted deftly, to be more realistic not only stands as a calculated maneuver designed to resist the imperially inflected realism that Daly was turning toward, but also helps us see how Miller's memory of the frontier—a place of communal transformation and fluid flourishing—would be forgotten in the progress toward modern American nationality and theatricality. Miller's retreat to melodrama sealed his play's fate: It would be forgotten in the history of an American theater turning toward realism. Its amplification of the melodramatic mode, which worked to distance it from realism, stands as a stark reminder of theatricality's importance in mapping and remapping the avenues of American progress. Not all theatrical projects, Miller's play reminds us, helped pave the road for imperialism. What exists in this play's failure is a frontier memory that, because it failed to align itself with the dominant history of imperialism, like Daly's play did so keenly, has often been firmly situated on the other side of the great divide of American memory.

As the two plays vied with each other, offering different memories of the frontier for a post–Civil War audience already witnessing the gradual diminishment of "uncivilized" lands in the West, what surfaced was a contest over which frontier memory would gain legitimacy. As Don Wilmeth and Rosemary Cullen note, Daly "knew little of the real West" (32), and what he did know, he loathed. In a letter he sent to his brother after a trip down the Mississippi on October 26, 1864, he writes, "I don't think much of that Mighty 'strame.' It is very narrow and very dirty" (qtd. in J. Daly 62–63). Although the Mississippi often served as a romantic inspiration for musing about the frontier and the West, Daly, like Fanny Trollope before him, sees nothing appealing about it, treating it with the withering specificity of a realist. For Daly, the frontier was there to be civilized, the land cultivated and the Indian eradicated, and the theater would be civilization's champion. In Daly's play, for instance, the Mayor of Rogue's Rest says, pointing his pistol at an Indian, "I've got my blotter handy, and we might as well wipe him off the records now" (115). Here, killing the Indian to erase him from the land and writing the Indian out of existence are joined in one metaphor, revealing not only Daly's imperialist leanings but also the way the theater itself could use its own writing to blot the Indian from the records. For Daly, the memory of the frontier should be one without the "dirty" Mississippi or the equally "dirty" Indian.

For Miller, on the other hand, remembering the frontier legitimately meant consciously remembering what Daly would have preferred forgotten. Whereas Daly wanted the Indian erased, Miller held the opposite view. Drawing from his own experience working with the Modocs in California, he pointed out, "If a trouble comes of this clashing together of the whites and the reds, we hear but one side of the story. The Indian daily papers are not read."[40] Miller's mission as a poet, storyteller, and playwright was not only to tell the Indians' side of the story but, in doing so, to tell the story of the frontier that Daly wanted to ignore. This alternative memory of the "plastic west," as Miller called the frontier (Life 27), was capable of sustaining alternative sexual identities, communal formations, and socially active theatricalities.

Writing about why the Southern Mines of California's gold rush years are not as memorable as the Northern Mines, Susan Lee Johnson argues that the Southern Mines "have been neglected because the area fits dominant cultural memory of the Gold Rush—as it has evolved in the United States—less well." She continues:

> The unruly history of the Southern Mines has proven more difficult to enlist in American narratives of success stories of progress and opportunity that are linked to financial gain and identified with people racialized as white and gendered as male. ... [T]he meaning-making process that occurred on a national level in the United States almost guaranteed that social change in the Southern Mines would not capture eastern imaginations, and hence would not figure in a reimagined, now continental American nation. (316)

I bring up Johnson's invaluable excavation of the history of the Southern Mines for two reasons. First, I see a similar historical phenomenon surrounding the representation of the frontier on the post–Civil War American stage. Miller's play, like the Southern Mines it represents, has been neglected because its memory of the frontier is at odds with the more dominant narratives of frontier imperialism epitomized by Daly's play. Second, while Johnson contends that the imagery and ideology of the Southern Mines failed to "capture eastern imaginations," what we have discovered in our exploration of Miller's play is that it thrilled audiences in the East, firing the imagination of eastern audiences who gathered at the theater to witness Miller's "plastic west."

What these two points underscore is how complicated the transmission of the memory of the frontier was on the post–Civil War stage, how deeply nuanced and complex the process of remembering was and continues to be today. Even though I chose to focus on similarly racialized and gendered playwrights (white and male) whose plays were produced in the same locale (New York City) and at similar moments in history (the 1870s and 1880s), we see not a rehearsing of identical memories of the frontier but rather a distinct pair of divergent frontier memories. Studying the staging of the frontier in post–Civil War theater as a "site of memory," therefore, helps demonstrate that the urban Northeast—the seat of American imperial power—was as invested in resisting the spread of empire westward as it was in assisting it, even if Daly's view would become the dominant one for the next century.

AFTERWORD

⌌⌍

Brokeback or Bushwhacked

The Legacies
of Pioneer Performances

The legacies of Daly's *Horizon* and Miller's *The Danites of the Sierras* and their intertwined ideological developments are realized in the performances described in the introduction—namely, Buffalo Bill's Wild West and Gowongo Mohawk's *The Wep-Ton-No-Mah, the Indian Mail Carrier.* Daly's twofold insistence on realism and the imperial ordering of the frontier becomes the framing device for Cody's incarnation of his Wild West, while Miller's espousal of an excessive, dissonant form of frontier theater is capitalized on by the cross-dressing Gowongo Mohawk and her racy frontier performance. The roughly half century of pioneer performances charted in this project—and redacted in the figures of Cody and Mohawk—thus ends where it began: the rupture of two ideological genealogies of performing the frontier that in their opposed aesthetic energies powered new forms of American theatrical expression.

Yet, for all of the ostensible balance between these contrasting performative formations in the nineteenth century, their subsequent theatrical histories are decidedly asymmetrical: Cody and Mohawk may have shared a similar spotlight at the end of the nineteenth century, but the Wild West muscled Mohawk's performance to the side at the beginning of the twentieth century. The reasons for this have as much to do with commerce as they do with ideology: while the Wild West's frontier fell in line more comfortably with the dominant ideology that defined the "American Century" than did *Wep-Ton-No-Mah's*, the sheer scale of Cody's spectacular production—with troops of horses and wagons, Indians and livestock—appealed more viscerally to the American public than Mohawk's more modest production did. It was this confluence of ideological mainstreaming and over-whelming production values that made Buffalo Bill's Wild West into *the* spectacle of American imperialism that people lined up to experience.

Yet, even if we bracket Mohawk's reactionary performance, the history of Buffalo Bill's Wild West itself belies the notion that he monopolized fron-tier representation in the twentieth century. While Cody's future looked bright at the World Columbian Exposition, it represented in many ways the apex of his popularity. In the succeeding decades, even as the nation continued to expand, engaging aggressively with the Dominican Republic, Panama, the Philippines, and China, Cody's star quickly faded. Part of the reason for this decline stems from his disastrous financial choices, for while he was generously recompensed for his role in the Wild West, he "spread himself too thin," recounts Kasson, "and his grip on his overall financial situation seemed tenuous"[1]—particularly his disastrous investment in the Cody-Dyer Mining and Milling Company in Arizona (130). He also suf-fered from some exploitive partnerships after the original Wild West broke up, including falling in with the cunning profiteer Harry Tammen (Kasson 156). In addition to his financial troubles, Cody's aesthetic investment in the live show was eclipsed by two major cultural developments that became dominant in the early twentieth century. First, Owen Wister published the first western novel, *The Virginian*, in 1902, indicating there would be other cowboys for the American populace to follow. While the staged frontiers-man we have explored in the introduction gave rise to the Wild West's invention of the cowboy, Wister's novel followed in this lineage of succes-sion by offering another popular cowboy—the nameless protagonist, the Virginian—a figure who challenged Cody's role as *the* representation of the frontier. Second, one year later, American audiences saw the first film to tell a complex story, *The Great Train Robbery*, which was also, as it turns out, the first narrative western film. While "not the first western or the first movie with a plot," as historian Paul Reddin has noted, the film still "energized the infant moving picture industry by bringing together plot, a chase on horse-back, gunplay, and justice triumphing."[2] Historian Tag Gallagher suggests even more: "Rather than the cinema inventing the western, it was the west-ern, already long existent in popular culture, that invented the cinema."[3] The spectacle and dynamic mise-en-scène of the frontier plays in the nine-teenth century fed into Cody's showmanship, which in turn helped struc-ture filmic westerns like *The Great Train Robbery*; but as critics like Nicholas Vardac have shown, film as an artistic medium could present spectacle bet-ter than the theater, whose own prizing of spectacular vision, as Marc Rob-inson relates, was persistently fractured by playwrights' manipulation of the aesthetics of interiority.[4] Moreover, the Wild West, as we have noted, sold its audiences authenticity, while early film, as Philip Deloria notes, sold its audience "illusion."[5] When Cody turned to film at the end of his career in *The Indian Wars*, his attachment to "real" Indians and "real" action detracted from its appeal to audiences, where the film floundered.[6] The Wild West's set piece of the Indian attack on the Deadwood Stagecoach, while convincing enough in the arena because of its tactile realness, would become much more appealing to early twentieth-century audiences in the illusory qualities of films such as John Ford's monumental *Stagecoach* (1939). In addition, unlike Cody's show, films like *The Great Train Robbery* and *Stagecoach* would be accessible to hundreds of thousands of people in multiple locations. When in a poignant reversal, Cody borrowed material from *The Great Train Robbery* for his own production in 1903, the persona named Buffalo Bill was indeed, as e. e. cummings's poem captured it, "defunct."

In rehearsing the eclipse of Buffalo Bill's popularity by the medium of film in the twentieth century, I do not want to document the heterogeneous formal apparatuses that proliferated around representing the frontier at the fin de siècle. Rather, I want to suggest that at least one way of taking the measure of the continuing complexity of nineteenth-century frontier performance in the twentieth—and twenty-first—centuries would be to spotlight one of the mediums that made Buffalo Bill defunct, film, and its representation of the frontier. Still, to generate even a brief account of the history of this frontier performance in the twentieth century would be to lose oneself in a thicket of film histories and historical revisions, monographs tackling the western, antiwestern, and neowestern and revisionist histories recontextualizing the western's place in American politics and policy, from Teddy Roosevelt to Dubya, from Cuba to Iraq.[7] To separate the tangled lines of the filmic western, much less to offer anything like a synoptic treatment of its history, lies well outside the scope of this project. Nevertheless, I want to use this afterword to explore two contemporary filmic "performances" of the frontier for the way they gesture back to this complex history of the film western in the twentieth century and, more crucially, to the double histories of frontier performance represented by Cody and Mohawk that I have explored in this study. One of these performances is the notorious set of photographed images of President George W. Bush, decked out in cowboy hat, boots, and jeans, clearing brush on his ranch in Crawford, Texas, in 2005, while the other is the much ballyhooed film of the same year *Brokeback Mountain*, a cultural flashpoint for discussions of the coupling of the quintessential western with a focused queer sensibility.

Within the parameters we have established, it is abundantly clear how Bush's brush-clearing performance draws on the history of frontier performance emblematized by Cody, while Ang Lee's gay western is an equally obvious surrogate for the kind of pioneer performance emblematized by Mohawk. While seemingly at odds with each other in terms of ideological investment, both of these frontier performances have nevertheless generated similar responses that have critiqued each performance's mobilization of frontier tropes in the service of crafting a compromised and conservative politics. Bush's brush clearing has become a symbol for the purposefully myopic, irresponsibly aggressive imperialism that defined Bush's post-9/11 America, while *Brokeback Mountain*, in its (mis)representation of the "gay frontier," has craftily reified the hypermasculine, homophobic positionality it purportedly works to overturn. Meanwhile, the critical discourse surrounding both frontier performances has participated in the flattening out of the varied and variegated understandings of the frontier that subtend both texts, constructing the frontier instead as a placeholder for essentially repressive, conservative values. To offer a thick description of the frontier that works against such misreading, therefore, means attempting to syncretize the competing representations of the frontier integrated into both performances while avoiding smoothing over the tensions that animate them. I want to do this in order to illustrate that this kind of critical thinning out of the frontier, particularly in popular performances, has two deleterious effects. First, it becomes unconsciously complicit in the same kind of forced homogenization of frontier representation that Bush is engaging in. Second, it engages in a misreading of the ideologically textured frontier landscape that Lee traffics in. To be sure, I am not attempting to quiet the roar of criticism leveled at Bush's repressive, imperialistic performance, nor am I content to read *Brokeback Mountain* as a misprized engine of radical political subversion. What I do want to suggest is that the politically and aesthetically rich body of frontier works in the nineteenth century that I have been exploring casts a very long shadow in the twentieth and twenty-first centuries. Reading these two performances in light of the critical field of inquiry I have been mapping accesses how the frontier continues to offer a way of negotiating conceptualizations of what it means to be American.

BUSHWHACKED: GEORGE BUSH AND LARRY MATTLAGE

There are myriad iconic images that surround George W. Bush as president of the United States from 2000 to 2008, and one might focus on any number of them, from his flight suit thumbs-up below the "Mission Accomplished" banner to his post-Katrina congratulating Michael D. "Brownie" Brown for doing a "heckuva" job—all telling symbols of his presidency's problems. One such image involves his brush-clearing "performance" outside his Crawford Ranch home in central Texas in winter 2005. While many of the images we associate with Bush's eight years record isolated one-time events, the image of his brush clearing is one that represents a continued obsession.

On any of the 365 days that he spent in Crawford at the "Western White House," as it was known, one could have seen him engaging in precisely this activity, for his "idea of paradise [was] to hop in his white Ford pickup truck in jeans and work boots, drive to a stand of cedars, and whack the trees to the ground."[8] Like Reagan's chopping wood and riding horses and George H. W. Bush's sailing off the shore of Kennebunkport, Maine, Bush's obsessive desire to clear cedar in the Texas hill country works to project an image of a "cowboy president, a tough rancher fighting the elements to survive," or as presidential historian Robert Dallek summarizes it, a "macho" figuration of the presidency (cited in Rein A03).

Bush's performance feels familiar to us not just because it caused such a firestorm in the media, becoming, like the images previously mentioned, a hallmark of his presidency's failings. Rather, as we see him accoutered in work boots, blue jeans, and aviator sunglasses (Figure A.1), he achieves his "macho" status by evoking a familiar representational lineage of the frontier stretching back to Buffalo Bill's Wild West, Augustin Daly's *Horizon*,

Figure A.1 President George W. Bush clearing brush, Crawford Ranch, Texas, 2005.
Source: The White House.

and the other works we have examined, a lineage of performance practices associated with a frontier of imperial conquest. Of course, Bush's contribution catalyzes these frontier performances by simultaneously evoking more recent iterations of the frontier as well, the filmic cowboy embodied by figures like John Wayne, Gary Cooper, and Clint Eastwood who also performed the frontier as a land to be settled. Its visceral symbolic power—and no doubt the reason why Bush chose to perform it—stems from the way it synthesizes these two established frontier traditions: Through a dense frontier performance of aggressive masculinity, rugged individualism, and imperial ordering, Bush creates an image around which a post-9/11 American audience was supposed to rally.

While Bush's performance powerfully evokes a defining American trope, everything that makes this frontier performance so politically useful for his presidency simultaneously opens it up to dissent. The performance has also been read as signaling Bush's deliberate disconnectedness from the American citizenry, his blatant disregard for a country embroiled in wars on two fronts. As Maureen Dowd acerbically put it after his long stay at Crawford for the 2005 winter holidays: "[H]e just spent six straight days mountain-biking and brush clearing in Crawford. He couldn't devote 60 minutes to getting our kids home rather than just a few for a 'Message: I care' photo-op faking sincerity?"[9] Galvanized by Cindy Sheehan's protest vigil outside the Bush compound, media opinion makers like Dowd have suggested that the president's retreat to Crawford is symbolic of his more general retreat from the work he should be doing as president. Rather than engaging in the hard work of leading the country, such criticism goes, he is engaging in a form of displaced manual labor, using his working-class performance of the frontier to avoid the tough policy decisions and public management he is responsible for as president. "He's the son of a rich man who doesn't have to spend his time cutting underbrush," Robert Dallek concludes (Rein A03); he was performing an unnecessary act that increased the value of his property as the rest of the property values in the United States started to deflate in 2005. Looking back at this performance in 2008, Frank Rich opined that "America belatedly learned the hard way that the brush-clearing cowboy of the Crawford 'ranch' (it's a country house, not a working ranch) was in reality an entitled Andover-Yale-Harvard oil brat whose arrogance has left us where we are now."[10] From this perspective, therefore, the Texan frontier Bush invokes in his brush-clearing performance is the perfect setting: It reveals how he uses political slumming to garner American support and express the pageantry of his "imperial presidency" as an "arrogant" attempt to hack down all impediments to ordering the world his way.

While the tenor of these critiques remains valid and the wrongs committed by Bush very real, this clutch of critical voices nevertheless misses another one of Bush's most damaging political maneuvers—the representational violence he commits by invoking the frontier in the way he does. In order to see this representational violence and to gauge its effects, you have to know something about cedar. Cedar, actually Ashe juniper (*Juniperus ashei*), is not native to central Texas but was an alien species that invaded after the Dust Bowl in the 1920s, and in some ways, it is a nuisance to landscapers precisely because of its tenacious resistance not only to drought and poor soil conditions but also to any attempts to remove or control it. Hacking at it is thus not only hard, backbreaking labor, it is futile. I bring this fact up not to suggest that Texans, particularly hill country ranchers, do not engage in such brush clearing but to draw attention to the staginess of Bush's frontier performance and to underscore the way it draws on the frontier lineage I have outlined at the expense of another frontier experience that exists right outside Bush's carefully manicured land on his neighbor's property. On that property three-quarters of a mile from Bush's ranch lives Larry Mattlage, a rancher whose family has been in Crawford since 1887. Unlike Bush, Mattlage keeps livestock, but they are not cattle; rather, they are goats and sheep, a fact that already troubles Bush's evocation of the *cow*boy in his Crawford performance. In Mattlage's view, brush clearing is just "for show. It's not necessary.... [Brush] is where the birds live. That's birdseed. That's deer food. That's cow food.... [Cedar] makes cedar posts. If they're grown properly, they make a good post that will last forever."[11] What is crucial to understand about Mattlage's pique at the president's brush clearing is not so much the fact that it is a kind of performative slumming or that it somehow emblemizes the monomania of Bush's own presidency. Mattlage is angry about those things as well, as we can see in his exasperation at Bush's performance as a "show," one that is "not necessary," but what strikes him as even more troubling is the fact that what Bush is doing is actually bad for the environment. His frontier performance, in short, damages the frontier stage on which Bush acts out his cowboy pantomime.

By pointing to the way that Bush's "show" damages the frontier landscape, Mattlage is suggesting the possibility of another kind of frontier performance that such a show necessarily forecloses. Mattlage's response to the brush-clearing incident suggests that there are at least two, if not more, different kinds of frontier plays that can be put on in the same setting that Bush is claiming as his own: a hypermasculine pageant of power and a more symbiotic, less aggressive drama involving humans and animals.

Even though Bush draws on a lineage of frontier performance that stretches back beyond Buffalo Bill Cody into the nineteenth century, this does not necessarily mean that Larry Mattlage is a surrogate for

Gowongo Mohawk. While not sharing the specific subversive social ideology that underpinned Mohawk's "weirdly sensational" act, Mattlage nevertheless offers an alternative representation of the frontier, both in his comments and in his actions, that suggests at least some connection with Mohawk. Both figures mobilize the frontier not simply to bolster American hegemony but also to explore alternatives to those power plays. The frontier emerges from this performative nexus as a decidedly multifaceted engine for political engagement, capable of both driving and derailing American imperial power. The same central Texas frontier landscape that allows Bush to perform his cowboy presidency at the same time contains within it an alternative to such a performance, as Larry Mattlage makes clear.

What the collection of conflicting frontiers contained within this one moment suggests is that the critical voices attacking Bush's brush-clearing performance have addressed only one of the nefarious aspects of this bit of political propaganda. It is, to be sure, political propaganda, but part of its deeper political agenda—as evidenced in Bush's attempt to imagine himself as a successor to figures like Cody and John Wayne—is its attempt to suppress other, competing representations of the frontier by perpetuating the cowboy image he wants to embody. Bush commits not only a kind of environmental damage but a form of representational violence as well, disabling other, dissenting frontier figurations. More crucial is the fact that the host of critical voices that have dissected the myriad problems with this event have equated Bush's performance uniformly and unequivocally with the frontier, thus confirming the same homogenizing logic that the president's performance perpetuates. The payoff here is not merely to understand how Bush has monopolized the frontier in his performance but also to understand how complicit we become in his performance's political logic if we do not recognize the alternative performative practices that he strives to obscure.

BROKEBACK'S DOUBLE VISION

Perhaps no frontier performance seems to oppose the ideology and politics of Bush's show more than Ang Lee's celebrated *Brokeback Mountain*, a film that tragically renders the queer relationship between two modern-day frontiersmen in Wyoming, Ennis Del Mar and Jack Twist, played by Heath Ledger and Jake Gyllenhaal, respectively. Produced in the same year as Bush's brush-clearing episode, the film is a provocative alternative to the president's performance: It laments the damaging masculinity of the traditional frontier, which the president's muscular show does all it can to prop up. If Bush's brush clearing was a critical bugaboo, then *Brokeback Moun-*

tain seemed to be a critical darling. The film's frontier imagery, as Jim Kitses argues, spoke to its "sophisticated play with Western conventions,"[12] and in a nuanced way, argues James R. Keller and Anne Goodwyn Jones, it worked consciously "to broaden the assumptions about traditional manhood." The film insists that "[m]en can fuck each other and still ride a bull, punch a cow, brawl, herd sheep, and make love to their wives."[13] The film's real achievement, it seems, is to foreground and make explicit the gay subtext running through other westerns, from the performances by Montgomery Cliff in *Red River* (1947) to James Dean's in *Giant* (1956) and, even more directly, from Jon Voight's cowboy hustler in *Midnight Cowboy* (1969) to Andy Warhol's fetishistic *Lonesome Cowboys* (1968).[14] Its novelty, as Susan Lee Johnson notes, lies in its fully illuminated depiction of same-sex desire not in the urban areas of the West but in its rural locations, sites that frame the traditionally coded representation of the frontier.[15]

Through the roar of applause celebrating the film's achievements, though, one can detect the whisper of a critique that condemns the film's depiction of exactly the kind of queer desire that Johnson applauds. As Roy Grundmann notes, "[r]ather than embodying homosexuality per se…Ennis' character's profile places Ledger in a dramatic tradition that articulates homosexuality not so much in terms of sex, but in terms of anguished masculinity in crisis—and that has always been a surefire recipe for success in American film and theater."[16] For Grundmann, this is a film less about queer sensibility than about the crisis of desire and identity evident in exactly the same kind of masculinity that Bush embodies in his brush-clearing performance—a fact perhaps intentionally highlighted in the film by having Heath Ledger accouter himself much like Dubya. Even Keller and Jones, who note the film's subversive qualities, concur that ultimately, it "does not challenge the central forceful prescriptions of American manhood" (24). This is a film whose "gay man" has already been prepared for us in a certain way: He is "white, masculine, straight-acting, good-looking, and, therefore, sympathetic."[17] Even more important, this gay man's queerness is represented in the film as a problem that needs to be worked through and managed; in the logic *Brokeback Mountain* espouses, queer desire is a "thing that takes hold of us," as Ennis calls it, a thing that ultimately has no future on the frontier. For all of its posturing about representing a more inclusive, less repressive frontier, *Brokeback Mountain* works subtly, these critics argue, to retrench that same vision of the frontier that someone like Bush traffics in.

The film is clearly a catalyst for a range of conflicting critical responses, but rather than simply rehashing these disagreements, I want to suggest that one way of dealing with them is to rethink how the film stages the frontier. Diana Ossana and her writing partner Larry McMurtry have admitted that they wanted to create a project that "subverts the myth of the American

West and its iconic heroes" (qtd. in Kitses 23), but the way they chose to do so, I am arguing, has little to do with its queer protagonists. In following how Ang Lee creates a bifurcated vision of the frontier in this film, we can witness how, as B. Ruby Rich claims, he "has taken one of the most sacred of American genres, the Western, and queered it" (qtd. in Clarke 30). What I argue is that *Brokeback Mountain* does not "queer" the notion of rugged masculinity on the frontier, for in many ways the film resuscitates a well-worn vision of embattled, roughneck manhood. Rather, it works actively to queer the idea that the only frontier that can exist is the one that stages this kind of masculinity. In the film's double vision, Lee explores the representational geography of the frontier, suggesting its complex figurative landscape that tragically curtails alternative subject relations even as it opens up a space that enables them. What makes this film progressive is not so much its overt political investments in queer male identity but rather its subtle representational queering of the frontier.

To get at Lee's double vision of the frontier in *Brokeback Mountain*, we need to attend to the way vision itself is deployed in this film. D. A. Miller cogently notes that, throughout the film's narrative, queerness is always an object of surveillance. He points to three different episodes that epitomize the way Ennis Del Mar, as queer male subject, is put on display: One is by Jack Twist at the beginning of the film when he takes in Ennis's image in his truck's side mirror; another occurs when Joe Aguirre uses his binoculars to focus on Jack and Ennis's romp; and the last one takes place when Alma, Ennis's wife, looks out her window and sees a passionate kiss between Jack and Ennis when the men are reunited after their initial encounter. As Miller notes, Lee underscores the importance of these three moments by framing them in similar ways; all three events take in the representation of queer identity through a kind of literalized lens—from Jack's mirror to Aguirre's binoculars to Alma's window. "Ennis is always being watched like a hawk," says Miller, and more importantly, "if not by Jack, or Joe Aguirre, or Alma, then, in a far more continuous surveillance than theirs combined, by us spectators."[18] Miller argues that the film's ostensible left-leaning politics are undone, in this instance, by its subtle displacement of the gaze from figures in the film to the spectators of the film; channeling Foucault, we use the gaze of surveillance to view homosexuality as something not only distinct and alien but also tragic. We are encouraged through the film's positioning of our vision and sympathies to forgive the "homosexual who doesn't mean to be homosexual" and thus to create a viewing subject "who doesn't mean for him to be either" (58). For Miller, this conservative technique helps explain part of the film's appeal, for "[e]ven as the storyline is busy destroying the Homosexual, the visuals work to safeguard this homoeroticism, which, on condition that it remain unowned, unnamed and unmeaning, need answer to nobody" (58).

As Miller has suggested, the film seems to create the spectator as a voyeur, placing him or her outside the action of the film and likewise outside a sphere of political involvement. I want to suggest that Lee's choice to frame the visuals in this way may also serve another purpose, one that works in a different direction than simply disengaging us from the queer subjectivity on display here. If the visuals are meant to heighten the sense of distance between the audience and what they gaze at, then this distance also works to forge—and map in terms of representation—separate spheres of action and identity within the film. Aguirre's binoculars magnify the large distance between his bigoted, repressive ideology and that of Jack and Ennis on Brokeback Mountain, whereas Alma's window shows how outside her domestic sphere Ennis and Jack really are. While Jack's use of the mirror in his visual framing does not signal his distance from Ennis as the other two episodes do, it nevertheless epitomizes the way Jack's queer leanings are reflected in Ennis. These lenses thus work to create visual cues suggesting the reciprocated desire between the two protagonists even as they likewise suggest the way the nature of this desire is separate from the regulatory worlds of Aguirre's labor and Alma's domesticity.

As spectators, moreover, we not only recognize the distance between these spheres, but we also are given access to each of them: If we are situated in Aguirre's trailer as a site for policing homosexuality, we are equally situated in the tent that Jack and Ennis share; if we share Alma's apartment and her sense of heartbreak at the sight of her husband's homosexual desire, we also share Jack and Ennis's alley where that desire expresses itself passionately. To claim that what Lee is doing is aligning his audience with Aguirre and Alma, or even with Jack as a sexual predator, is to misread the way that we are made to encounter and experience very different spheres. We are forced, in other words, to share space with Ennis and Jack as well as with Aguirre and Alma.

As energizing to the plot as this kind of shuttling between alienation and intimacy might be, it is not, in itself, an expression of any kind of vanguard sensibility. After all, the kind of idyllic love affair between Ennis and Jack in the sphere of Brokeback Mountain is not radically new, nor is the kind of overbearing, homophobic town sphere that Aguirre represents in Riverton, Wyoming. What is radically new is the way Lee works diligently to give both spheres a chance to stake their claims as authentic versions of the frontier. On Brokeback, Jack and Ennis ride horses, tend sheep, hunt, fish, and camp, all of which Lee overtly codes as representing the frontier, and yet subtending all these frontier activities is not rugged manhood but queer pleasure. Likewise, Riverton has none of the trappings of some nostalgic version of the frontier and is, instead, full of depressing grocery stores, grimy apartments, and dilapidated pickup trucks. It is, nevertheless, the core of the action from which the entire narrative unfolds—the place of social reality rather than some idyllic and fleeting utopia, and we read it, therefore, as a version of the "real" frontier to which Ennis and Jack must return. Even if we want to share Jack's hazy pipedream of "getting a little place" with Ennis and disdain Riverton's violent homophobia that quashes such a dream, we likewise understand Riverton as the space of Ennis's fraught marriage and his strained relationship to his children. If Brokeback represents the tragedy of dashed dreams, in other words, then Riverton represents the tragedy of broken families. What makes this film important, therefore, is the way that Lee uses the symbols of vision—a mirror, binoculars, a window—to suggest how distant these frontier worlds are from each other, even as he presents both of them as embodiments of the frontier.

Brokeback Mountain is really a western that contains a clutch of different frontiers, and while Lee's manipulation of symbols of vision works to distance these frontiers from each other, it is his attention to the visuals involving food—and particularly those involving meat—that dramatizes the differences between these versions of the frontier. As a symbol, meat might seem a strange object on which to hang a reading of the film, but its connection to the ecology of the frontier is deep and pervasive. The notions of the hunt, of sustaining oneself from the land, and of the relationship between man and animal are some of the most important tropes of the traditional frontier, stretching back at least as far as James Fenimore Cooper's revealingly titled Leatherstocking novel *Deerslayer* (1841). In *Brokeback Mountain*, this same notion of hunting and living off of the land is narratively broached when Ennis is charged with leading mules carrying supplies up the mountain. It is a quintessential frontier image, but one that is disrupted by another, equally quintessential frontier image when he confronts a bear. In this scene, when Ennis comes across the animal at a stream crossing, it rears and roars, causing the mules to be spooked and run away, thus eliminating most of Ennis and Jack's supplies. When Ennis returns to the camp, he suggests that the two of them must hunt to sustain themselves, and we then cut to Ennis sighting an elk along his rifle and killing it.

What happens next is startling, for rather than just show Jack and Ennis eating the food by firelight, which Lee does, he also pictures row upon row of elk meat drying on a homemade rack by the fire pit at the camp. This is startling because it not only registers the way Jack and Ennis plan to use every bit of the elk after their initial meal, rather than wasting it, but also because it arrests one's vision with its excessiveness. Lee clearly wants the drying meat to signal the men's ability to survive by their wits and skills on the frontier, but it is a symbol that seems overly deliberate. If Lee merely meant to signify the men's ability to live off the land, or if he somehow wanted to make an argument about their difference from previous iterations of the profligate frontiersman squandering the resources of the wild frontier, then he might have signaled this in a more condensed fashion. By contrast, this symbol's excessiveness makes the spectator hyperaware of its significance as a symbol.

In the scene by the fire that night, what is significant about this drying elk becomes clear. The two men share their kill, but their dialogue turns to the past, to Jack's troubled history with his father, and to Ennis's orphaned childhood. Framed by the drying elk meat, and in some sense by the way it reads as an excessive symbol of frontier machismo, the two men not only share sustenance, but they also share sympathetic personal stories about their upbringing. The scene is thus ironic, for in the midst of such excessive gesturing to a traditional form of frontier masculinity, the film also points to the initial moment of Ennis and Jack's falling in love with each other. Jack even remarks on Ennis's garrulousness, particularly since Ennis has been and will continue to be the taciturn version of the frontiersman for the rest of the film. It is a breakthrough scene, in other words, but what Lee does by using the prop of the elk is to signal his own breaking up of a trope of the western. The film creates a homology between the animal-as-food motif that runs through the western and the first moments of homosexual love and its community building that will undergird the rest of the scenes in this film. Meat, in this sense, becomes identical with "meet," thus disrupting the usual symbology of the frontier.

The film never returns to this rather primal scene of hunting elk and eating the kill on Brokeback, but it does revisit the symbol of meat in two other scenes that occur in the frontier town—at both men's Thanksgiving dinners—where meat again takes on symbolic value. At the beginning of Jack's Thanksgiving, which takes place not in Riverton but in Texas, the ultimate version of the frontier space, Lee provides a close-up of Jack basting a turkey. Like the scene of the drying elk, we are confronted, as viewers, with an almost hypercoded symbol. The turkey represents those values that American audiences associate with Thanksgiving—home, family, communion— but Lee's close attention to the meat itself deflates its symbolic value. The scene moves on to Jack's contretemps with his father-in-law about Jack's son watching television during dinner. In a choreographed scene of one-upmanship, the two patriarchs square off; Jack insisting that the television depicting a football game be turned off during dinner, and Jack's father-in-law insisting that watching football is important if, as he brays, "you want your son to grow up to be a man." The scene ends in a feel-good moment of Jack's turning off the television and his dressing down of his father-in-law for abusing Jack's hospitality. Yet this scene that centers on the Thanks-giving turkey—on meat—registers more than Jack's frustration with his father-in-law's social boorishness. In a bit of irony reminiscent of the scene on Brokeback, the Thanksgiving turkey becomes not a sign of familial bliss but one of familial dysfunction, of fathers-in-law who despise their sons-in-law, of quiet, mousy women steamrolled by their husbands, of spoiled children who would rather watch television than engage with the family. If the scene of the elk on the mountain undercuts the frontier mythology associated with the hunt, then this scene subverts the idea of the frontier town as a legitimate alternative to Brokeback's "perversion" by undercut-ting its notion of "family."

This idea is magnified in Ennis's Thanksgiving, which he spends with his ex-wife, Alma, his two daughters, and Alma's new husband, Monroe. This scene also begins with a tight focus on the Thanksgiving turkey, this time with Monroe hacking away at it with an electric knife. This shot ironically restages Ennis and Jack's rough-and-tumble hunting on Brokeback Moun-tain, substituting the ersatz quality of the frontier town for the natural, "real" quality of the country frontier. Lee undercuts this already destabi-lized image of frontier value even more when, after dinner, while Alma and Ennis wash the dishes at the sink, Alma all but accuses Ennis of homosexu-ality with "Jack Nasty." Ennis grabs her violently by the arm, threatens to knock her teeth out, and then flees the house, taking out his anger at being discovered by pulling a man out of a truck (who then beats him up). Again, as in Jack's scene, this moment is ironic for all of the ways that it presents the tropes associated with Thanksgiving—again, centered on the turkey—against the deep-seated resentments and emotional wreckage that defines the family. This scene also signifies familial dysfunction and a lack of com-munity, as well as Alma's deep-seated rage manifested as homophobia.

Taken together, these three scenes depicting meat define the competing spaces of the frontier that *Brokeback Mountain* envisions, as well as encode the different social values of those frontiers. Each scene ironically plays against its traditional frontier coding, and while the film definitely wants us to sympathize with the plight of Ennis and Jack on Brokeback and to free ourselves from the deadening pull of small town life, the film likewise sug-gests the interlocked qualities of these two frontier spaces. If Jack and Ennis share the idyllic frontier fantasy of Brokeback Mountain, where social pre-scriptions are shed, Lee also works to suggest how hard it is to mix this frontier fantasy with the alternate fantasy of the frontier in Riverton.

This double bind is perfectly captured in yet another scene involv-ing meat in the film, this time the image of the gutted sheep lying on the mountainside after Jack and Ennis's first passionate night in the tent. As a portent, it could not be clearer. Jack and Ennis have neglected their responsibility to Aguirre to guard the sheep, and a coyote has gotten into the herd. Ennis's reaction to the eviscerated sheep registers exactly the weight of social force that defines his relationship to his own queer desire. The kind of sexual "perversion" he has engaged in with Jack, his look conveys, is a dereliction of his social duty and will lead inevitably to his destruction. After all, the gutted carcass of the sheep—the sheep as a piece of meat—cannot fail to remind Ennis of the final image of meat that the film supplies for us. In a confessional moment, Ennis explains why he cannot get a place with Jack. In a voiceover, Ennis recalls how his father took him and his little brother to view the body of a frontiersman, who had "shacked up" with another man and was then beaten to death as a warning to others against engaging in any kind of homosexual behavior. Foreshadowing Jack's death, Lee tracks with the two young boys as they come across the body of the dead homosexual, and as spectators, we encounter the arresting visual image of a twisted, bloodied body, whose penis and testicles have been "pulled off." We are forced to look at yet another image of meat, this one linking quite explicitly to the gutted sheep as the meat we saw earlier, suggesting that no matter which space Jack and Ennis inhabit, their homosexuality will end violently in death. In the social reality that encompasses both Jack and Ennis on Brokeback and Jack and Ennis in the frontier town, homosexual passion is subject to a kind of deadly predation by the forces of intolerance.

The symbol of meat, therefore, both registers how different these frontier spaces of Brokeback and Riverton are and yet how tragically interlaced they are. One can no more escape to Brokeback Mountain permanently, the film demonstrates, than one can escape from the wreck of familial relations or the enslavement of capitalism. One might read this as a pessimistic vision of homosexuality on the frontier, or even as Lee's conservative predilections, suggesting that the queer double bind depicted in the movie is the inevitable fate of homosexuality on the frontier. What I want to argue, however, is that the movie's real achievement is the way it works assiduously to create two competing, mutually exclusive frontier spaces, legitimizes both of them, and then rather than elide one in favor of the other, keeps these frontier visions in tension. Unlike Bush's brush-clearing performance, which attempts to erase other, less repressive visions of the frontier in its imperialistic grandstanding, *Brokeback Mountain* creates a clearing where one can encounter competing, resistant frontiers in all of their messy interconnectedness. By drawing our attention to the way our vision is framed, Lee drives a wedge into a monolithic incarnation of the frontier. He then repeatedly invokes the frontier trope of meat to explore the dissonant social landscapes of his competing frontiers while suggesting, in sum, how mutually constructed and concomitantly produced they really are.

I want to conclude with the notion that *Brokeback Mountain* is not a revolutionary film. Its politics are centrist and safe, and even as Lee spools out the idea of a queer frontier, he ultimately reels it back in tightly. Yet, as we have seen in the plays we explored in the previous chapters, the film turns to the frontier not as a way of consolidating hegemonic power but rather of figuring alternative forms of empowerment even as it disfigures the kind of power politics utilized by Bush in his brush-clearing performance. Again, as with the previous performances we have encountered, the film likewise works to explore new aesthetic figurations by disfiguring the kind of encoding of the frontier as a space of hypermasculine imperialism that Bush's performance trades in. These two performances thus show the lengthy, complex, and mutually sustained legacies of pioneer performances we have encountered starting in Jacksonian America, continuing through the late nineteenth century, and inflecting our own moment at the dawn of the new millennium. While the end of the Bush presidency might seem to signal the end of this kind of conservative rehashing of a frontier defined by its repressive social politics, the American obsession with the frontier guarantees that this representation will appear again. Yet as much as this imperial frontier will, like Ennis's memory of frontier violence, shadow our future, it will likewise give rise to new visions of the frontier that will work politically and aesthetically to upstage and upend this repressive fantasy. Anticipating these future "border wars," while looking back over the various fields of battle I have been charting, one gets a full measure of how important the frontier has been in defining the aesthetic and social borders of an American nation, one that includes both Bush's Crawford Ranch and Lee's Brokeback Mountain.

NOTES

INTRODUCTION

1. Martin Ridge argues that Turner's "themes regarding American society and character as depicted in fiction, art, drama, and film have so effectively captured the American public's imagination and are now so deeply woven into the American consciousness that it may still be a part of the American mentality a century from now"; see Martin Ridge, "The Life of an Idea: The Significance of Frederick Jackson Turner's Frontier Thesis" in *Does the Frontier Experience Make America Exceptional?*, ed. Richard W. Etulain (Boston: Bedford/ St. Martin's, 1999) 75.

2. For more on the history of the World Columbian Exposition and its politics, see Alan Trachtenberg, *The Incorporation of America: Culture and Society in the Gilded Age* (New York: Hill and Wang, 1982) 13–32, and Robert W. Rydell, *All the World's a Fair: Visions of Empire at American International Expositions, 1876–1916* (Chicago: University of Chicago Press, 1987) 38–71.

3. Joy S. Kasson, *Buffalo Bill's Wild West: Celebrity, Memory, and Popular History* (New York: Farrar, Straus and Giroux, 2001) 114.

4. For more on the historical and ideological similarities between Roosevelt and Turner, see Richard Slotkin, *Gunfighter Nation: The Myth of the Frontier in Twentieth-Century America* (Norman: University of Oklahoma Press, 1992) 33.

5. Rosemarie K. Bank, "Representing History: Performing the Columbian Exposition," *Theatre Survey* 54:5 (December 2002): 601.

6. Frederick Jackson Turner, "The Significance of the Frontier in American History," in *The Frontier in American History* (New York: Dover, 1996) 3.

7. Richard White, *The Middle Ground: Indians, Empires, and Republics in the Great Lakes Region, 1650–1815* (Cambridge, UK: Cambridge University Press, 1991) ix-xvi, and Mary Louise Pratt, "Arts of the Contact Zone," *Profession* 91 (1991): 33–40.

8. For more on Turner, Manifest Destiny, and American imperial efforts after 1893, see Anders Stephanson, *Manifest Destiny: American Expansion and the Empire of Right* (New York: Hill and Wang, 1995) 75.

9. Paul Reddin, *Wild West Shows* (Urbana: University of Illinois Press, 1999) 61. See Philip J. Deloria, *Indians in Unexpected Places* (Lawrence: University Press of Kansas, 2004) for his assessment of how the Wild West "proved a far more effective popular vehicle than Turner's conference paper" because of its popular appeal and "linked lessons about empire, conquest, character, and social order" (62).

10. Richard White has also noted this same discrepancy, for if Turner's story was one of free land, the nonviolent occupation of a continent, and the hammering out of a truly "American" character, Buffalo Bill's was one of violent conquest, the antagonistic conquering of Native Americans who were on the land. "Turner took as his theme the conquest of nature; he considered savagery incidental. Buffalo Bill made the conquest of savages central; the conquest of nature was incidental." Yet, as White continues, both stories "taught the same lessons" of conquest and domination; see Richard White, "Frederick Jackson Turner and Buffalo Bill," in *The Frontier in American Culture*, ed. James R. Grossman (Berkeley: University of California Press, 1994) 11.

11. Several critics and historians have suggested that the Wild West provided a space—a Foucaultian heterotopia, to use Rosemarie K. Bank's term ("Representing" 591)—for subverting and enriching the show's depiction of Native Americans. Philip Deloria argues that Native Americans who traveled with the show, showing up backstage playing table tennis or learning to ride a bicycle, told a story about "Indian modernity," for "beneath all the mocking static ... such tales were first and foremost, Indian stories about Indian encounters with and actions on a modern world" (68; for a similar argument, see also Louis Warren's depiction of Indian performances in Wild West shows [194, 407]). Similarly, Rosemarie K. Bank argues that this attempt to privilege the racism involved in the Wild West merely creates another damaging binary about the show's real heterotopic possibilities (598), since working for the Wild West "offered reasonable pay, a chance to travel, and an opportunity to interact with a large variety of non-Indian people" (Kasson 163). In particular, if we look at the divergent politics of the Wild West and the Indian Bureau in the late nineteenth century, suggests L. G. Moses, we can see how the Wild West may have, indeed, benefited Indians. The Wild West portrayed the Indians as heroic, while in the hands of the Indian Bureau, these same Indians "became either barbarian[s] best forgotten or measure[s] of the progress made by worthy members of the Indian race. Thus, at the world's fair, the image of the vanishing Indian was set beside the aspiring Indian who, through the government's efforts on behalf of civilization, would presumably vanish one day into mainstream society" (149). This subordinated history needs to be told, but its reinterpolation into the history of the Wild West does not alter the ideological effect and political thrust of Cody's show, which may have propped up Native Americans but just as easily did so to make them worthy opponents, potent savages equal to the powerful frontiersman who inevitably, in the show's performative narrative, vanquished them. Moreover, while the Wild West afforded Native Americans, like Sitting Bull, opportunities at mobility—both economic and geographical—denied them on reservations, it also seemed to instruct them, as it did Sitting Bull, "not to challenge American authority. And, if Kicking Bear and Short Bull welcomed their release from the stockade," Deloria continues, "they were sentenced to the Wild West in order that they might suffer placelessness and anomie, learn to fear and respect America's might, and be renounced from any position of influence among their people" (71). Thus, both the performative narrative of the show and the economic and political realities of performing this narrative suggest that Cody created the situation for both representational and financial violence.

12. This critical and historical field has been assiduously worked over already. See the essays contained in Clyde A. Milner II, ed., *A New Significance: Re-envisioning the History of the American West* (New York: Oxford University Press, 1996). For more on the legacy of Buffalo Bill's Wild West, see Louis S. Warren, *Buffalo Bill's America: William Cody and the Wild West Show* (New York: Knopf, 2005) and Robert W. Rydell and Rob Kroes, *Buffalo Bill in Bologna: The Americanization of the World, 1869–1922* (Chicago: University of Chicago Press, 2005).

13. Michel Foucault, "Nietzsche, Genealogy, History," in *Language, Counter-Memory, Practice: Selected Essays and Interviews*, tr. Donald F. Bouchard and Sherry Simon, ed. Donald F. Bouchard (Ithaca, NY: Cornell University Press, 1977) 160.

14. See a review of her play in Chicago's *Sunday Inter Ocean*, 6 December 1891.

15. The reviewer for the *Baltimore Sun* noted on September 27, 1892, that her week's engagement at the Howard Auditorium would be her "last visit to Baltimore prior to a tour of England." For more on the Wild West in Europe, see Kasson, 65–93, as well as, more generally, Robert W. Rydell, *Buffalo Bill in Bologna: The Americanization of the World, 1869–1922* (Chicago: University of Chicago Press, 2005).

16. *Philadelphia Inquirer*, 28 October 1890.

17. *Wheeling Register*, 28 October 1891.

18. One of the attractions of the Wild West, in fact, was its ostensible "authenticity," the chance to see real Indians, real buffalo, and real frontier artifacts, such as Sitting Bull's cabin and the Deadwood Stagecoach, and one might argue that part of the legacy of the frontier in aesthetic representation, particularly in the late nineteenth century, is the way the frontier itself codes as a wellspring of the "real." See Alex Nemerov, "Doing the 'Old America': The Image of the American West, 1880–1920," in *The West as America: Reinterpreting Images of the Frontier, 1820–1920* (Washington, DC: Smithsonian Institution Press, 1991).

19. *Wheeling Register*, 28 October 1891.

20. On Mohawk's challenge to the boundaries of ethnicity and sexuality, see Roger A. Hall, *Performing the American Frontier, 1870–1906* (Cambridge, UK: Cambridge University Press, 2001) 157.

21. *Baltimore Sun*, 24 September 1892.

22. *Philadelphia Inquirer*, 4 October 1891.

23. *Philadelphia Inquirer*, 4 October 1891.

24. *Sunday Inter Ocean*, 6 December 1891.

25. This not only distinguishes Mohawk from Oakley, but it also differentiates Mohawk's performance from that other nineteenth-century cross-dressing celebrity, Adah Isaacs Menken. Menken, like Mohawk, also achieved a kind of titillating celebrity by cross-dressing, but while Menken constructed a kind of drag pleasure in the available, sensual female body by, in the climactic scene from *Mazeppa*, being lashed spread eagle in flesh-colored tights to the back of a horse, Mohawk purposely obscured her gender identity, and thus the sexual pleasure derived from that identity, by performing virile masculinity. If Menken's cross-dressing was mere pretense for a sanctioned striptease focused on the female body, Mohawk's ambiguous performance manufactured a distinctly different kind of spectacular pleasure—the pleasure of illicit visual consumption of the female form versus the pleasure of continuously obscured revelation of gender. For more on Menken, see Kim Marra, *Strange Duets: Impresarios and Actresses in the American Theatre, 1865–1914* (Iowa City: University of Iowa Press, 2006) 17–19.

26. Gowongo Mohawk and Charlie Charles, *Wep-Ton-No-Mah, The Indian Mail Carrier*, copyrighted 1892 (Rare Book and Manuscript Collection, Library of Congress) 2.

27. Patricia Nelson Limerick, *The Legacy of Conquest: The Unbroken Past of the American West* (New York: Norton, 1987) 21.

28. Donald Worster, *Under Western Skies: Nature and History in the American West* (New York: Oxford University Press, 1992) 11–12.

29. It is worth noting that this definition implicitly incorporates Slotkin's privileging of violence as a crucial aspect of frontier interaction while building on White's notion of the "middle ground" and Pratt's idea of the "contact zone" in its definition of a "zone of interpenetration," and thus nicely condenses a number of similarly oriented critiques; see

Howard Lamar and Leonard Thompson, eds., *The Frontier in History: North America and South America Compared* (New Haven, CT: Yale University Press, 1981) 7.

30. Limerick rightly notes that "[a]nytime one is tempted to refer to 'the Indian,' two considerations should hold off the temptation. First, one must remember the diversity of language, culture, and economy.... Second, one must keep in mind the variations in historical development. Tribes made contact with Euro-Americans at different times and under different circumstances.... Some tribes followed the course of clear, armed resistance; other allied themselves with the Euro-Americans, fighting together against a shared Indian enemy" (215–216).

31. Patricia Nelson Limerick, "The Adventures of the Frontier in the Twentieth Century," in James R. Grossman, ed., *The Frontier in American Culture* (Berkeley: University of California Press, 1994) 73. Limerick makes a similar maneuver in her "Disorientation and Reorientation: The American Landscape Discovered from the West," *The Journal of American History* 79:3, Discovering America: A Special Issue (December 1992), where she speaks of "white men" as the "people in power" while condemning "conventional studies" of the frontier for concentrating "wholeheartedly on the thinking of English-speaking, westward-moving, literate, record-keeping, middle- and upper-class, pre-twentieth century, white men" (1031, 1022).

32. Susan Lee Johnson, *Roaring Camp: The Social World of the California Gold Rush* (New York: Norton, 2000) 51.

33. Daniel Walker Howe offers a thorough exploration of the rise of Jacksonian democracy and, in particular, points to the way improvements in communications—what he calls the "communication revolution"—led both to these improvements and to the period's zeitgeist; see Daniel Walker Howe, *What Hath God Wrought?: The Transformation of America, 1815–1848* (New York: Oxford University Press, 2007)

34. Howe's argument for the primacy of the "communications revolution" differs from that of Charles Sellers's, who makes a case for the importance of the generation of the free market during the Age of Jackson, the "market revolution," as he calls it. Yet, it seems that looking at the period through both lenses simultaneously, as I want to do, allows us to see both the economic foundations of Jacksonian democracy and the ways that economic base paved the way for revolutionizing the communication process in the United States, particularly if we consider the theater as being one of the key organs of communication in the nineteenth century. See Charles Sellers, *The Market Revolution: Jacksonian America, 1815–1846* (New York: Oxford University Press, 1994).

35. Bruce A. McConachie, *Melodramatic Formations: American Theatre and Society, 1820–1870* (Iowa City: University of Iowa Press, 1992) 31–32.

36. Jeffrey H. Richards, *Drama, Theatre, and Identity in the American New Republic* (Cambridge, UK: Cambridge University Press, 2005) 31. For more on the prerevolutionary prejudice against the theater in the colonies for being British and for being too extravagant for the nascent colonial economy, see Odai Johnson, *Absence and Memory in Colonial American Theatre: Fiorelli's Plasters* (New York: Palgrave Macmillan, 2006) 73–91, and Tice L. Miller, *Entertaining the Nation: American Drama in the Eighteenth and Nineteenth Centuries* (Carbondale: University of Southern Illinois Press, 2007) 1–3.

37. Heather S. Nathans, *Early National Theatre from the Revolution to Thomas Jefferson: Into the Hands of the People.* (Cambridge, UK: Cambridge University Press, 2003) 37.

38. Robert C. Allen, *Horrible Prettiness: Burlesque and American Culture* (Chapel Hill: University of North Carolina Press, 1991) 51.

39. One tangible way that we can chart this is by noting the groundswell of interest in the 1830s and 1840s with playwriting contests looking for original work on native themes (Allen 82).

40. Alexis de Tocqueville, *Democracy in America*, tr. George Lawrence, ed. J. P. Mayer (New York: Harper Collins, 1969) 489.

41. See Lawrence Levine, *Highbrow/Lowbrow: The Emergence of Cultural Hierarchy in America* (Cambridge, MA: Harvard University Press, 1990), 26–27

42. Philip J. Deloria, *Playing Indian* (New Haven, CT: Yale University Press, 1998) 5–6.

43. Gordon M. Sayre, *The Indian Chief as Tragic Hero* (Chapel Hill: University of North Carolina Press, 2005) 2–6.

44. David Grimsted, *Melodrama Unveiled: American Theater and Culture, 1800–1850* (Berkeley: University of California Press, 1987) 171–205.

45. In fact, for all of the critical energy devoted to New Western History since the 1970s, there has been only one assessment of frontier representation, Roger Hall's *Performing the Frontier*, which for all of its historical detailing and archival depth, tells a rather univocal story about the theater as the mouthpiece for Manifest Destiny. While other critics have assessed specific frontier echoes in nineteenth-century performance—Indian plays, tragic mulatta plays, melodramas of race, freak shows, blackface minstrelsy—they have tended to echo Hall's idea of frontier performance as an essentially hegemonic enterprise. See the chapters that follow for a more detailed examination of these critics.

46. These definitions are, respectively, Limerick's (35), Worster's ("New West" 93), and Johnson's (12).

47. For more on this notion of a constructed West, see Leo Marx's familiar, but nevertheless useful *The Machine in the Garden: Technology and the Pastoral Ideal in America* (Oxford, UK: Oxford University Press, 1964). For a more recent account that suggests the connections between industrialism, environmentalism, and the frontier, see William Cronon's *Nature's Metropolis: Chicago and the Great West* (New York: Norton, 1991) and *Under an Open Sky: Rethinking America's Western Past* (New York: Norton, 1994). For a more overarching view, see Raymond Williams's classic, *The City and the Country* (Oxford, UK: Oxford University Press, 1975).

CHAPTER 1

1. In the introduction to his book on makeup, Maurice Hageman recalls that before the advent of grease paint, actors like Forrest who played "Indians, gypsies, [and] mulattoes" darkened up their faces not with burnt cork, which was used for portraying "negroes," but with "[b]urnt umber or balsamenia, commonly called '*Bollamenia*' by professionals." *Hageman's Make-Up Book* (Chicago: Dramatic Publishing Company, 1898), 6.

2. Walt Whitman, "The Gladiator—Mr. Forrest—Acting" (1846), in *The American Theatre as Seen by Its Critics, 1752–1934*, eds. Montrose J. Moses and John Mason Brown (New York: W. W. Norton, 1934), 69.

3. George William Curtis, the editor of *Harper's*, critiqued Forrest's acting style for its "rant, roar, and rigmarole." Qtd. in Lawrence Levine, *Highbrow/Lowbrow: The Emergence of Cultural Hierarchy in America* (Cambridge, MA: Harvard University Press, 1990), 57.

4. Larzer Ziff, *Writing in the New Nation: Prose, Print, and Politics in the Early United States* (New Haven, CT: Yale University Press, 1991), 105.

5. Michael Warner, *The Letters of the Republic: Publication and the Public Sphere in Eighteenth-Century America* (Cambridge, MA: Harvard University Press, 1990), 61.

6. Christopher Looby, *Voicing America: Language, Literary Form, and the Origins of the United States* (Chicago: University of Chicago Press, 1996), 3.

7. John A. Schutz and Douglas Adair, eds. *The Spur of Fame: Dialogues of John Adams and Benjamin Rush, 1805–1813* (San Marino, CA: Huntington Library, 1966), 42–43.

8. See Kenneth Cmiel, *Democratic Eloquence: The Fight over Popular Speech in Nineteenth-Century America* (New York: William Morrow, 1990); Jay Fliegelman, *Declaring Independence: Jefferson, Natural Language, and the Culture of Performance* (Palo Alto, CA: Stanford University Press, 1993); Thomas Gustafson, *Representative Words: Politics, Literature,*

and the American Language, 1776–1865 (Cambridge, UK: Cambridge University Press, 1992); Michael P. Kramer, *Imagining Language in America: From the Revolution to the Civil War* (Princeton, NJ: Princeton University Press, 1992); and James Perrin Warren, *Culture of Eloquence: Oratory and Reform in Antebellum America* (University Park: Pennsylvania State University Press, 1999).

9. I take the last part of Jay Fliegelman's suggestive, but ultimately unsubstantiated, subtitle to his work—*Declaring Independence: Jefferson, Natural Language, and the Culture of Performance*—as the exception that proves the rule: None of these critics spend much time treating performance qua performance.

10. Tending to Forrest's performance thus grounds Philip J. Deloria's trenchant argument that "playing Indian" allowed early Americans to "imagine and perform an identity of revolution," *Playing Indian* (New Haven, CT: Yale University Press, 1998) 14, by mapping out exactly how that playing Indian was performed and of what that identity of revolution entailed.

11. See Sandra M. Gustafson, *Eloquence Is Power: Orality and Performance in Early America* (Chapel Hill: University of North Carolina Press, 2000) and her discussion of the role the Native American played in reconditioning and recoding oratory in the early national period, 8, 118.

12. Theresa Strouth Gaul, " 'The Genuine Indian Who Was Brought upon the Stage': Edwin Forrest's Metamora and White Audiences," *Arizona Quarterly* 56:1 (Spring 2000): 1.

13. Renato Rosaldo, "Imperialist Nostalgia," *Representations* 26 (Special Issue: Memory and Counter-Memory) (Spring 1989): 108.

14. Developing this idea, numerous modern critics have suggested that the elegiac mode of imperialist nostalgia in these plays eased white guilt about the genocidal eradication of a people. See Marilyn J. Anderson, "The Image of the Indian in American Drama During the Jacksonian Era, 1829–1845," *Journal of American Culture* 1:4 (Winter 1978): 800; Shari M. Huhndorf, *Going Native: Indians in the American Cultural Imagination* (Ithaca, NY: Cornell University Press, 2001) 5; and Susan Scheckel, *The Insistence of the Indian: Race and Nationalism in Nineteenth-Century American Culture* (Princeton, NJ: Princeton University Press, 1998) 5–13. Even James Nelson Barker's frontier operetta, *The Indian Princess* (1808), which created different characterizations of Indians for white audiences—the nefarious Grimosco and Miami versus the sympathetic but weak Powhatan—still pushes the Indian to the margins at the end of the play as the march of civilization continues. For more on Barker's complex, but nonetheless imperialist, dramaturgy, see Jeffrey H. Richards, *Drama, Theatre, and Identity in the American New Republic* (Cambridge, UK: Cambridge University Press, 2005) 181.

15. Werner Sollors, *Beyond Ethnicity: Consent and Descent in American Culture* (New York: Oxford University Press, 1986) 124.

16. Gordon M. Sayre, *The Indian Chief as Tragic Hero* (Chapel Hill: University of North Carolina Press, 2009) 8.

17. Lauren Berlant defines the national symbolic as "the order of discursive practices whose reign within a national space produces, and also refers to, the 'law' in which the accident of birth within a geographic/political boundary transforms individuals into subjects of a collectively-held history. Its traditional icons, its metaphors, its heroes, its rituals, and its narratives provide an alphabet for a collective consciousness or national subjectivity; through the National Symbolic the historical nation aspires to achieve the inevitability of the status of natural law, a birthright. This pseudo-genetic condition not only affects profoundly the citizen's subjective experience of her/his political rights, but also of civil life, private life, the life of the body itself." *The Anatomy of National Fantasy: Hawthorne, Utopia, and Everyday Life* (Chicago: University of Chicago Press, 1991) 20.

18. Jill Lepore, *The Name of War: King Philip's War and the Origins of American Identity* (New York: Vintage, 2001) 191.

19. In Don Wilmeth's extensive survey of the figure of the Indian on the American stage, he finds that "[n]o other actor was as successful essaying an Indian [as Forrest was], although John McCullough, D. H. Harkins, and a few others, with very limited success, attempted Metamora after Forrest." "Noble or Ruthless Savage?: The American Indian on Stage and in the Drama," *Journal of American Drama and Theatre* 1 (Spring 1989): 49.

20. William Rounseville Alger, *Life of Edwin Forrest, The American Tragedian*, Volume 1 (Philadelphia: J. B. Lippincott, 1877) 245.

21. Gabriel Harrison, *Edwin Forrest: The Actor and the Man* (Brooklyn, NY: N.V., 1889) 39.

22. See Nan Johnson, "The Popularization of Nineteenth-Century Rhetoric: Elocution and the Private Learner," in *Oratorical Culture in Nineteenth-Century America: Transformations in the Theory and Practice of Rhetoric*, eds. Gregory Clark and S. Michael Halloran (Carbondale: Southern Illinois University Press, 1993) 144.

23. Thomas Sherdian, *A Course of Lectures on Elocution* (London: W. Strahan, 1762) x. See also James Burgh, who was totally surprised that any actor could "bring out ... *strong and pathetic* expressions ... in [a] cold and *un-animated* ... manner." *The Art of Speaking* (Danbury, CT: Printed for Edmund and Ephram Washburn, 1795) 15.

24. As Merritt Caldwell, a prominent elocutionist, suggested, the study and practice of elocution provides "a theoretical knowledge ... of natural language" that insures that "the learner [is] sufficiently in possession of all his natural peculiarities." Yet this promotion of a "natural language" disguises its policing power by insisting on its "naturalness," for the object of elocution, continues Caldwell, is "to refine and perfect nature; not to pervert it" (Qtd. Johnson 144–145).

25. Eric Cheyfitz, *The Poetics of Imperialism: Translation and Colonization from* The Tempest *to* Tarzan (New York: Oxford University Press, 1991) xx.

26. Benjamin Rush, "Of the Mode of Education Proper in a Republic" (1798), in *The Selected Writings of Benjamin Rush*, ed. Dagobert D. Runes (New York: Philosophical Library, 1947), 93–94.

27. Gilbert Austin's *Chironomia; or a Treatise on Rhetorical Delivery* (London: W. Bulmer, and Co., 1806) draws on and expands John Bulwer's *Chironomia; or, The art of manual rhetoricke*, a "fraternal treatise," as Joseph R. Roach calls it, with *Chirologia: or, the Natural Languages of the Hand* published together with *Chironomia* in 1644, works that systematically explore the ways the hands could be used to communicate the passions. Austin was an amateur chemist and member of the Royal Irish Academy, and as such, he knew Antoine Lavoisier, the father of modern chemistry, and, more importantly, Lavoisier's famous *Methods of Chemical Nomenclature* (1787), which outlines the method and meaning of chemical terms. It is not incredible to suggest that *Chironomia* is a kind of scientific textbook of the passions, treating them empirically as Lavoisier treats chemical elements and processes. For more on Bulwer and Austin's treatment of the "rhetoric of the passions," see Joseph R. Roach, *The Player's Passion: Studies in the Science of Acting* (Ann Arbor: University of Michigan Press, 1985) 33–34.

28. For a more detailed enumeration of these tropes, see Jonas Barish's seminal work, *The Antitheatrical Prejudice* (Berkeley: University of California Press, 1981).

29. James Rees, *The Life of Edwin Forrest: With Reminiscences and Personal Recollections* (Philadelphia: T. B. Peterson, 1874) 173–174.

30. Forrest studied the precepts of the elocution revolution with teachers like Lemuel G. White, who was a pupil of the European actor James Fennell. For more on Forrest's relationship to elocutionists, see Alfred Ayres, *Acting and Actors, Elocution and Elocutionists: A Book About Theater Folk and Theater Art* (New York: D. Appleton, 1894) 31, and Unknown Author, *The History of Edwin Forrest, The Celebrated American Tragedian, From*

His Childhood to His Present Elevated Station as a Performer (New York: Published at No. 29 Ann Street, 1837), Harvard Theatre Collection, Houghton Library, 7.

31. Philip Fisher, *The Vehement Passions* (Princeton, NJ: Princeton University Press, 2002) 2.

32. Intriguingly, Forrest had an English translation of Descartes's work in his personal library, a London edition from 1650 called *The Passions of the Sowle*. See Joseph Sabin, Comp. *Catalogue of the Library of Edwin Forrest* (Philadelphia: Collins, 1863) 127.

33. As noted earlier, Indians were seen as wellsprings of rhetorical power starting in the late eighteenth century (Gustafson 8, 118), and thus Forrest's "wonder" at the Indian's rhetorical power is not without precedents. However, Forrest's attempts to articulate his own version of Americanness through the Indian and the aesthetic choices and consequences precipitating out from this event outstripped how previous versions of Indian rhetoric were treated.

34. Advertising the first of many playwriting competitions in the November 28, 1828, *New York Courier*, Forrest had issued a call for "the best tragedy, in five acts, of which the hero, or principal character, shall be an aboriginal of this country." From the fourteen submissions for the competition, Stone's *Metamora* was chosen, and by late December, Forrest was playing the Indian chieftain in New York City: see *New York Courier*, 28 November 1828.

35. John Augustus Stone, *Metamora; or, The Last of the Wampanoags* in *Staging the Nation: Plays from the American Theater, 1787–1909*, ed. Don B. Wilmeth (Boston: Bedford, 1998) 77–78.

36. Jeffrey D. Mason also notes the patriotic overtones of this soliloquy, pointing out its echoing of Patrick Henry; see *Melodrama and the Myth of America* (Bloomington: Indiana University Press, 1993) 44.

37. Tyler Ansbinder, *Five Points: The 19th-Century New York City Neighborhood That Invented Tap Dance, Stole Elections, and Became the World's Most Notorious Slum* (New York: Free Press, 2001) 14–37.

38. Sollors's idea benefits from that of Arnold Krupat, who argues that once the idea of the noble savage made its way across the ocean, "it became attractive (at least in the east) to think of Indians as standing in for America's missing feudal past, to hear their chants as 'poetic' (rather than satanic, or as gibberish), finally, as constituting a 'literature' it only remained to establish in writing." "Identity and Difference in the Criticism of Native American Literature." *Diacritics* 13:2 (Summer 1983): 2.

39. Jeffrey D. Mason notes that, while Forrest performed in Charleston on March 2, and 5, 1831, there is no record of his performing in Augusta until 1847. "The tale," he admits, "may be either inaccurately dated or even apocryphal" (204, n. 24). However, given that Murdoch was in Georgia at the same time as Forrest and his recollection is quite detailed, it is possible, even probable, that Forrest experienced such a reception in Georgia.

40. James E. Murdoch, *The Stage, or, Recollections of Actors and Acting* (Philadelphia: J. M. Stoddart, 1880) 298–299.

41. Jeffrey H. Richards notes how a delegation of Cherokee chiefs had attended the John Street Theatre in New York in 1767 (9).

42. George C. D. ODell, *Annals of the New York Stage*, Volume 3: 1821–1834 (New York: Columbia University Press, 1928) 18.

43. Rosemarie K. Bank, *Theatre Culture in America, 1825–1860* (Cambridge, UK: Cambridge University Press, 1997) 64.

44. While we may not consider Penobscots actors in the sense that Forrest was an actor in a staged theatrical text, it would be "folly," argues Deloria, "to imagine that white Americans blissfully used Indianness to tangle with their ideological dilemmas while native people stood idly by, exerting no influence over the resulting images. Throughout a long history of Indian play, native people have been present at the margins, insinuating their way into

Euro-American discourse, often attempting to nudge notions of Indianness in directions they found useful. As the nineteenth and twentieth centuries unfolded, increasing numbers of Indians participated in white people's Indian play, assisting, confirming, co-opting, challenging, and legitimating the performative tradition of aboriginal American identity" (8). For more on the sophistication of Indian performance, see Louis S. Warren, *Buffalo Bill's America: William Cody and the Wild West Show* (New York: Alfred A. Knopf, 2005) 194–195.

45. See Pauleena MacDougall, *The Penobscot Dance of Resistance: Tradition in the History of a People* (Durham: University of New Hampshire Press, 2004) 68, 107

46. Philip J. Deloria, *Indians in Unexpected Places* (Lawrence: University Press of Kansas, 2006) 57.

47. Rosemarie K. Bank describes the way that John Ross, the famous Cherokee chieftain and political figure, refuted the newspaper accounts of his attendance at the National Theatre in Washington, D.C., in 1836 because he did not want his image as Indian to be manipulated by white audiences. She highlights how cognizant native populations were of how their theater attendance could be maneuvered for political ends, a point I am extending to the Penobscots as well (67–68). For more on this event, see Sayre, 16.

48. See Michael Paul Rogin, *Fathers and Children: Andrew Jackson and the Subjugation of the American Indian* (New York: Alfred Knopf, 1975).

CHAPTER 2

1. Nelson F. Adkins, "James Kirke Paulding's *Lion of the West*," *American Literature* 3:3 (November 1931): 249.

2. Paulding's biographer, Amos Herold, and his son William I. Paulding do not make any of the claims about *The Lion of the West* that Adkins does. Consult Amos Lee Herold, *James Kirke Paulding, Versatile American* (New York: Columbia University Press, 1926) and William I. Paulding, *Literary Life of James K. Paulding* (New York: Scribner and Co., 1867).

3. Tidwell's copy of the play was the one submitted to the Lord Chamberlain's Office for approval before its European premiere at the Theatre Royal, Covent Garden in 1833.

4. James Kirke Paulding, *The Lion of the West*, ed. James N. Tidwell (Palo Alto, CA: Stanford University Press, 1954) 7. All quotations from the play use this edition's pagination.

5. Larry J. Reynolds, *James Kirke Paulding* (Boston: Twayne Publishing, 1984) and Lorman Ratner, *James Kirke Paulding: The Last Republican* (Westport, CT: Greenwood, 1992).

6. Tice L. Miller, *Entertaining the Nation: American Drama in the Eighteenth and Nineteenth Centuries* (Carbondale: University of Southern Illinois Press, 2007) 49.

7. Francis Hodge, *Yankee Theatre: The Image of America on the Stage, 1825–1850* (Austin: University of Texas Press, 1964) 239.

8. Rosemarie K. Bank, *Theatre Culture in America, 1825–1860* (Cambridge, UK: Cambridge University Press, 1997) 39.

9. Raymond Williams, *Marxism and Literature* (New York: Oxford University Press, 1977) 135, 133–134.

10. See David Grimsted, *Melodrama Unveiled: American Theatre and Culture, 1800–1850* (Berkeley: University of California Press, 1987) and Peter Brooks, *The Melodramatic Imagination: Balzac, Henry James, and the Mode of Excess* (New Haven, CT: Yale University Press, 1976).

11. One example of his interest in natural wonders can be found in his experimental long poem, *The Backwoodsman* (Philadelphia: M. Thomas, 1818), where he depicts a "wild romantic scene" of the Hudson River valley set off by a "sea of mingling hills" and the "winding," "majestic" Hudson (30), a *locus classicus* for several important works by later members of the Hudson River School, such as Robert Havell, Jr.'s *West Point from Fort*

Putnams (ca. 1850) and John Ferguson Weir's *View of the Highlands from West Point* (1862). Coupled with this scene of tempestuous beauty, however, Paulding provides an eagle that surveys the landscape, resting in his "high abode" and "defying the World's accumulated shock." In the preface to the poem, Paulding states that his object "was to indicate to the youthful writers of his native country, the rich poetic resources with which it abounds, as well as to call their attention *home*, for the means of attaining novelty of subject, if not to originality in style or sentiment" (6). To call home the attention of the native artist is the purpose for Paulding's writing this poetic "experiment," and his eagle thus serves dual purposes, calling attention to the landscape but also emphasizing its Americanness.

12. Edgar Allan Poe, Review in *Southern Literary Messenger* 2 (April 1836): 338.
13. For more on the dominance of melodrama, see Jeffrey D. Mason, *Melodrama and the Myth of America* (Bloomington: Indiana University Press, 1993) 15.
14. Rosemarie K. Bank, *Theatre Culture in America, 1825–1860* (Cambridge, UK: Cambridge University Press, 1997) 111.
15. Daniel Gerould, "Russian Formalist Theories of Melodrama" *Journal of American Culture* 1:1 (Spring 1978): 164. See Peter Brooks for his description of Denis Diderot's *drame* in relation to the charting of the development of classical melodrama (14).
16. Jeffrey D. Mason makes a parallel point about melodrama, stressing its capacity to focus our attention, at various moments along a cultural genealogy, on a range of "villains," both domestic and foreign, aristocratic and working class, white and black or "aboriginal;" see *Melodrama and the Myth of America* (Bloomington: Indiana University Press, 1993) 16.
17. Matthew S. Buckley, "Refugee Theatre: Melodrama and Modernity's Loss," *Theatre Journal* 61:2 (May 2009): 181.
18. Carolyn Williams, "Moving Pictures: George Eliot and Melodrama," in *Compassion: The Culture and Politics of an Emotion*, ed. Lauren Berlant (New York: Routledge, 2004) 110.
19. See David Grimsted for a thorough articulation of how, as he states, "[v]irtue and the heroine stood almost indistinguishable at the center of melodrama, the one a personification of the other" (172).
20. *The New-York Mirror* applauded the "new petit comedy," noting that it "was received by a numerous audience with decided marks of approbation." It went on to congratulate Hackett for his portrayal of Nimrod Wildfire, calling him an "able and very successful representative, who kept the house in a row by his comical and characteristic narrations" (30 April 1831). Constance Rourke, in her seminal *American Humor: A Study of National Character* (New York: Harcourt, Brace and Company, 1931), noted that Nimrod Wildfire's "reception in New York was uproarious.... [H]is eccentricities were considered not only western but American, and he was warmly applauded therefore" (71). Rourke actually conflates the notion of western and America in her consideration of Wildfire.
21. The play is summarized in *The Morning Courier and New-York Enquirer*, 27 April 1831.
22. This summary of Stone's version of the play appears in Arthur Hobson Quinn's *A History of the American Drama: From the Beginning to the Civil War* (New York: Harper and Brothers, 1923): 293–294.
23. Bruce McConachie, *Melodramatic Formations: American Theatre and Society, 1820–1870* (Iowa City: Iowa University Press, 1992) 68.
24. Jeffrey Mason suggests that the Manichean vision of melodrama contributed to melodrama's bourgeois appeal (16–17), and David Grimsted mentions that melodrama's basic plot structure "bore the impress of democratic society. Love was the great emotion experienced by all classes, the great leveler that equalized 'the prince's palace with the cottage, and the noble with the shepherd.' ... [T]he theme was almost exactly the same: the victory of the forces of morality, social restraint and domesticity over what was dark, passionate, and anti-social" (220).

25. Gary A. Richardson, "Plays and Playwrights: 1800–1865," in *The Cambridge History of American Theatre: Volume 1, Beginnings to 1870*, eds. Don B. Wilmeth and Christopher Bigsby (Cambridge, UK: Cambridge University Press, 1998) 260.

26. Rosemarie K. Bank argues that the frontier characterization of Wildfire was "employed to alleviate the rectitude of more genteel frontier heroes" throughout the antebellum period (72), which shows how popular this kind of frontier characterization was, as well as how vital a character like Wildfire was for challenging and retooling the melodramatic imagination.

27. Robert B. Heilman, *Tragedy and Melodrama* (Seattle: University of Washington Press, 1968) 85.

28. James Kirke Paulding, "The American Drama," *American Quarterly Review* 2 (June 1827): 341.

29. James Kirke Paulding, "National Literature," revised in *Salmagundi, Second Series* (1835) (New York: AMS Press) 2:266. Entitled "The Wreck of Genius" in *Salmagundi, Second Series* (1819–1820) 3:264–288.

30. René Descartes, *Les Passions de l'aime* in *Ouevres et Lettres* (Paris: Libraire Gallimard, 1953) 728. The original French is: *"une subite surprise de l'âme, qui fait qu'elle se parte à considérer avec attention les objets qui lui semblant rares et extraordinaires."* The translations above are mine.

31. *"par le mouvement des espirits qui sont disposés par cette impression à tendre avec grande force vers l'endroit du cerveau où elle est pour l'y fortifier et conserver"*

32. *"fait que tout le corps demeure immobile comme une statue, et qu'on ne peut apercevoir de l'objet que la première face qui s'est présentée, ni par conséquent en acquérir une plus particulière connaissance."*

33. Philip Fisher, *Wonder, the Rainbow, and the Aesthetics of Rare Experiences* (Cambridge, MA: Harvard University Press, 1998) 42.

34. Alan Wallach, "Thomas Cole: Landscape and the Course of Empire," in *Thomas Cole: Landscape into History*, ed. William H. Truettner and Alan Wallach (New Haven, CT: Yale University Press, 1994) 29.

35. Edmund Burke, *A Philosophical Enquiry into the Origins of Our Ideas of the Sublime and Beautiful*, in *A Philosophical Enquiry into the Sublime and Beautiful and Other Pre-Revolutionary Writings*, ed. David Womersley (London: Penguin, 1998) 86.

36. See Barbara Novak's now classic description of this phenomenon in the landscape painting of the Hudson River School—particularly Thomas Cole, who was a contemporary of James Kirke Paulding—in *Nature and Culture: American Landscape and Painting, 1825–1875* (Oxford, UK: Oxford University Press, 1980) 29–40.

37. See Tom Furniss, *Edmund Burke's Aesthetic Ideology: Language, Gender, and Political Economy* (Cambridge, UK: Cambridge University Press, 1993) 1–2, 20–21; Frances Ferguson, "Legislating the Sublime," in *Studies in Eighteenth-Century British Art and Aesthetics*, ed. Ralph Cohen (Berkeley: University of California Press, 1985) 128–147; and C. B. Macpherson, *Burke* (Oxford, UK: Oxford University Press, 1980) 5.

38. *"on peut dire en particulier de l'admiration qu'elle est utile en ce qu'elle fait que nous apprenons et retenons en notre mémoire les choses que nous avons auparavant ignorées; car nous n'admirons que ce qui nous paraît rare et extraordinaire, et rien ne nous peut paraître tel que pour ce que nous l'avons ignoré, ou même aussi on pour ce qu'il est différent des choses que nous avons sues; car c'est une différence qui fait qu'on le nomme extraordinaire."*

39. Even as the great American artist Thomas Cole immortalized Niagara Falls in "A Distant View of the Falls of Niagara," the falls themselves became an immensely successful tourist site with as many as 60,000 tourists coming each year in the 1820s. Responding to the artist's images and gift books in the early nineteenth century and utilizing the newly completed Erie Canal in 1825, "a new set of curiosity-seekers descended on Niagara. Even

travelers who went west in search of fertile lands and new opportunities took time out to view Niagara. In the 1800s, American travelers on the roads leading westward could be assured of encountering fellow Americans on pilgrimages to the Falls. Visiting Niagara Falls became a primary goal of travel in North America;" see William Irwin, *The New Niagara: Tourism, Technology, and the Landscape of Niagara Falls, 1776–1917* (University Park: Pennsylvania State University Press, 1996) xix.

40. Martin Meisel, "Speaking Pictures," in *Melodrama*, ed. Daniel Gerould (New York: New York Literary Forum, 1980) 7: 54.

41. The relationship between painting and drama is addressed and expounded on in relation to French melodrama in Denis Diderot's two early texts *Entretiens sur le fils naturel* (1757) and the *Discours de la poesie* (1758), where, as Michael Fried has suggested, he "called for the development of a new stage dramaturgy that would find in painting, or in certain exemplary paintings, the inspiration for a more convincing representation of action than any provided by the theater of his time." To achieve this new stage dramaturgy, argued Diderot, meant seeking stage tableaux, "which if properly managed he believed were capable of moving an audience to the depth of their collective being;" see *Absorption and Theatricality: Painting and Beholder in the Age of Diderot* (Chicago: University of Chicago Press, 1980) 77–78.

42. Rosemarie K. Bank, "Mrs. Trollope Visits the Theatre: Cultural Diplomacy and Historical Appropriation," *Journal of American Drama and Theatre* 5:3 (Fall 1993): 16.

43. Francis Milton Trollope, *Domestic Manners of the Americans* (London: Whittaker, Treacher, and Co., 1832) 25.

44. All of James Kirke Paulding's quotations about the Mississippi come from this biography by his son and use its pagination.

45. James Kirke Paulding, Letter to Lewis J. Cist, January 16, 1837, in *The Letters of James Kirke Paulding*, ed. Ralph M. Aderman (Madison: University of Wisconsin Press, 1962) 190.

46. James Kirke Paulding, Letter to Daniel Drake, January 1, 1835, in *The Letters of James Kirke Paulding*, ed. Ralph M. Aderman (Madison: University of Wisconsin Press, 1962) 158–159.

47. Interestingly, Paulding's validation of the swamp as a true measure of American quality is later repeated by Henry David Thoreau, whose long essay on the wonders of the frontier, "Walking" (1862), capitalizes on the same trope of the swamp. It becomes a "sacred space,—a *sanctum sanctorum*" where Thoreau can "recreate himself." Thoreau relates that "[h]ope and the future for me are not in lawns and cultivated fields, not in towns and cities, but in the impervious and quaking swamps. ... That was the jewel that dazzled me. I derive more of my subsistence from the swamps which surround my native town than from the cultivated gardens in the village"; see Henry David Thoreau, "Walking," in *"Walden" and Other Writings of Henry David Thoreau*, ed. Brooks Atkinson (New York: Modern Library, 1992) 646–647.

48. Judith Butler, "The Force of Fantasy: Mapplethorpe, Feminism, and Discursive Excess," in *The Judith Butler Reader*, ed. Sara Selih with Judith Butler (Oxford, UK: Blackwell, 2004) 285.

CHAPTER 3

1. David R. Roediger, *The Wages of Whiteness: Race and the Making of the American Working Class*, revised edition, (London: Verso, 1991) 118.

2. *Negro Minstrelsy in New York*, vol. 2 (New York: Collected and Illustrated by Chalres C. Morneau, n.d.) Harvard Theatre Collection, Houghton Library.) n.p.

3. Carl Wittke, *Tambo and Bones: A History of the American Minstrel Stage* (Durham, NC: Duke University Press, 1930) 31.

4. Eric Lott, *Love and Theft: Blackface Minstrelsy and the American Working Class* (New York: Oxford University Press, 1993) 51.

5. W. T. Lhamon, Jr., *Raising Cain: Blackface Performance from Jim Crow to Hip Hop* (Cambridge, MA: Harvard University Press, 1998) 6.

6. See Marvin McAllister who argues that "[m]ore than constructing stereotypes to explain the unfamiliar, this nation's earliest blackface practitioners produced a performance tradition based on revealing, but then ridiculing, Afro-America;" *White People Do Not Know How to Behave at Entertainments Designed for Ladies and Gentlemen of Colour* (Chapel Hill: University of North Carolina Press, 2003) 150. See as well Daphne A. Brooks who localizes this critique to the way blackface minstrelsy insisted on and sought to naturalize a "spectacularly abject and hyperexcessive black body in nineteenth-century theatre;" *Bodies in Dissent: Spectacular Performances of Race and Freedom, 1850–1910* (Durham, NC: Duke University Press, 2006) 28.

7. Saidiya V. Hartman, *Scenes of Subjection: Terror, Slavery, and Self-Making in Nineteenth-Century America* (New York: Oxford University Press, 1997) 22. She explains in more detail that the "affiliation of performance and blackness can be attributed to the spectacularization of black pain and racist conceptions of Negro nature as carefree, infantile, hedonistic, and indifferent to suffering and to an interested misreading of the interdependence of labor and song common among the enslaved. The constitution of blackness as an abject and degraded condition and the fascination with the other's enjoyment went hand in hand. Moreover, blacks were envisioned fundamentally as vehicles for white enjoyment, in all of its sundry and unspeakable expressions; this was as much the consequence of the chattel status of the captive as it was of the excess enjoyment imputed to the other, for those forced to dance on the decks of slave ships crossing the Middle Passage, step it up lively on the auction black, and amuse the master and his friends were seen as the purveyors of pleasure" (22–23).

8. Joseph Roach notes that "[p]erformance genealogies draw on the idea of expressive movements as mnemonic reserves, including patterned movements made and remembered by bodies, residual movements retained implicitly in images or words (or in silences between them), and imaginary movements dreamed in minds, not prior to language but constitutive of it, a psychic rehearsal for physical actions drawn from a repertoire that culture provides," *Cities of the Dead: Circum-Atlantic Performance* (New York: Columbia University Press, 1996) 26. He also argues that a genealogy of performance, like the one I am tracing, by its definition "also attend[s] to 'counter-memories,' or the depositories between history as it is discursively transmitted and memory as it is publicly enacted by bodies that bear its consequences" (26).

9. See Robert C. Toll, *Blacking Up: The Minstrel Show in Nineteenth-Century America* (London: Oxford University Press, 1974) 40, and William J. Mahar, *Behind the Burnt Cork Mask: Early Blackface and Antebellum American Popular Culture* (Urbana: University of Illinois Press, 1999) 88. For a more general investigation of the political culture of antebellum American, see Anne Norton, *Alternative Americans: A Reading of Antebellum Political Culture* (Chicago: University of Chicago Press, 1986).

10. Edward Said, *Beginnings: Intention and Method* (New York: Columbia University Press, 1985) 51.

11. Conner's account comes from a collection of (generally) undated newspaper clippings in the T. D. Rice Clipping File, Harvard Theatre Collection, Houghton Library.

12. One sees the penumbra of this story shadowing Rice's contemporary, F. C. Wemyss, and his history of minstrelsy in his *Theatrical Biography; or, The Life of an Actor and Manager* (Glasgow: R. Griffin, 1848); it also makes its way into later theater historians' accounts,

like Brander Mathews, "The Rise and Fall of Negro Minstrelsy" *Scribner's Magazine* 57:6 (1915): 754–759, and Arthur Hornblow, *A History of the Theater in America* (Philadelphia: J. B. Lippincott, 1919).

13. These emerging conventions found performative outlets in, among other forms, Calathumpian bands in the early nineteenth century in such urban locales as Philadelphia and New York, where working-class whites blacked up for carnivalesque transgressions on New Year's Day. These "demons of disorder," as Dale Cockrell calls them, who blacked up using chimney soot or grease paint, took to the streets demanding food and drink from the socially elite while continuing to objectify the black subjects they came across; see Dale Cockrell, *Demons of Disorder: Early Blackface Minstrels and Their World* (Cambridge, UK: Cambridge University Press, 1997) 30–62. While Calathumpian bands tended to be isolated as rituals and limited to certain parts of the calendar, black dance and, in particular, Pinkster, with its sensual moves emphasizing the hips and the pelvis, were consistently available as sources for blackface minstrelsy, as Raymond Knapp argues; see *The American Musical and the Formation of National Identity* (Princeton, NJ: Princeton University Press, 2005) 51. Even the American circus lent its artistic influence to mainstage blackface performers, for its blackface clowns entertained audiences, leading Russell Sanjek to dub the circus the "incubator of the minstrel show;" see Russell Sanjek, *American Popular Music and Its Business: The First Hundred Years*, vol. 2 (New York: Oxford University Press, 1988) 166–170. For more on the history of minstrelsy in relation to popular performative forms, see also Sarah Meer, *Uncle Tom Mania: Slavery, Minstrelsy, and Transatlantic Culture in the 1850s* (Athens: University of Georgia Press, 2005) 10–24.

14. While Dale Cockrell outlines minstrelsy's descent from the "Yankee impersonator" (24), and while he gestures to Jim Crow's "Southwest 'roaring' and 'whooping' tradition" (71), this aspect of minstrelsy's genealogy remains relatively unexplored.

15. David Roediger also suggests the strong relationship between blackface minstrelsy— particularly abolitionist politics—and the songs of the American West (118).

16. Broadside for an unnamed Philadelphia theater in *Minstrel Playbills and Broadsides*, Box R, Harvard Theatre Collection, Houghton Library.

17. Constance Rourke outlines a number of American comic archetypes, including the minstrel, backwoodsman (or frontiersman), and Yankee; see *American Humor: A Study of National Character* (New York: Doubleday, 1931).

18. *Eastern Argus*, 7 May 1834.

19. *Boston Morning Post*, 8 May 1834, and 8 September 1835.

20. *Philadelphia Sun*, 8 May 1834.

21. James Kirke Paulding, *The Lion of the West*, ed. James N. Tidwell (Palo Alto, CA: Stanford University Press, 1954) 54.

22. Carroll Smith-Rosenberg, *Disorderly Conduct: Visions of Gender in Victorian America* (New York: Knopf, 1985) 96.

23. Like Wildfire, the sensationally popular Crockett of the almanacs between 1830 and 1850 was "loose, liminal, and wild ... without boundaries or limits" (Smith-Rosenberg 95).

24. I borrow the term *surrogate* from Joseph Roach's foundational definition of surrogacy as the attempt to fit "satisfactory alternates" into the cavities created by the loss of the original, a term he also reads as synonymous with the term *performance,* or, as he phrases it, "the doomed search for originals by continuously auditioning stand-ins" (2–3).

25 A disclaimer in the *New-York Mirror* makes Paulding's fear clear: "It having been erroneously stated in some of the public papers, that the hero of this piece was intended to represent a late member of congress from the state of Tennessee, we are authorized, and requested, by the author, to say *that it is not so.* The design was to embody certain peculiar

characteristics of the west in one single person, who should thus represent, not an individual, but the species" (18 December 1830).

26. Although Paulding's letter to Crockett is now lost, the congressman's response is available. In it, the congressman says that he has not seen the newspaper publications that charged Paulding with plagiarizing Crockett's character, "and if I had," Crockett continues, "I should not have taken the reference to myself in exclusion of many who fill offices and who are as untaught as I am. I thank you however for your civility in assuring me that you had no reference to my peculiarities;" qtd. in Larry J. Reynolds, *James Kirke Paulding* (Boston: Twayne Publishing, 1984) 97.

27. Nelson F. Adkins, "James Kirke Paulding's *Lion of the West*," *American Literature* 3:3 (November 1931): 7–8.

28. T. D. Rice, "Jim Crow," in "Jim Crow's Ramble!" (London: Z.T. Purday, n.d.), Minstrel Sheet Music Collection, Harvard Theatre Collection, Houghton Library.

29. T. D. Rice, "Jim Crow," Verse 7 (New York: E. Riley, n.d.), Minstrel Sheet Music Collection, Harvard Theatre Collection, Houghton Library.

30. T. D. Rice, "Jim Crow," Verse 8, in "Jimmy Crow" (New York: Atwill's Music Saloon, n.d., in Minstrel Sheet Music Collection, Harvard Theatre Collection, Houghton Library.

31. See Marvin Carlson, *The Haunted Stage: The Theatre as Memory Machine* (Ann Arbor: University of Michigan Press, 2001), and in particular his notion of "recycling and recollection" as a stand-in for performance (2).

32. *Boston Morning Post*, 10 May 1834.

33. James Kirke Paulding, *Slavery in the United States* (New York: Harper and Brothers, 1836) 280.

34. For more on the relationship between physiology and racism, see Dana D. Nelson, *National Manhood: Capitalist Citizenship and the Imagined Fraternity of White Men* (Durham, NC: Duke University Press, 1998) 102–134. On the racialization of anatomy, see Michael Sappol, *A Traffic in Dead Bodies: Anatomy and Embodied Social Identity in Nineteenth-Century America* (Princeton, NJ: Princeton University Press, 2004); Robert J. C. Young, *Colonial Desire: Hybridity in Theory, Culture, and Race* (London: Routledge, 1995); and Robyn Wiegman, *American Anatomies: Theorizing Race and Gender* (Durham, NC: Duke University Press, 1995).

35. Lorenzo Dow Turner, "The Transition Period (1808–1881)," *Journal of Negro History* 14:4 (October 1929): 410.

36. Floyd C. Watkins, "James Kirke Paulding and the South," *American Quarterly* 5:3 (Autumn 1958): 228. It is worth adding that James H. Hackett, who played Wildfire in Paulding's play, shared Paulding's sentiment. In 1863, Hackett wrote in a commentary on Shakespearean performance that the "great moral lesson of the tragedy of *Othello* is, that Black and white blood cannot be intermingled in marriage without a gross outrage upon the laws of Nature; and that, in such violations, Nature will vindicate her laws;" see James Henry Hackett, *Notes and Comments upon Certain Plays and Actors of Shakespeare, with Criticism and Correspondence* (New York: Carleton, 1863) 224.

37. T. D. Rice, *The Virginia Mummy*, in W. T. Lhamon, Jr., *Jump Jim Crow: Lost Plays, Lyrics, and Street Prose of the First Atlantic Popular Culture* (Cambridge, MA: Harvard University Press, 2003): 159. All quotations from the play use this edition.

38. For instance, in a performance of Rice's *The Virginia Mummy* at the National Theatre in Cincinnati, Ohio, on May 9, 1846, the broadside advertising the show states that "in the course of the above piece, MR. RICE will sing the celebrated Song of 'SICH A GITTEN UP STAIRS;'" see Minstrel Broadsides and Playbills, Box R, Harvard Theatre Collection, Houghton Library.

39. T. D. Rice, "Such a Getting Up Stairs," London: T.E. Purday, n.d., in Minstrel Sheet Music Collection, Harvard Theatre Collection, Houghton Library.

40. Scott Trafton, *Egypt Land: Race and Nineteenth-Century American Egyptomania* (Durham, NC: Duke University Press, 2004) 124. On the museum culture, see also *Mermaids, Mummies, and Mastodons: The Emergence of the American Museum*, ed. William T. Alderson (Washington, D.C.: American Association of Museums, 1992).

41. Trafton also notes the way that Ginger Blue's performance, at this moment, is a "highly self-conscious reference to the very act of blacking up" (123).

42. This is a variation on the similar theme explored by Karen Sanchez-Eppler in her discussion of the way white female abolitionists deployed blackness and the black body as a tool for establishing white women's equal rights; see *Touching Liberty: Abolition, Feminism, and the Politics of the Body* (Berkeley: University of California Press, 1993).

43. For more on Catlin's popularity and for its performative qualities as a "wild west show," see Paul Reddin, *Wild West Shows* (Urbana: University of Illinois Press, 1999) 1–52.

44. See Steven Conn, *History's Shadow: Native Americans and Historical Consciousness in the Nineteenth Century* (Chicago: University of Chicago Press, 2006).

45. Theodore Weld, *American Slavery As It Is* (New York: American Anti-Slavery Society, 1839) 77.

46. Marcus Wood, *Blind Memory: Visual Representations of Slavery in England and America, 1780–1865* (New York: Routledge, 2000) 246–247.

47. Frederick Douglass, *My Bondage and My Freedom* (New York: Dover, 1955) 359, my emphasis.

48. Peggy Phelan, *Unmarked: The Politics of Performance* (New York: Routledge, 1993) 6–11.

49. Newspaper article, "T. D. Rice—'Jim Crow,'" in Joseph N. Ireland, *Records of the New York Stage from 1750 to 1860*, vol. 2, part 2 (New York: T. H. Morrell, 1867) n.p., Harvard Theatre Collection, Houghton Library.

CHAPTER 4

1. *New York Times*, 15 December 1859: 4.

2. The term *miscegenation*, with which we are more familiar, originated after Boucicault's play, in 1864. Boucicault's audience would have known the kind of interracial identity that Zoe represents, therefore, not as miscegenation but as amalgamation. For more on these terms, see Debra J. Rosenthal, *Race Mixture in Nineteenth-Century U.S. and Spanish American Fiction: Gender, Culture, and Nation Building* (Chapel Hill: University of North Carolina Press, 2004) 4.

3. Richard Fawkes, *Dion Boucicault: A Biography* (London: Quartet Books, 1979) 107.

4. Dion Boucicault, "Letter from the Author of 'The Octoroon' to the Editor of the Herald," *New York Herald*, 7 December 1859: 5.

5. Dion Boucicault, "Letter to the Editor," *London Times*, 20 November 1861: 5.

6. "A young and wealthy planter in Louisiana," Boucicault recalls, "fell deeply and sincerely in love with a Quadroon girl of great beauty and purity. The lovers found their union opposed by the law; but love knows no obstacles. The young man, in the presence of two friends, who served as witnesses, opened a vein in his arm and introduced into it a few drops of his mistress's blood; thus he was able to make oath that he had black blood in his veins, and being attested the marriage was performed," Dion Boucicault, unpublished manuscript, Theatre Museum, Covent Garden, London, 1861.

7. *Spirit of the Times*, 17 December 1859: 529.

8. Joseph Jefferson, *The Autobiography of Joseph Jefferson* (New York: Century, 1890) 162.

9. Review, *New York Times*, 15 December 1859.

10. Nancy Bentley argues that while the mulatta has "a potentially disruptive" character, a tragic mulatta like Zoe uses the "humiliation" of her body as a kind of social policing; see

"White Slaves: The Mulatto Hero in Antebellum Fiction," *American Literature* 65:3 (September 1993): 503, 505. P. Gabrielle Foreman suggests that Boucicault's play popularized a "scheme of racial difference" that demanded the suicide of Zoe at the end; see "Who's Your Mama? 'White' Mulatta Genealogies, Early Photography, and Anti-Passing Narratives of Slavery and Freedom," *American Literary History* 14:3 (Fall 2002): 521. According to Jennifer Devere Brody, *The Octoroon* is a play that is "continually concerned with the maintenance and production of civilized subjects," and by disappearing from the play's final scene, the potentially problematic Zoe "ultimately serves to establish the establishment" (55–57). Daphne A. Brooks underscores this point by suggesting that the text's potentially disruptive critique is smoothed over by its "visually policing racial liminality." As Brooks summarizes, "Boucicault's play aims to rein in the very excess it had produced in its title character. ... *The Octoroon* worked toward the ultimate reinstatement of social stability and 'clarity'"; Daphne A. Brooks, *Bodies in Dissent: Spectacular Performances of Race and Freedom, 1850–1910* (Durham, NC: Duke University Press, 2006) 38, 41.

11. Dion Boucicault, *The Octoroon; or, Life in Louisiana*, in *Early American Drama*, ed. Jeffrey H. Richards (New York: Penguin, 1997) 491. All further quotations from the play come from this edition and use its pagination.

12. Joseph Roach, *Cities of the Dead: Circum-Atlantic Performance* (New York: Columbia University Press, 1996) 179.

13. Like its source text, Mayne Reid's *The Quadroon*, which in one of its early editions changed its subtitle from *A Lover's Adventures in Louisiana* to *Adventures in the Far West*, Boucicault's work consistently references itself as a frontier play. Salem Scudder, one of the key figures in it, defines the "here" of the play as the "wilds of the West" (486), and unhesitatingly dubs its action as "our Western life" (485).

14. Saidiya V. Hartman, *Scenes of Subjection: Terror, Slavery, and Self-Making in Nineteenth-Century America* (New York: Oxford University Press, 1997) 27.

15. See Werner Sollors's treatment of the Indian play in *Beyond Ethnicity: Consent and Descent in American Culture* (New York: Oxford University Press, 1986) and, particularly, Roger Hall's assessment of mid-nineteenth-century stagings of the frontier as only helping to bolster American's "own sense of righteousness and destiny," *Performing the American Frontier, 1870–1906* (Cambridge, UK: Cambridge University Press, 2001) 228.

16. Robert B. Heilman, *Tragedy and Melodrama* (Seattle: University of Washington Press, 1968) 85.

17. Peter Brooks, *The Melodramatic Imagination: Balzac, Henry James, Melodrama, and the Mode of Excess* (New Haven, CT: Yale University Press, 1976) 4–5. Also see theater historian David Grimsted, who notes melodrama's "black-or-white" formation. "No one argued that melodrama was true to life," Grimsted insists, "but the moral was always there, writ large and obviously. Every spectator knew who was good and who bad and how the final chips of poetical justice would fall," *Melodrama Unveiled: American Theater and Culture, 1800–1850* (Berkeley: University of California Press, 1987) 41.

18. Linda Williams, *Playing the Race Card: Melodramas of Black and White from Uncle Tom to O.J. Simpson* (Princeton, NJ: Princeton University Press, 2001) 40.

19. For more on the influence of Pixérécourt and other French melodramatists on the American theater, see Bruce A. McConachie, *Melodramatic Formations: American Theatre and Society, 1820–1870* (Iowa City: University of Iowa Press, 1992) 29–68.

20. Marc Robinson, *The American Play, 1787–2000* (New Haven, CT: Yale University Press, 2009) 28.

21. Williams's assessment of melodrama's dependence on pain builds on Saidiya V. Hartman's argument that blackness in antebellum America was frequently established—and managed—by the violence enacted on the black body. In melodrama, she writes, "the

battle of good and evil was waged at the site of the tortured and chaste black body; suffering announced virtue" (28).

22. It is worth noting that in Reid's novel, Edward Rutherford, the melodramatic hero, responds to the lament of the tragic mulatta, Aurore, by boldly dismissing her "stigma" of mixed-race identity, saying, "In the eyes of Love, rank loses its fictitious charm—titles seemed trivial things;" see Mayne Reid, *The Quadroon; or, A Lover's Adventures in Louisiana* (New York: Robert M. De Witt, 1856) 97.

23. Russ Castronovo, *Necro Citizenship: Death, Eroticism, and the Public Sphere in the Nineteenth-Century United States* (Durham, NY: Duke University Press, 2001) 42.

24. Lauren Berlant, "Poor Eliza," *American Literature* 70:3 (1998): 636. See also Berlant, "The Subject of True Feeling: Pain, Privacy, and Politics," in *Cultural Studies and Political Theory*, ed. Jodi Dean (Ithaca, NY: Cornell University Press, 2000) 42–62.

25. For more on this, see Bentley 503–504.

26. See McConachie, 225–227.

27. Dion Boucicault, "The Decline of the Drama," *North American Review* 125 (September 1877): 236.

28. Dion Boucicault, "The Art of Dramatic Composition," *North American Review* 126 (January 1878): 52.

29. *New York Herald*, 15 September 1859: 7. By 1873, suggests Bruce McConachie, most urban playhouses had "eliminated the pit, shoved the remaining boxes nearer the proscenium, and adopted orchestra/balcony seating for most spectators. The pricing and reserve seating policies of the bourgeois theatres kept most of the orchestra and first balcony seats within the reach of modest business-class households, but beyond the means and the planning of most workers, who sat in the upper balcony if they attended at all" (200).

30. Walt Whitman, "The Old Bowery," *November Boughs* in *Walt Whitman: Complete Poetry and Collected Prose*, ed. Justin Kaplan (New York: Library of America, 1982) 1189.

31. For more on this phenomenon, consult Karen Halttunen, *Confidence Men and Painted Women: A Study of Middle-Class Culture in America, 1830–1870* (New Haven, CT: Yale University Press, 1986), Lawrence Levine, *Highbrow/Lowbrow: The Emergence of Cultural Hierarchy in America* (Cambridge, MA: Harvard University Press, 1990), and David Nasaw, *Going Out: The Rise and Fall of Public Amusements* (Cambridge, MA: Harvard University Press, 1999).

32. William Winter, *Other Days: Being Chronicles and Memoirs of the Stage* (New York: Moffat, Yard, and Company, 1908) 132.

33. See David C. Miller, *Dark Eden: The Swamp in Nineteenth-Century American Culture* (Cambridge, UK: Cambridge University Press, 1989) 77–104.

34. Michael Paul Rogin insists that during and after the Indian Removal Act of 1830, "Indians were the bogeymen who frightened children in early America," and it was their supposed savagery that was the key to this representational scare tactic; see *Fathers and Children: Andrew Jackson and the Subjugation of the American Indian* (New York: Knopf, 1975) 120. Jeffrey D. Mason suggests that the history of the printing of Henry Trumball's *History of the Discovery of America* indexes exactly how prevalent the notion of the savage, bloodthirsty Indian was in the mid-nineteenth century. Between 1802 and 1831, this work, which details the savage atrocities enacted by Native American peoples, went through thirteen printings, and its successor, *History of the Indian Wars*, went through seven printings between 1841 and 1854; see *Melodrama and the Myth of America* (Bloomington: Indiana University Press, 1993) 31. Competing with the noble savage, in other words, was the ruthless savage, epitomized onstage by works like Louisa Medina's staging of Robert Montgomery Bird's *Nick of the Woods* (1837), which Bird imagined as a rebuttal of James Fenimore Cooper's Uncas and Chingachgook. For more on this distinction, see Don B. Wilmeth, "Noble or Ruthless Savage?: The American Indian on Stage and in the

Drama," *Journal of American Drama and Theatre* 1 (Spring 1989): 39–78. Rosemarie K. Bank argues that this distinction structures the ideology of the frontier in the antebellum period, but as Wahnotee's characterization suggests, this firm binary between "noble" and "ruthless" savage did not entirely define frontier representation; see Rosemarie K. Bank, *Theatre Culture in America, 1825–1860* (Cambridge, UK: Cambridge University Press, 1997) 71–72.

35. On the staging of the noble savage, see Shari M. Huhndorf, *Going Native: Indians in the American Cultural Imagination* (Ithaca, NY: Cornell University Press, 2001) and Susan Scheckel, *The Insistence of the Indian: Race and Nationalism in Nineteenth-Century American Culture* (Princeton, NJ: Princeton University Press, 1998). For more on the symbolic architecture of the noble savage narrative, see Werner Sollors, *Beyond Ethnicity: Consent and Descent in American Culture* (New York: Oxford University Press, 1986) 102–130.

36. George C. D. Odell, *Annals of the New York Stage*, Volume 8: 1857–1865, (New York: Columbia University Press, 1931) 254.

37. James W. Cook, *The Arts of Deception: Playing with Fraud in the Age of Barnum* (Cambridge, MA: Harvard University Press, 2001) 133. For more on how What is It? was produced as a frontier piece, consult Joy S. Kasson, *Buffalo Bill's Wild West: Celebrity, Memory, and Popular History* (New York: Hill and Wang, 2000) where she notes that while Barnum later described his freak as African, "in the decade after Catlin's exhibitions Barnum claimed American Indian status for his performer" (68).

CHAPTER 5

1. Louis S. Warren, *Buffalo Bill's America: William Cody and the Wild West Show* (New York: Alfred A. Knopf, 2005) 6.

2. Roger A. Hall, *Performing the American Frontier, 1870–1906* (Cambridge, UK: Cambridge University Press, 2001) 13.

3. Pierre Nora, "Between Memory and History: Les Lieux de Mémoire." *Representations* 26 (Spring 1989): 23.

4. Paul Gilroy, *The Black Atlantic: Modernity and Double Consciousness* (Cambridge, MA: Harvard University Press, 1993) 4, 28.

5. As Brenda Murphy argues, *Horizon* was a key text in moving theater toward realism while *The Danites* was one of the most successful "Western" plays. For more on the importance of these two plays, see Brenda Murphy, *American Realism and American Drama, 1880–1940* (Cambridge, UK: Cambridge University Press, 1987) 11–13. See also Kim Marra, *Strange Duets: Impresarios and Actresses in the American Theatre, 1865–1914* (Iowa City: University of Iowa Press, 2000) 2.

6. Joseph Francis Daly, *The Life of Augustin Daly* (New York: Macmillan, 1917) 90.

7. George Parson Lathrop, "An American School of Dramatic Art: The Inside Working of the Theatre." *Century Magazine* 56:2 (June 1898): 273.

8. Bruce A. McConachie, *Melodramatic Formations: American Theatre and Society, 1820–1870* (Iowa City: University of Iowa Press, 1992) 204–205.

9. Marvin Felheim, *The Theater of Augustin Daly: An Account of the Late Nineteenth Century American Stage* (New York: Greenwood, 1969) 28.

10. Augustin Daly, "The American Dramatist," *North American Review* 142 (May 1886): 491.

11. Augustin Daly, "American Playwrights on the American Drama," *Harper's Weekly*, 2 February 1889: 97.

12. Kim Marra, "Taming America as Actress: Augustin Daly, Ada Rehan, and the Discourse of Imperial Frontier Conquest," in *Performing America: Cultural Nationalism in American Theater*, eds. Jeffrey D. Mason and J. Ellen Gainor (Ann Arbor: University of Michigan Press, 1999) 54. For more on Daly's efforts to tame wild actresses, see Barbara Wallace

Grossman, *A Spectacle of Suffering: Clara Morris on the American Stage* (Carbondale: University of Southern Illinois Press, 2009) 85–87.

13. Augustin Daly, *Horizon*, in *Plays by Augustin Daly*, eds. Don B. Wilmeth and Rosemary Cullen (Cambridge, UK: Cambridge University Press, 1984): 121. All future quotations from the play use this edition's pagination.

14. Joaquin Miller, *Overland in a Covered Wagon: An Autobiography*, ed. Sidney G. Firman (New York: D. Appleton, 1931) 9. For more on Miller's life, consult Miller's biography, Harr Wagner, *Joaquin Miller and His Other Self* (San Francisco: Harr Wagner Publishing, 1929).

15. Elbert Hubbard, *So Here Then Is a Little Journey to the Home of Joaquin Miller* (East Aurora, NY: Roycrafters, 1903) 6.

16. Joaquin Miller, *Joaquin Miller's Poems*, 6 vols. (San Francisco: Whitaker and Ray, 1909) II: 91.

17. Nathaniel Lewis, "Authentic Reproduction: The Picturesque Joaquin Miller," *Arizona Quarterly* 57:2 (Summer 2001): 9.

18. Joaquin Miller, *First Families of the Sierras* (London: George Routledge, 1975) 33, 67.

19. Edmund Booth, *Edmund Booth, Forty-Niner: The Life Story of a Deaf Pioneer* (Stockton, CA: San Joaquin Pioneer and Historical Society, 1953) 21.

20. Susan Lee Johnson, *Roaring Camp: The Social Life of the California Gold Rush* (New York: W. W. Norton, 2000) 121.

21. Joaquin Miller, *The Danites in the Sierras* in *American Plays*, ed. Allan Gates Halline (New York: American Book Company, 1976): 389. All further quotations from the play use this edition's pagination.

22. George C. D. Odell, *Annals of the New York Stage*, Volume 10 (New York: Columbia University Press, 1938) 401.

23. Mary Jane Megquier, *Apron Full of Gold: The Letters of Mary Jane Megquier*, ed. Robert Cleland (Albuquerque: University of New Mexico Press, 1994) 120.

24. Louise Amelia Knapp Smith Clappe, *The Shirley Letters from the California Mines in 1851–1852*, ed. Thomas C. Russell (San Francisco: Thomas C. Russell, 1922) 349.

25. Robert M. Utley, *The Indian Frontier of the American West, 1846–1890* (Albuquerque: University of New Mexico Press, 1984) 164.

26. For a detailed account of the political and psychological contours of this familial metaphor, see Michael Paul Rogin, *Fathers and Children: Andrew Jackson and the Subjugation of the American Indian* (New York: Knopf, 1975).

27. See Terryl L. Givens, *The Viper on the Hearth: Mormons, Myths, and the Construction of Heresy* (New York: Oxford University Press, 1997) 135.

28. Will Bagley, *Blood of the Prophets: Brigham Young and the Massacre at Mountain Meadows* (Norman: University of Oklahoma Press, 2002) 190.

29. I take this distinction between mimesis and diegesis from Roland Barthes's *The Responsibility of Forms: Critical Essays on Music, Art, and Representation*, tr. Richard Howard (Berkeley: University of California Press, 1991).

30. Daniel Gerould, "Russian Formalist Theories of Melodrama," *Journal of American Culture* 1:1 (Spring 1978): 158.

31. I have taken the liberty in this instance of spelling out the names of the characters, regularizing capitalization, and deitalicizing the script in order to clarify, to the best of my abilities, who is doing what to whom.

32. Martin Meisel, "Speaking Pictures," in *Melodrama*, ed. Daniel Gerould (New York: New York Literary Forum, 1980) 7: 58.

33. The reviewer for the *New York Herald* complained about the play's faulty melodramatic effects as well as the play's defective stage effects, noting that the setup for the play was the "usual story" and not very interesting; see *New York Herald*, 22 March 1871. While the

play ran for seven weeks, it never toured the country the way other successful Daly pieces did, and given the rage for frontier plays in post–Civil War America, its relatively short run, limited to New York City, attests to the fact that it was not as satisfying to audiences as other pieces were (Felheim 68).

34. George Bernard Shaw, *Our Theatres in the Nineties*, 3 Vols. (London: Constable, 1932) 1:166.

35. Jean Cutler quoted in Wilmeth and Cullen, 17.

36. Kim Marra makes a similar point about Daly's imperialist leanings: "Like Andrew Carnegie, he advanced through conquest in the business sphere. Rather than land and ore, the theater, and especially its putatively wayward and seductive leading ladies, became the raw matter he cultivated for profit" (*Strange* 3).

37. Arthur Hobson Quinn, *A History of the American Drama: From the Civil War to the Present Day* (New York: Appleton-Century-Crofts, 1936) 1.

38. Playbill for the McCauley Theatre, n.d., programs and clippings for *The Danites in the Sierras*, New York Public Library's Billy Rose Theater Collection, New York City.

39. Playbill for the Grand Opera House, New York City, 1881, programs and clippings for *The Danites in the Sierras*, New York Public Library's Billy Rose Theater Collection, New York City.

40. Joaquin Miller, *Life Amongst the Modocs: Unwritten History* (London: Richard Bentley and Sons, 1873) 160.

AFTERWORD

1. Joy S. Kasson, *Buffalo Bill's Wild West: Celebrity, Memory, and Popular History* (New York: Farrar, Straus and Giroux, 2001) 130.

2. Paul Reddin, *Wild West Shows* (Urbana: University of Illinois Press, 1999) 151.

3. Quoted in Robert V. Hine and John Mack Faragher, *The American West: A New Interpretive History* (New Haven, CT: Yale University Press, 2000) 503.

4. See Nicholas Vardac, *From Stage to Screen: Theatrical Origins of Early Film: David Garrick to D.W. Griffith* (Cambridge, MA: Harvard University Press, 1949) for a detailed discussion of the relationship between nineteenth-century theater and the birth of the cinema. See also Marc Robinson, *The American Play, 1787–2000* (New Haven, CT: Yale University Press, 2009) 106–214, for an analysis of the relationship between theatrical realism and the field of vision.

5. Philip Deloria, *Indians in Unexpected Places* (Lawrence: University of Kansas Press, 2006) 106.

6. L. G. Moses, *Wild West Shows and the Images of American Indians, 1883–1933* (Albuquerque: University of New Mexico Press, 1996) 223–224.

7. A suggestive, but by no means thorough, list would include general cultural histories, such as Jane Tompkins, *West of Everything: The Inner Life of Westerns* (New York: Oxford University Press, 1993), Richard Slotkin, *Gunfighter Nation: The Myth of the Frontier in Twentieth-Century America* (Norman: University of Oklahoma Press, 1998), and Amy Kaplan, *The Anarchy of Empire in the Making of U.S. Culture* (Cambridge, MA: Harvard University Press, 2005). For more on just the western, see Lee Clark Mitchell, *Westerns: Making the Man in Fiction and Film* (Chicago: University of Chicago Press, 1998), Scott Simmon, *The Invention of the Western Film: A Cultural History of the Genre's First Half Century* (Cambridge, UK: Cambridge University Press, 2003), and Jon Kitses, *Horizons West: Directing the Western from John Ford to Clint Eastwood* (New York: Palgrave Macmillan, 1969).

8. Lisa Rein, "Down on the Ranch, President Wages War on the Underbrush," *Washington Post*, 31 December 2005: A03.

9. Maureen Dowd, "Reach Out and Touch No One," *New York Times*, 7 January 2006.

10. Frank Rich, "Shoddy! Tawdry! A Televised Train Wreck," *New York Times*, 20 April 2008.

11. Evgenia Peretz, "Highnoon in Crawford," *Vanity Fair* (November 2005): 231.

12. Jim Kitses, "All That Brokeback Allows," *Film Quarterly* 60:3 (March 2007): 23.

13. James R. Keller and Anne Goodwyn Jones, "*Brokeback Mountain*: Masculinity and Manhood," *Studies in Popular Culture* 30:2 (Spring 2008): 33.

14. For more on the queer subtexts to filmic westerns, see Roger Clarke, "Lonesome Cowboys," *Sight and Sound* 16:1 (January 2006): 32, and Corey K. Creekmur, "*Brokeback*: The Parody," *GLQ* 13:1 (2007): 106.

15. Susan Lee Johnson, Review of *Brokeback Mountain*, by Ang Lee, *The Journal of American History* 93:3 (December 2006): 989.

16. Roy Grundmann, "*Brokeback Mountain*: Good Social Intentions but Not Great Filmmaking," *Cineaste* 31:3 (Summer 2006): 84.

17. Dwight A. McBride, "Why I Hate That I Loved *Brokeback Mountain*," *GLQ* 13:1 (2007): 97.

18. D. A. Miller, "On the Universality of *Brokeback*," *Film Quarterly* 60:3 (March 2007): 56–58.

WORKS CITED

Adkins, Nelson F. "James Kirke Paulding's *Lion of the West.*" *American Literature* 3:3 (November 1931): 249–258.

Alderson, William T., Ed. *Mermaids, Mummies, and Mastodons: The Emergence of the American Museum.* Washington, D.C.: American Association of Museums, 1992.

Alger, William Rounseville. *Life of Edwin Forrest, The American Tragedian.* Volume 1. Philadelphia: J. B. Lippincott, 1877.

Allen, Robert C. *Horrible Prettiness: Burlesque and American Culture.* Chapel Hill: University of North Carolina Press, 1991.

Anderson, Marilyn J. "The Image of the Indian in American Drama During the Jacksonian Era, 1829–1845." *Journal of American Culture* 1:4 (Winter 1978): 800–810.

Anonymous. *The History of Edwin Forrest, The Celebrated American Tragedian, from His Childhood to His Present Elevated Station as a Performer.* New York: Published at No. 29 Ann Street, 1837.

Ansbinder, Tyler. *Five Points: The 19th-Century New York City Neighborhood That Invented Tap Dance, Stole Elections, and Became the World's Most Notorious Slum.* New York: Free Press, 2001.

Austin, Gilbert. *Chironomia; or a Treatise on Rhetorical Delivery.* London: W. Bulmer, and Co., 1806.

Ayres, Alfred. *Acting and Actors, Elocution and Elocutionists: A Book about Theater Folk and Theater Art.* New York: D. Appleton, 1894.

Bagley, Will. *Blood of the Prophets: Brigham Young and the Massacre at Mountain Meadows.* Norman: University of Oklahoma Press, 2002.

Baltimore Sun, September 24, 1892.

Baltimore Sun, September 27, 1892.

Bank, Rosemarie K. "Representing History: Performing the Columbian Exposition." *Theatre Survey* 54:4 (December 2002): 589–606.

———. *Theatre Culture in America, 1826–1860.* Cambridge, UK: Cambridge University Press, 1997.

Barish, Jonas. *The Antitheatrical Prejudice.* Berkeley: University of California Press, 1981.

Barthes, Roland. *The Responsibility of Forms: Critical Essays on Music, Art, and Representation.* Tr. Richard Howard. Berkeley: University of California Press, 1991.

Bentley, Nancy. "White Slaves: The Mulatto Hero in Antebellum Fiction." *American Literature* 65 (1993): 501–522.

Berlant, Lauren. *The Anatomy of National Fantasy: Hawthorne, Utopia, and Everyday Life.* Chicago: University of Chicago Press, 1991.

———. "Poor Eliza." *American Literature* 70:3 (1998): 635–668.

———. "The Subject of True Feeling: Pain, Privacy, and Politics." In *Cultural Studies and Political Theory.* Ed. Jodi Dean. Ithaca, NY: Cornell University Press, 2000: 42–62.

Booth, Edmund. *Edmund Booth, Forty-Niner: The Life Story of a Deaf Pioneer*. Stockton, CA: San Joaquin Pioneer and Historical Society, 1953.

Boston Morning Post, May 8, 1834.

Boston Morning Post, May 10, 1834.

Boston Morning Post, September 8, 1835.

Boucicault, Dion. "The Art of Dramatic Composition." *North American Review* 126 (January–February 1878): 40–52.

———. "The Decline of the Drama." *North American Review* 125 (September 1877): 235–245.

———. "Letter from the Author of 'The Octoroon' to the Editor of the Herald." *New York Herald*, December 7, 1859.

———. "Letter to the Editor." *London Times*. November 20, 1861.

———. *The Octoroon; or, Life in Louisiana*. In *Early American Drama*. Ed. Jeffrey H. Richards. New York: Penguin, 1997.

———. Unpublished manuscript. Theatre Museum, Covent Garden, London, 1861.

Brody, Jennifer Devere. *Impossible Purities: Blackness, Femininity, and Victorian Culture*. Durham, NC: Duke University Press, 1998.

Brooks, Daphne A. *Bodies in Dissent: Spectacular Performances of Race and Freedom, 1850–1910*. Durham, NC: Duke University Press, 2006.

Brooks, Peter. *The Melodramatic Imagination: Balzac, Henry James, Melodrama, and the Mode of Excess*. New Haven, CT: Yale University Press, 1976.

Buckley, Matthew S. "Refugee Theatre: Melodrama and Modernity's Loss." *Theatre Journal* 61:2 (May 2009): 175–190.

Burgh, James. *The Art of Speaking*. Danbury, CT: Printed for Edmund and Ephram Washburn, 1795.

Burke, Edmund. *A Philosophical Enquiry into the Origins of Our Ideas of the Sublime and Beautiful*. In *A Philosophical Enquiry into the Sublime and Beautiful and Other Pre-Revolutionary Writings*. Ed. David Womersley. London: Penguin, 1998: 49–200.

Butler, Judith. "The Force of Fantasy: Mapplethorpe, Feminism, and Discursive Excess." In *The Judith Butler Reader*. Ed. Sara Selih with Judith Butler. Oxford, UK: Blackwell, 2004: 183–202.

Carlson, Marvin. *The Haunted Stage: The Theatre as Memory Machine*. Ann Arbor: University of Michigan Press, 2001.

Castronovo, Russ. *Necro Citizenship: Death, Eroticism, and the Public Sphere in the Nineteenth Century United States*. Durham, NC: Duke University Press, 2001.

Cheyfitz, Eric. *The Poetics of Imperialism: Translation and Colonization from The Tempest to Tarzan*. New York: Oxford University Press, 1991.

Clappe, Louise Amelia Knapp Smith. *The Shirley Letters from the California Mines in 1851–1852*. Ed. Thomas C. Russell. San Francisco: Thomas C. Russell, 1922.

Clarke, Roger. "Lonesome Cowboys." *Sight and Sound* 16:1 (January 2006): 28–33.

Cmiel, Kenneth. *Democratic Eloquence: The Fight over Popular Speech in Nineteenth-Century America*. New York: William Morrow, 1990.

Cockrell, Dale. *Demons of Disorder: Early Blackface Minstrels and Their World*. Cambridge, UK: Cambridge University Press, 1997.

Conn, Steven. *History's Shadow: Native Americans and Historical Consciousness in the Nineteenth Century*. Chicago: University of Chicago Press, 2006.

Cook, James W. *The Arts of Deception: Playing with Fraud in the Age of Barnum*. Cambridge, MA: Harvard University Press, 2001.

Creekmur, Corey K. "*Brokeback*: The Parody." *GLQ* 13:1 (2007): 105–107.

Cronon, William. *Nature's Metropolis: Chicago and the Great West*. New York: Norton, 1991.

———. *Under an Open Sky: Rethinking America's Western Past*. New York: Norton, 1994.

Daly, Augustin. "The American Dramatist." *North American Review*, 142 (May 1886): 485–492.

———. "American Playwrights on the American Drama." *Harper's Weekly*, February 2, 1889: 97–99.

———. *Horizon*. In *Plays by Augustin Daly*. Eds. Don B. Wilmeth and Rosemary Cullen. Cambridge, UK: Cambridge University Press, 1984.

Daly, Joseph Francis. *The Life of Augustin* Daly. New York: Macmillan, 1917.

Deloria, Philip J. *Indians in Unexpected Places*. Lawrence: University Press of Kansas, 2004.

———. *Playing Indian*. New Haven, CT: Yale University Press, 1998.

Descartes, René. *Les passions de l'âme*. In *Ouevres et lettres*. Paris: Librairie Gallimard, 1953: 695–802.

de Tocqueville, Alexis. *Democracy in America*. Tr. George Lawrence. Ed. J. P. Mayer. New York: Harper Collins, 1969.

Douglass, Frederick. *My Bondage and My Freedom*. New York: Dover, 1955.

Dowd, Maureen. "Reach Out and Touch No One." *New York Times*, January 7, 2006.

Eastern Argus, May 7, 1834.

Fawkes, Richard. *Dion Boucicault: A Biography*. London: Quartet Books, 1979.

Felheim, Marvin. *Theater of Augustin Daly: An Account of the Late Nineteenth Century American Stage*. New York: Greenwood, 1969.

Ferguson, Francis. "Legislating the Sublime." In *Studies in Eighteenth-Century British Art and Aesthetics*. Ed. Ralph Cohen. Berkeley: University of California Press, 1985: 128–147.

Fisher, Philip. *The Vehement Passions*. Princeton, NJ: Princeton University Press, 2002.

———. *Wonder, the Rainbow, and the Aesthetics of Rare Experiences*. Cambridge, MA: Harvard University Press, 1998.

Fliegelman, Jay. *Declaring Independence: Jefferson, Natural Language, and the Culture of Performance*. Palo Alto, CA: Stanford University Press, 1993.

Foreman, P. Gabrielle. "Who's Your Mama? 'White' Mulatta Genealogies, Early Photography, and Anti-Passing Narratives of Slavery and Freedom." *American Literary History* 14:3 (Fall 2002): 505-539.

Foucault, Michel. "Nietzsche, Genealogy, History." In *Language, Counter-Memory, Practice: Selected Essays and Interviews*. Tr. Donald F. Bouchard and Sherry Simon. Ed. Donald F. Bouchard. Ithaca, NY: Cornell University Press, 1977.

Fried, Michael. *Absorption and Theatricality: Painting and Beholder in the Age of Diderot*. Berkeley: University of California Press, 1980.

Furniss, Tom. *Edmund Burke's Aesthetic Ideology: Language, Gender, and Political Economy*. Cambridge, UK: Cambridge University Press, 1993.

Gaul, Theresa Strouth. "'The Genuine Indian Who Was Brought upon the Stage': Edwin Forrest's Metamora and White Audiences." *Arizona Quarterly* 56:1 (Spring 2000): 1–27.

Gerould, Daniel. "Russian Formalist Theories of Melodrama." *Journal of American Culture*, 1:1 (Spring 1978): 152–168.

Gilroy, Paul. *The Black Atlantic: Modernity and Double Consciousness*. Cambridge, MA: Harvard University Press, 1993.

Givens, Terryl L. *The Viper on the Hearth: Mormons, Myths, and the Construction of Heresy*. New York: Oxford University Press, 1997.

Grimsted, David. *Melodrama Unveiled: American Theater and Culture, 1800–1850*. Berkeley: University of California Press, 1987.

Grossman, Barbara Wallace. *A Spectacle of Suffering: Clara Morris on the American Stage*. Carbondale: University of Southern Illinois Press, 2009.

Grundmann, Roy. "*Brokeback Mountain*: Good Social Intentions but Not Great Filmmaking." *Cineaste* 31:3 (Summer 2006): 84–85.

Gustafson, Sandra M. *Eloquence Is Power: Orality and Performance in Early America*. Chapel Hill: University of North Carolina Press, 2000.

Gustafson, Thomas. *Representative Words: Politics, Literature, and the American Language, 1776–1865*. Cambridge, UK: Cambridge University Press, 1992.

Hackett, James Henry. *Notes and Comments upon Certain Plays and Actors of Shakespeare, with Criticism and Correspondence*. New York: Carleton, 1863.

Hageman, Maurice. *Hageman's Make-Up Book*. Chicago: Dramatic Publishing Company, 1898.

Hall, Roger A. *Performing the American Frontier, 1870–1906*. Cambridge, UK: Cambridge University Press, 2001.

Halttunen, Karen. *Confidence Men and Painted Women: A Study of Middle-Class Culture in America, 1830–1870*. New Haven, CT: Yale University Press, 1986.

Harrison, Gabriel. *Edwin Forrest: The Actor and the Man*. Brooklyn: N.V., 1889.

Hartman, Saidiya V. *Scenes of Subjection: Terror, Slavery, and Self-Making in Nineteenth-Century America*. New York: Oxford University Press, 1997.

Heilman, Robert B. *Tragedy and Melodrama*. Seattle: University of Washington Press, 1968.

Herold, Amos Lee. *James Kirke Paulding, Versatile American*. New York: Columbia University Press, 1926.

Hine, Robert V., and John Mack Faragher. *The American West: A New Interpretive History*. New Haven, CT: Yale University Press, 2000.

Hodge, Francis. *Yankee Theatre: The Image of America on the Stage, 1825–1850*. Austin: University of Texas Press, 1964.

Hornblow, Arthur. *A History of the Theater in America*. Philadelphia: J.B. Lippincott, 1919.

Howe, Daniel Walker. *What Hath God Wrought?: The Transformation of America, 1815–1848*. New York: Oxford University Press, 2007.

Hubbard, Elbert. *So Here Then Is a Little Journey to the Home of Joaquin Miller*. East Aurora, NY: Roycrafters, 1903.

Huhndorf, Shari M. *Going Native: Indians in the American Cultural Imagination*. Ithaca, NY: Cornell University Press, 2001.

Irwin, William. *The New Niagara: Tourism, Technology, and the Landscape of Niagara Falls, 1776–1917*. University Park, PA: Pennsylvania State University Press, 1996.

Jefferson, Joseph. *The Autobiography of Joseph Jefferson*. New York: Century, 1890.

Johnson, Nan. "The Popularization of Nineteenth-Century Rhetoric: Elocution and the Private Learner." In *Oratorical Culture in Nineteenth-Century America: Transformations in the Theory and Practice of Rhetoric*. Eds. Gregory Clark and S. Michael Halloran. Carbondale: Southern Illinois University Press, 1993: 139–157.

Johnson, Odai. *Absence and Memory in Colonial American Theatre: Fiorelli's Plasters*. New York: Palgrave Macmillan, 2006.

Johnson, Susan Lee. Review of *Brokeback Mountain*, by Ang Lee. *The Journal of American History* 93:3 (December 2006): 988–990.

———. *Roaring Camp: The Social World of the California Gold Rush*. New York: Norton, 2000.

Kaplan, Amy. *The Anarchy of Empire in the Making of U.S. Culture*. Cambridge, MA: Harvard University Press, 2005.

Kasson, Joy S. *Buffalo Bill's Wild West: Celebrity, Memory, and Popular History*. New York: Hill and Wang, 2000.

Keller, James R., and Anne Goodwyn Jones. "*Brokeback Mountain*: Masculinity and Manhood." *Studies in Popular Culture* 30:2 (Spring 2008): 21–36.

Kitses, Jim. "All That Brokeback Allows." *Film Quarterly* 60:3 (March 2007): 22–27.

———. *Horizons West: Directing the Western from John Ford to Clint Eastwood*. New York: Palgrave Macmillan, 1969.

Knapp, Raymond. *The American Musical and the Formation of National Identity*. Princeton, NJ: Princeton University Press, 2005.

Kramer, Michael P. *Imagining Language in America: From the Revolution to the Civil War*. Princeton, NJ: Princeton University Press, 1992.

Krupat, Arnold. "Identity and Difference in the Criticism of Native American Literature." *Diacritics* 13:2 (Summer 1983): 2–13.

Lamar, Howard, and Leonard Thompson, eds. *The Frontier in History: North America and South America Compared*. New Haven, CT: Yale University Press, 1981.

Lathrop, George Parson. "An American School of Dramatic Art: The Inside Working of the Theatre." *Century Magazine* 56:2 (June 1898): 265–275.

Lepore, Jill. *The Name of War: King Philip's War and the Origins of American Identity*. New York: Vintage, 2001.

Levine, Lawrence. *Highbrow/Lowbrow: The Emergence of Cultural Hierarchy in America*. Cambridge, MA: Harvard University Press, 1990.

Lewis, Nathaniel. "Authentic Reproduction: The Picturesque Joaquin Miller." *Arizona Quarterly* 57:2 (Summer 2001): 1–31.

Lhamon, Jr., W. T. *Jump Jim Crow: Lost Plays, Lyrics, and Street Prose of the First Atlantic Popular Culture*. Cambridge, MA: Harvard University Press, 2003.

———. *Raising Cain: Blackface Performance from Jim Crow to Hip Hop*. Cambridge, MA: Harvard University Press, 1998.

Limerick, Patricia Nelson. "The Adventures of the Frontier in the Twentieth Century." In *The Frontier in American Culture*. Ed. James R. Grossman. Berkeley: University of California Press, 1994.

———. "Disorientation and Reorientation: The American Landscape Discovered from the West." *The Journal of American History* 79:3, Discovering America: A Special Issue (December 1992): 1021-1049.

———. *The Legacy of Conquest: The Unbroken Past of the American West*. New York: Norton, 1987.

Looby, Christopher. *Voicing America: Language, Literary Form, and the Origins of the United States*. Chicago: University of Chicago Press, 1996.

Lott, Eric. *Love and Theft: Blackface Minstrelsy and the American Working Class*. New York: Oxford University Press, 1993.

MacDougall, Pauleena. *The Penobscot Dance of Resistance: Tradition in the History of a People*. Durham, NH: University of New Hampshire Press, 2004.

MacPherson, C. B. *Burke*. Oxford, UK: Oxford University Press, 1980.

Mahar, William J. *Behind the Burnt Cork Mask: Early Blackface and Antebellum American Popular Culture*. Urbana: University of Illinois Press, 1999.

Marra, Kim. *Strange Duets: Impresarios and Actresses in the American Theatre, 1865–1914*. Iowa City: University of Iowa Press, 2006.

———. "Taming America as Actress: Augustin Daly, Ada Rehan, and the Discourse of Imperial Frontier Conquest." In *Performing America: Cultural Nationalism in American Theater*. Eds. Jeffery D. Mason and J. Ellen Gainor. Ann Arbor: University of Michigan Press, 1999: 52–72.

Marx, Leo. *The Machine in the Garden: Technology and the Pastoral Ideal in America*. Oxford, UK: Oxford University Press, 1964.

Mason, Jeffrey D. *Melodrama and the Myth of America*. Bloomington: Indiana University Press, 1993.

Mathews, Brander "The Rise and Fall of Negro Minstrelsy" *Scribner's Magazine* 57:6 (1915): 754–759.

McAllister, Marvin. *White People Do Not Know How to Behave at Entertainments Designed for Ladies and Gentlemen of Colour*. Chapel Hill: University of North Carolina Press, 2003.

McBride, Dwight A. "Why I Hate That I Loved *Brokeback Mountain*." *GLQ* 13:1 (2007): 95–97.

McConachie, Bruce A. *Melodramatic Formations: American Theatre and Society, 1820–1870.* Iowa City: University of Iowa Press, 1992.

Meer, Sarah. *Uncle Tom Mania: Slavery, Minstrelsy, and Transatlantic Culture in the 1850s.* Athens: University of Georgia Press, 2005.

Megquier, Mary Jane. *Apron Full of Gold: The Letters of Mary Jane Megquier.* Ed. Robert Cleland. Intro. Polly Welts Kaufman. Albuquerque: University of New Mexico Press, 1994.

Meisel, Martin. "Speaking Pictures." In *Melodrama.* Ed. Daniel Gerould. Vol. 7. New York: New York Literary Forum, 1980.

Miller, D. A. "On the Universality of *Brokeback.*" *Film Quarterly* 60:3 (March 2007): 50–60.

Miller, David C. *Dark Eden: The Swamp in Nineteenth-Century American Culture.* Cambridge, UK: Cambridge University Press, 1989.

Miller, Joaquin. *The Danites in the Sierras.* In *American Plays.* Ed. Allan Gates Halline. New York: American Book Company, 1976.

———. *First Families of the Sierras.* London: George Routledge, 1875.

———. *How I Became Chief of the Scalplocks.* Los Angeles: Bird in Hand Press, 1970.

———. *Joaquin Miller's Poems.* 6 vols. San Francisco: Whitaker and Ray, 1909.

———. *Life Amongst the Modocs: Unwritten History.* London: Richard Bentley and Sons, 1873.

———. *Overland in a Covered Wagon: An Autobiography.* Ed. Sidney G. Firman. New York: D. Appleton, 1931.

Miller, Tice L. *Entertaining the Nation: American Drama in the Eighteenth and Nineteenth Centuries.* Carbondale: University of Southern Illinois Press, 2007.

Milner II, Clyde A., ed. *A New Significance: Re-envisioning the History of the American West.* New York: Oxford University Press, 1996.

Mitchell, Lee Clark. *Westerns: Making the Man in Fiction and Film.* Chicago: University of Chicago Press, 1998.

Mohawk, Gowongo, and Charlie Charles. *Wep-Ton-No-Mah, The Indian Mail Carrier.* Copyrighted 1892. Rare Book and Manuscript Collection, Library of Congress.

Morning Courier and New-York Enquirer, April 27, 1831.

Moses, L. G. *Wild West Shows and the Images of American Indians, 1883–1933.* Albuquerque: University of New Mexico Press, 1996.

Murdoch, James E. *The Stage, or, Recollections of Actors and Acting.* Philadelphia: J. M. Stoddart, 1880.

Murphy, Brenda. *American Realism and American Drama, 1880–1940.* Cambridge, UK: Cambridge University Press, 1987.

Nasaw, David. *Going Out: The Rise and Fall of Public Amusement.* Cambridge, MA: Harvard University Press, 1999.

Nathans, Heather S. *Early National Theatre from the Revolution to Thomas Jefferson: Into the Hands of the People.* Cambridge, UK: Cambridge University Press, 2003.

Negro Minstrelsy in New York. Vol. 2. New York: Collected and Illustrated by Charles C. Morneau, n.d. Harvard Theatre Collection, Houghton Library.

Nelson, Dana D. *National Manhood: Capitalist Citizenship and the Imagined Fraternity of White Men.* Durham, NC: Duke University Press, 1998.

Nemerov, Alex. "Doing the 'Old America:' The Image of the American West, 1880–1920." In *The West as America: Reinterpreting Images of the Frontier, 1820–1920.* Washington, D.C.: Smithsonian Institution Press, 1991.

New York Herald, September 15, 1859: 7.

New York Herald, March 22, 1871.

New-York Mirror, December 18, 1830.

New-York Mirror, April 30, 1831.

New York Times, December 15, 1859.

Nora, Pierre. "Between Memory and History: *Les Lieux de Mémoire.*" *Representations* 26 (Spring 1989): 7–25.

Norton, Anne. *Alternative Americans: A Reading of Antebellum Political Culture.* Chicago: University of Chicago Press, 1986.

Novak, Barbara. *Nature and Culture: American Landscape and Painting, 1825–1875.* Oxford, UK: Oxford University Press, 1980.

Odell, George C. D. *Annals of the New York Stage.* Vol. 8. New York: Columbia University Press, 1931.

———. *Annals of the New York Stage.* Vol. 10. New York: Columbia University Press, 1938.

Paulding, James Kirke. "The American Drama." *American Quarterly Review* 2 (June 1827): 331–357.

———. *The Backwoodsman.* Philadelphia: M. Thomas, 1818.

———. Letter to Lewis J. Cist, January 16, 1837. In *The Letters of James Kirke Paulding.* Ed. Ralph M. Aderman. Madison: University of Wisconsin Press, 1962: 189–190.

———. Letter to Daniel Drake, January 1, 1835. In *The Letters of James Kirke Paulding.* Ed. Ralph M. Aderman. Madison: University of Wisconsin Press, 1962: 158–161.

———. *The Lion of the West; or a Trip to Washington.* Ed. James N. Tidwell. Palo Alto, CA: Stanford University Press, 1954.

———. "National Literature." Revised in *Salmagundi, Second Series* (1835), New York: AMS Press, 2: 265–272. Entitled "The Wreck of Genius" in *Salmagundi, Second Series* (1819–1820), 3: 264–288.

———. *Slavery in the United States.* New York: Harper and Brothers, 1836.

Paulding, William I. *Literary Life of James K. Paulding.* New York: Scribner and Co., 1867.

Peretz, Evgenia. "Highnoon in Crawford." *Vanity Fair* (November 2005): 222–236.

Phelan, Peggy. *Unmarked: The Politics of Performance.* New York: Routledge, 1993.

Philadelphia Inquirer, October 4, 1891.

Philadelphia Inquirer, October 28, 1890.

Philadelphia Sun, May 8, 1834

Poe, Edgar Allan. Review in *Southern Literary Messenger* 2 (April 1836): 337–338.

Pratt, Mary Louise. "Arts of the Contact Zone." *Profession* 91 (1991): 33–40.

Quinn, Arthur Hobson. *A History of the American Drama: From the Beginning to the Civil War.* New York: Harper and Brothers, 1923.

———. *A History of the American Drama: From the Civil War to the Present Day.* New York: Appleton, Century, Crofts, 1936.

Ratner, Lorman. *James Kirke Paulding: The Last Republican.* Westport, CT: Greenwood, 1992.

Reddin, Paul. *Wild West Shows.* Urbana: University of Illinois Press, 1999.

Rees, James. *The Life of Edwin Forrest: With Reminiscences and Personal Recollections.* Philadelphia: T. B. Peterson, 1874.

Reid, Mayne. *The Quadroon; or, Adventures in the Far West.* Ridgewood, NJ: Gregg Press, 1967 [1856].

———. *The Quadroon; or, A Lover's Adventures in Louisiana.* New York: Robert M. De Witt, 1856.

Rein, Lisa. "Down on the Ranch, President Wages War on the Underbrush." *Washington Post,* December 31, 2005: A03.

Reynolds, Larry J. *James Kirke Paulding.* Boston: Twayne Publishing, 1984.

Rice, T. D. "Jim Crow." In "Jim Crow's Ramble!" (London: Z.T. Purday, n.d.), Minstrel Sheet Music Collection, Harvard Theatre Collection, Houghton Library.

———. "Jim Crow," Verse 7 (New York: E. Riley, n.d.), Minstrel Sheet Music Collection, Harvard Theatre Collection, Houghton Library.

———. "Jim Crow," Verse 8, in "Jimmy Crow" (New York: Atwill's Music Saloon, n.d.), in Minstrel Sheet Music Collection, Harvard Theatre Collection, Houghton Library.

————. "Such a Getting Up Stairs," London: T.E. Purday, n.d. In Minstrel Sheet Music Collection, Harvard Theatre Collection, Houghton Library.

————. *The Virginia Mummy*. In W. T. Lhamon, Jr., *Jump Jim Crow: Lost Plays, Lyrics, and Street Prose of the First Atlantic Popular Culture*. Cambridge, MA: Harvard University Press, 2003: 159–177.

Rich, Frank. "Shoddy! Tawdry! A Televised Train Wreck." *New York Times*, April 20, 2008.

Richards, Jeffrey H. *Drama, Theatre, and Identity in the American New Republic*. Cambridge, UK: Cambridge University Press, 2005.

Richardson, Gary A. "Plays and Playwrights: 1800–1865." In *The Cambridge History of American Theatre: Volume 1, Beginnings to 1870*. Eds. Don B. Wilmeth and Christopher Bigsby. Cambridge, UK: Cambridge University Press, 1998: 250–302.

Ridge, Martin. "The Life of an Idea: The Significance of Frederick Jackson Turner's Frontier Thesis." In *Does the Frontier Experience Make America Exceptional?* Ed. Richard W. Etulain. Boston: Bedford/St. Martin's, 1999.

Roach, Joseph. *Cities of the Dead: Circum-Atlantic Performance*. New York: Columbia University Press, 1996.

————. *The Player's Passion: Studies in the Science of Acting*. Ann Arbor: University of Michigan Press, 1985.

Robinson, Marc. *The American Play, 1787–2000*. New Haven, CT: Yale University Press, 2009.

Roediger, David R. *The Wages of Whiteness: Race and the Making of the American Working Class*. Revised Edition. London: Verso, 1991.

Rogin, Michael Paul. *Fathers and Children: Andrew Jackson and the Subjugation of the American Indian*. New York: Alfred Knopf, 1975.

Rosaldo, Renato. "Imperialist Nostalgia." *Representations* 26 Special Issue: Memory and Counter-Memory (Spring 1989): 107–122.

Rosenthal, Debra J. *Race Mixture in Nineteenth-Century U.S. and Spanish American Fiction: Gender, Culture, and Nation Building*. Chapel Hill: University of North Carolina Press, 2004.

Rourke, Constance. *American Humor: A Study of National Character*. New York: Doubleday, 1931.

Rush, Benjamin. "Of the Mode of Education Proper in a Republic" (1798). In *The Selected Writings of Benjamin Rush*. Ed. Dagobert D. Runes. New York: Philosophical Library, 1947.

Rydell, Robert W. *All the World's a Fair: Visions of Empire at American International Expositions, 1876–1916*. Chicago: University of Chicago Press, 1987.

Rydell Robert W. and Rob Kroes. *Buffalo Bill in Bologna: The Americanization of the World, 1869–1922*. Chicago: University of Chicago Press, 2005.

Sabin, Joseph. *Catalogue of the Library of Edwin Forrest*. Philadelphia: Collins, 1863.

Said, Edward. *Beginnings: Intention and Method*. New York: Columbia University Press, 1985.

Sanchez-Eppler, Karen. *Touching Liberty: Abolition, Feminism and the Politics of the Body*. Berkeley: University of California Press, 1993.

Sanjek, Russell. *American Popular Music and Its Business: The First Hundred Years*. Vol. 2. New York: Oxford University Press, 1988.

Sappol, Michael. *A Traffic in Dead Bodies: Anatomy and Embodied Social Identity in Nineteenth-Century America*. Princeton, NJ: Princeton University Press, 2004.

Sayre, Gordon M. *The Indian Chief as Tragic Hero: Native Resistance and the Literatures of America, from Moctezuma to Tecumseh*. Chapel Hill: University of North Carolina Press, 2005.

Scheckel, Susan. *The Insistence of the Indian: Race and Nationalism in Nineteenth-Century American Culture*. Princeton, NJ: Princeton University Press, 1998.

Schutz, John A., and Douglas Adair, eds. *The Spur of Fame: Dialogues of John Adams and Benjamin Rush, 1805–1813*. San Marino, CA: Huntington Library, 1966.

Sellers, Charles. *The Market Revolution: Jacksonian America, 1815–1846*. New York: Oxford University Press, 1994.

Shaw, George Bernard. *Our Theatres in the Nineties*. 3 Vols. London: Constable, 1932.

Sheridan, Thomas. *A Course of Lectures on Elocution*. London: W. Strahan, 1762.

Simmon, Scott. *The Invention of the Western Film: A Cultural History of the Genre's First Half Century*. Cambridge, UK: Cambridge University Press, 2003.

Slotkin, Richard. *Gunfighter Nation: The Myth of the Frontier in Twentieth-Century America*. Norman: University of Oklahoma Press, 1992.

Smith-Rosenberg, Carroll. *Disorderly Conduct: Visions of Gender in Victorian America*. New York: Knopf, 1985.

Sollors, Werner. *Beyond Ethnicity: Consent and Descent in American Culture*. New York: Oxford University Press, 1986.

Spirit of the Times, December 17, 1859.

Stephanson, Anders. *Manifest Destiny: American Expansion and the Empire of Right*. New York: Hill and Wang, 1995.

Stone, John Augustus. *Metamora, or the Last of the Wampanoags*. In *Staging the Nation: Plays from the American Theater, 1787–1909*. Ed. Don B. Wilmeth. Boston: Bedford, 1998.

Sunday Inter Ocean, December 6, 1891.

"T. D. Rice—'Jim Crow.'" In Joseph N. Ireland, *Records of the New York Stage from 1750 to 1860*, Vol. 2. Part 2. New York: T. H. Morrell, 1867, Harvard Theatre Collection, Houghton Library.

Thoreau, Henry David. "Walking." In *Walden and Other Writings of Henry David Thoreau*. Ed. Brooks Atkinson. New York: Modern Library, 1992: 625–664.

Toll, Robert C. *Blacking Up: The Minstrel Show in Nineteenth-Century America*. London: Oxford University Press, 1974.

Tompkins, Jane. *West of Everything: The Inner Life of Westerns*. New York: Oxford University Press, 1993.

Trachtenberg, Alan. *The Incorporation of America: Culture and Society in the Gilded Age*. New York: Hill and Wang, 1982.

Trafton, Scott. *Egypt Land: Race and Nineteenth-Century American Egyptomania*. Durham, NC: Duke University Press, 2004.

Trollope, Frances Milton. *Domestic Manners of the Americans*. London: Whittaker, Treacher, and Co., 1832.

Turner, Frederick Jackson. "The Significance of the Frontier in American History." In *The Frontier in American History*. New York: Dover, 1996.

Turner, Lorenzo Dow. "The Transition Period (1808–1881)" *Journal of Negro History* 14:4 (October 1929): 403–416.

Utley, Robert M. *The Indian Frontier of the American West, 1846–1890*. Albuquerque: University of New Mexico Press, 1984.

Vardac, Nicholas. *From Stage to Screen: Theatrical Origins of Early Film: David Garrick to D.W. Griffith*. Cambridge, MA: Harvard University Press, 1949.

Wagner, Harr. *Joaquin Miller and His Other Self*. San Francisco: Harr Wagner Publishing Company, 1929.

Wallach, Alan. "Thomas Cole: Landscape and the Course of Empire." In *Thomas Cole: Landscape Into History*. Eds. William H. Truettner and Alan Wallach. New Haven, CT: Yale University Press, 1994: 23–112.

Warner, Michael. *The Letters of the Republic: Publication and the Public Sphere in Eighteenth-Century America*. Cambridge, MA: Harvard University Press, 1990.

Warren, James Perrin. *Culture of Eloquence: Oratory and Reform in Antebellum America*. University Park, PA: Pennsylvania State University Press, 1999.

Warren, Louis S. *Buffalo Bill's America: William Cody and the Wild West Show*. New York: Knopf, 2005.

Watkins, Floyd C. "James Kirke Paulding and the South." *American Quarterly* 5:3 (Autumn 1958): 219–230.

Weld, Theodore. *American Slavery As It Is*. New York: American Anti-Slavery Society, 1839.

Wemyss, F.C. *Theatrical Biography; or, The Life of An Actor and Manager*. Glasgow: R. Griffin, 1848.

Wheeling Register, October 28, 1891.

White, Richard. "Frederick Jackson Turner and Buffalo Bill." In *The Frontier in American Culture*. Ed. James R. Grossman. Berkeley: University of California Press, 1994: 7–66.

———. *The Middle Ground: Indians, Empires, and Republics in the Great Lakes Region, 1650–1815*. Cambridge, UK: Cambridge University Press, 1991.

Whitman, Walt. "The Gladiator—Mr. Forrest—Acting" (1846). In *The American Theatre as Seen by Its Critics, 1752–1934*. Eds. Montrose J. Moses and John Mason Brown. New York: W. W. Norton, 1934: 69–70.

———. "The Old Bowery." *November Boughs*. In *Walt Whitman: Complete Poetry and Collected Prose*. Ed. Justin Kaplan. New York: Library of America, 1982: 1189.

Wiegman, Robyn. *American Anatomies: Theorizing Race and Gender*. Durham, NC: Duke University Press, 1995.

Williams, Carolyn. "Moving Pictures: George Eliot and Melodrama." In *Compassion: The Culture and Politics of an Emotion*. Ed. Lauren Berlant. New York: Routledge, 2004: 105–145.

Williams, Linda. *Playing the Race Card: Melodramas of Black and White from Uncle Tom to O.J. Simpson*. Princeton, NJ: Princeton University Press, 2001.

Williams, Raymond. *The City and the Country*. Oxford, UK: Oxford University Press, 1975.

———. *Marxism and Literature*. New York: Oxford University Press, 1977.

Wilmeth, Don B. "Noble or Ruthless Savage?: The American Indian on Stage and in the Drama." *Journal of American Drama and Theatre* 1 (Spring 1989): 39–78.

Winter, William. *Other Days: Being Chronicles and Memoirs of the Stage*. New York: Moffat, Yard, and Company, 1908.

Wittke, Carl. *Tambo and Bones: A History of the American Minstrel Stage*. Durham, NC: Duke University Press, 1930.

Wood, Marcus. *Blind Memory: Visual Representations of Slavery in England and America, 1780–1865*. New York: Routledge, 2000.

Worster, Donald. *Under Western Skies: Nature and History in the American West*. New York: Oxford University Press, 1992.

Young, Robert J.C. *Colonial Desire: Hybridity in Theory, Culture, and Race*. London: Routledge, 1995.

Ziff, Larzer. *Writing in the New Nation: Prose, Print, and Politics in the Early United States*. New Haven, CT: Yale University Press, 1991.

INDEX